KENNIKAT PRESS SCHOLARLY REPRINTS

Dr. Ralph Adams Brown, Senior Editor

Series in
**AMERICAN HISTORY AND CULTURE
IN THE NINETEENTH CENTURY**
Under the General Editorial Supervision of
Dr. Martin L. Fausold
Professor of History, State University of New York

© Paul Thompson

THEODORE ROOSEVELT

From Harrison to Harding

A Personal Narrative, Covering
a Third of a Century

1888–1921

By

Arthur Wallace Dunn

In Two Volumes

With Portraits

Volume II

KENNIKAT PRESS
Port Washington, N. Y./London

FROM HARRISON TO HARDING

First published in 1922
Reissued in 1971 by Kennikat Press
Library of Congress Catalog Card No: 78-137908
ISBN 0-8046-1476-8

Manufactured by Taylor Publishing Company   Dallas, Texas

KENNIKAT SERIES ON AMERICAN HISTORY AND
CULTURE IN THE NINETEENTH CENTURY

CONTENTS

Contents

Contents

Contents

Contents

Contents

Contents

ILLUSTRATIONS

From Harrison to Harding

From Harrison to Harding

CHAPTER I

AN EVENTFUL YEAR

The Busiest Period in Roosevelt's Career—Railroad Rate Legislation—
The "Ananias Club" Established—Free Passes Abolished—Pure
Food Law—Simplified Spelling Has a Short Life—La Follette's
Reception—Uncle Joe's Birthday—Woodrow Wilson Mentioned
for President.

THE year 1906 was marked by more important
events than any other between the Spanish war
and the great war in Europe. It was the year of the
railroad rate legislation and the foundation of the
"Ananias Club." Free railroad passes were abolished.
Early in that year Nicholas Longworth and Alice Roosevelt were married. Oklahoma and Indian Territories
were united and admitted as a state. General Leonard
Wood fought the battle of Dojo in the Moro country.
Prof. Woodrow Wilson was for the first time mentioned
as a Presidential possibility. It was the year of the
famous Bellamy Storer recall and "Dear Maria" letters.
Roosevelt delivered his celebrated muckrake speech.
The San Francisco earthquake occurred. The pure
food bill was passed, which made possible the Dr. Wiley

3

imbroglio in after years. William H. Taft wavered
several times as to a seat on the Supreme bench. Uncle
Joe Cannon had one of his many birthdays, and some
one got him to say that he would rather be Speaker
than President. The meat packers met Roosevelt and
went down to defeat. James K. Jones announced that
Bryan was "the great conservative force" and would be
elected President in 1908. Bryan returned from a world
tour and dampened Democratic ardor by proclaiming
government ownership of railroads as a Democratic
principle. Elihu Root made his remarkable South
American friendship speech at Rio de Janeiro.
President Roosevelt adopted simplified spelling
and Congress by legislation caused him to revoke
his order. Secretary Taft made his celebrated
speech at Bath, Maine, in favor of tariff revision. Taft
was sent to Cuba to "sit on the lid" of that new Republic, which showed revolutionary tendencies. Roosevelt had Charles Evans Hughes nominated for Governor
of New York, and Hughes defeated William Randolph
Hearst.

It was a year of Cabinet changes. Brownsville,
Texas, was shot up, on which account Roosevelt dismissed a battalion of colored troops. Roosevelt went
to Panama and shook up the entire force. Captain
Peary and Dr. Cook were honor guests at the same dinner. John J. Pershing was jumped over 1,200 other
army officers and made a brigadier general. William
H. Taft published an announcement that he was not
seeking a Presidential nomination. Woodrow Wilson

was brought out as a Presidential possibility for the nomination in 1908.

There were many more happenings of minor interest, but I have only indicated the most important. It was the greatest year of President Roosevelt's life, and the wonder of it all is that he could do so much in twelve months.

The railroad rate legislation in itself was not so very important, but it was given a prominence far beyond its after effect. The House passed the Hepburn bill, so-called because Colonel Wm. P. Hepburn was Chairman of the Committee on Interstate and Foreign Commerce and reported the measure. It was really the Esch-Townsend bill, a combination measure prepared by Congressman Esch of Wisconsin and Congressman Townsend of Michigan. As it passed the House, it gave the Interstate Commerce Commission authority to fix railroad rates.

While the bill was pending in the House Hepburn had frequent conferences with President Roosevelt. On one of these occasions one of the Roosevelt boys entered the office and sought help from his father. One of the snakes he had captured that day had crawled up his coat sleeve, and although the boy had a firm grasp upon its tail the snake could not be pulled out.

"Let me take off your coat," said the President.

As he did so another snake was flung from the boy's coat pocket and landed on Hepburn's knee. As President and son struggled with the coat and the other snake, Hepburn went out, remarking:

"You seem to be pretty busy, Mr. President; I will call another time."

"I fear Colonel Pete thought it was going to be menagerie day at the White House," the President gleefully exclaimed, in telling of the incident.

The struggle over the rate bill was in the Senate. It seemed to be certain that, if the Hepburn Bill was reported out of the committee, it would pass about as it came from the House. The effort of the conservative element was to get an amendment providing for a court review of rates fixed by the commission.

Senator Elkins was Chairman of the Interstate Commerce Committee, and was one of the supposed ultra conservative Senators who were holding up the bill. On one occasion a muckraking writer asked him about the bill, and Elkins said they were trying to draft a provision in regard to courts.

"I have no use for courts, myself," remarked the writer.

"In that case," said Elkins, briskly, "I will put my hands on my watch and pocket book and bid you good day. I have known people before who had no use for courts."

And he disappeared into his committee room.

One day the conservative members of the committee were in the room and discussing what they should do.

"I am going to vote to report the bill," said Elkins.

"What!" the others almost shouted.

"Yes," replied Elkins. "When a team is going to

run away I prefer to be on the wagon rather than in front of it."

Senator Dolliver of Iowa made the fight for the Hepburn bill in the committee, and it was natural to suppose that when it was reported he would have charge of it. But as soon as the committee voted to report the bill, Senator Aldrich moved that it be reported by Senator Tillman. The Rhode Island Senator had a double purpose in this move. He wanted to slap Dolliver in the face because of his activity on lines antagonistic to what Aldrich desired, and he also thought it would be annoying to President Roosevelt, who, on account of the Prince Henry dinner incident, was not on speaking terms with Tillman. All the Democrats, with Aldrich, Foraker, Crane, and Kean, carried the motion, and thus was presented the incongruous situation of an Administration measure being in charge of the Administration's most implacable enemy, and of a Democrat having charge of the most important bill of the session in a Senate with a large Republican majority. It was these petty characteristics of Aldrich which prevented him from being a great Senator.

And now we come to the first appearance of the "Ananias Club."

Former Senator Wm. E. Chandler couldn't keep out of things as long as he lived. He at once enlisted as a go-between, the line of communication, so to speak, between the President in the White House and Tillman in the Senate. Soon there was an explosion. Tillman told the Senate that the President had made certain

statements about the pending bill. Lodge telephoned
the White House and went back into the Senate, and on
the authority of the President denied Tillman's statement. Tillman explained that, owing to the lack of
relations between himself and the President, former
Senator Chandler had been carrying messages, and it
was from Chandler that he learned the President's
position as he had stated it.

Quickly came a denial from the White House.
Chandler in a letter stood by Tillman and said that
Roosevelt had authorized the communication. Roosevelt
denounced Chandler as a liar, thus making him the
first member of the "Ananias Club." But he was not
lonesome long. The "Club" was rapidly filled by
those who went forth from the White House and
undertook to repeat what the President had said.

One day the whole controversy over the rate bill was
cleared up. Senator Allison came from the White
House with a court review provision. It was soon incorporated in the bill, and not long afterwards the
measure was passed.

That rate bill contained the provision which abolished
passes save to railroad employees and a favored few
others. The manner in which passes came to be abolished is an interesting story. For years everybody
who had the least claim or a "pull" could obtain a
pass. No road was more generous than the Pennsylvania, particularly with Senators, Representatives,
newspaper men, and others who had influence in
Washington. At that time the passenger station of

the Pennsylvania was on a government reservation, and for a considerable distance the tracks ran through a government park.

In those good old days of passes nearly everybody got about what they wanted. Not only were Senators and Representatives given passes, but their families, employees, and relatives also traveled free. As to the Washington newspaper men, the Pennsylvania not only gave them passes, but took them in special trains to national conventions, and every year there was a seaside trip of several days given by the railroad to the newspaper men and their wives.

"I came down to Washington," a newspaper correspondent once said, "to fight the corporations, and especially the Pennsylvania railroad. But I had not been here very long before I had a pass home and back, two or three free trips to New York, a trip to Cape May for several days, and now, so far as I am concerned, if the Pennsylvania road wants the Capitol rotunda for a round house they can have it."

Some time before this rate legislation was considered Congress passed a bill providing for a Union Station in Washington, and the Pennsylvania station was removed from the government reservation. Congress appropriated $1,500,000 to help the roads build the Union Station.

When all this was done, biff, bang, came the announcement of no more passes. The Pennsylvania led the movement, which was followed by the Baltimore & Ohio, the Chesapeake & Ohio, and the Norfolk

& Western. With the exception of the Southern Railway, Washington was practically cut off. Congressmen coming to Washington by way of St. Louis, Chicago, Pittsburgh, Buffalo, or from northern points, had to pay their fares.

"If we have to pay fares everybody else 'll have to do the same," they said, and so they put the anti-pass section in the rate bill.

Foraker's antagonistic attitude towards Roosevelt was shown in the rate legislation. It began when Foraker opposed the uniting of New Mexico and Arizona as one state; then followed disagreements over patronage, and the position Foraker took on the rate legislation was so earnest, so intense, that it practically ended his relations with the White House. Foraker was the only Republican who voted against the rate bill.

Quite as important in its effect was the pure food bill. This law bears no one man's name, although it came near having Hepburn's name because it was reported from the committee of which he was chairman. The pure food bill passed because Roosevelt was for it, and because there were two persistent and vigorous supporters of the measure in the Senate. They were Heyburn of Idaho and McCumber of North Dakota. They passed the bill in the Senate, although there never was a majority actually for it, if a vote could have been dodged or avoided. But with Roosevelt and the country demanding the legislation, Senators were obliged to vote for it. For twenty years a pure food

bill had been kicking about Congress. The southern
men did not want it because they feared it would interfere with cotton seed oil. Northern men were opposed
to it because of the opposition of food manufacturers.
But James R. Mann of Illinois put the bill through the
House, and Heyburn kept it before the Senate and forced
a vote in spite of all efforts to sidetrack it, as had been
done for a score of years.

The meat inspection bill was made a part of the agricultural appropriation bill. This was another Roosevelt measure. Senator Beveridge handled it in the
Senate. There was a sharp contest in the House.
James W. Wadsworth of New York, who was chairman
of the agricultural committee, opposed the meat inspection measure, and thereby incurred the displeasure of Roosevelt. He was made to feel it, too, for
Roosevelt caused Wadsworth's defeat at the Fall
election.

While President Roosevelt was able to have his own
way in the more important matters of legislation, he
was confronted with a solid opposition in the matter of
simplified spelling. It was during the year 1906 that
Andrew Carnegie was creating a diversion by champion-
ing the spelling of English words as they sounded.
President Roosevelt approved the idea and ordered all
government documents printed with the new spelling.
Congress revolted, and in one of the first bills passed
after the order was issued, provided by legislation for
the restoration of the spelling theretofore in vogue.
Roosevelt had to sign the bill and then he revoked his

former order.   He could yield in little things and never
fought for a barren victory.

In the long session of the Fifty-ninth Congress the
Smoot case was heard, and in connection with this case
an incident occurred which indicated the attitude of the
Senate towards Senator La Follette.   The Wisconsin
Senator showed that he was antagonistic to the Republican majority as then constituted.   In after years he said
that he stood alone when he entered the Senate, but that
he had thirteen supporters before his first term ended.
When La Follette first spoke in the Senate there was
not a very large attendance of Senators and he
was inclined to scold about it.   In later years he
adopted the plan which seemed to suit him.   He rarely
listened to speeches in the Senate, and was indifferent
whether Senators listened to him when he made
speeches.

Senator Burrows, Chairman of the Committee on
Privileges and Elections, was opposed to Smoot, and reported a resolution declaring Smoot's seat vacant.   One
day Senator Spooner, who was decidedly bitter against
La Follette, went to Burrows and said:

"I can tell you how you can get one vote for your
resolution; strike out the name Smoot and insert La
Follette."   Then he added: "You can get enough
amendments of that kind to pass your resolution."

But La Follette stood well with the President.   Never
was this quite so apparent as on the closing day of the
session when Roosevelt went to the Capitol to sign bills
so as to hasten adjournment.   Many Senators and

Representatives wanted to see him, and there was a distinct effort to get the Presidential ear. It was observed that La Follette was particularly favored by Roosevelt. When others crowded around he would go apart with La Follette, turning his back on Vice President Fairbanks and others in order to have a more confidential chat with the Wisconsin Senator.

An interesting episode of that Congress was the grand "blowout" in honor of Speaker Cannon on his 70th birthday. It was given at the old Arlington hotel. It was not a dinner, but a reception, and in every part of the large dining room were well supplied refreshment stands. President Roosevelt was one of the guests and in excellent spirits. He circulated among the other guests, and in a democratic way clinked glasses with friends whom he warmly greeted.

Later in the evening friends of Senator Clark of Montana persuaded him to sing the *Star Spangled Banner*. Standing on a table in one of the reception rooms this man of millions sang in a high tenor the national anthem. Nay, more, a little later he sang the *Marseillaise* in French.

These incidents illustrate the whole-hearted manner in which the friends of Uncle Joe celebrated the fact that he was still a young man at three-score-and-ten.

Colonel George Harvey nominated Prof. Woodrow Wilson of Princeton University for President of the United States at a dinner in the Lotus Club, New York City, on February 3, 1906. So far as I know that was the first public mention of Wilson for the high office he afterwards filled for eight years.

The marriage of Miss Roosevelt and Mr. Longworth was one of the notable events of the season. For the second time a President's daughter was married in the White House; Nellie Grant having been the first.

Not long after the wedding Mr. and Mrs. Longworth went abroad. They dined with King Edward VII in England, and were entertained by Emperor Wilhelm II of Germany on board his yacht. Everywhere in Europe they were given attentions such as no other American bridal couple has ever received.

CHAPTER II

The Storer Correspondence—Muckrakers Attacked—Bryan Returns
from Abroad and Dampens Democratic Ardor by Proclaiming
Government Ownership—Root in South America—Cuba in Erup-
tion—Taft Declares for Tariff Revision—Roosevelt Makes Hughes
Governor—The Brownsville Affair.

THEODORE ROOSEVELT was firm in the belief
that an incident which did not affect a man's
integrity could not be more than a nine days' wonder at
most. That was apparently his view in regard to the
celebrated Storer correspondence. It seems rather
strange, considering the great to-do that was made
over the Storer affair, that it was so soon forgotten.

Bellamy Storer was a member of Congress from Cin-
cinnati when Roosevelt was Civil Service Commissioner.
His wife was Maria Longworth, an aunt of Nicholas
Longworth. In those early days Roosevelt and the
Storers were close friends. Roosevelt remembered them
when he became President. He made Storer Ambassador to Italy and later Ambassador to Austria. There
was a lively correspondence between Mr. Roosevelt and
Mrs. Storer, and later, when the correspondence was
published, the "Dear Maria" letters, as they were
called, made interesting reading.

The break came when Mrs. Storer went too far. The President, like a great many others, wanted to see Archbishop Ireland of St. Paul made a cardinal of the Church of Rome, but the Storers, ardent Catholics and friends of the Archbishop, went further than they were warranted in using the President's name in the affair, and the whole matter blew up with a bang that was heard in every diplomatic center of the world.

Storer was recalled. Mrs. Storer wrote letters and gave out parts of the correspondence and there was a public scandal which might have been confined to personal controversy. Finally, it was determined by the President to send the entire correspondence to Congress and have it published.

I was in the President's room the morning the correspondence was to be sent in. The mass of papers lay on his desk. Senator Lodge came in and saw it. It was a painful occasion for the Massachusetts Senator.

"It is too bad," he said, "that all this must be made public."

"It is too bad," assented Roosevelt, and his teeth snapped as he closed his jaw.

He picked up the sheaf of papers and began turning over sheet after sheet, with a frown upon his face. "It is too bad," he repeated. Then something caught his eye. The frown faded and the teeth gleamed. "But some of this is delicious," he almost shouted.

Only once afterwards did I ever hear him make a reference to the Storer correspondence. He was talking at a dinner party. "I recently saw," he said, "an advertisement of two volumes entitled *Indiscreet Diplomatic Correspondence.* I hastened to acquire the volumes and read the books. Imagine my disappointment when I found that it did not compare in interest or indiscretion with the Storer correspondence."

President Roosevelt in one of his many speeches used the word "muckraker," and applied it to a class of writers whose articles were published in popular periodicals, the main motive of such articles being to criticize and vilify public men. Many of his sincere and admiring friends were shocked and grieved, for quite a number of them were doing a great deal of "muckraking" in writing about Roosevelt's supposed enemies.

The speech was first delivered at a Gridiron dinner. The members of the Club wondered why. They were not muckrakers; the correspondents in Washington could not defame and lie about men, misrepresent them, misconstrue their motives, and get away with it. They would be exposed as fakers, falsifiers, and slanderers. But as to the men whom Roosevelt rebuked, they were employed to write only one side of a situation and did not have any scruples. Even though many of these muckraking articles were intended to help Roosevelt, to sustain him against men who disagreed with him, the unfairness of it all caused him to revolt. His muckrake speech was not printed and caused no comment. The White House announced that President Roosevelt would pay his respects to muckrakers in a speech to be delivered at Norfolk, Virginia, during the summer.

But he could not wait. At the laying of the corner-stone of the House office building he again delivered the famous muckrake speech.

The return from abroad of William J. Bryan marked an epoch in the history of the Democratic party. It was confidently asserted that his long ramble around the world had made him conservative. He was frequently referred to by Democrats as the "great conservative force." Roosevelt was then the radical, and had been accused by Bryan of having stolen the planks of the Bryan platform.

Before Bryan left Europe John Sharp Williams went to England and met him. It was understood that the mission of Williams was to urge Bryan to take a conservative course, and especially to omit references to government ownership in his public utterances, that idea being particularly unpalatable to southern men. That Williams was unsuccessful was shown in Bryan's celebrated Madison Square Garden speech, his first public appearance upon his return. It was not at all a conservative speech, and he declared rather emphatically for government ownership, which dampened the ardor of Democrats, as it was then believed that he was to be the nominee in 1908.

Perhaps it was this declaration which caused eastern Democrats to seek another candidate. At all events late in the year 1906 a story was published in a New Haven, Conn., paper giving an account of a "recent meeting in New York at which it was determined by a number of leading Democrats to support Woodrow

Wilson, President of Princeton University, for the Democratic nomination in 1908."

After the San Francisco earthquake that city was in charge of United States troops, hence it was under the control of the President. Edward H. Harriman of the Southern Pacific railroad was greatly interested and went out to San Francisco where he found James D. Phelan, appointed by Roosevelt to take charge of the civic end, in control of affairs. Harriman wanted something done which did not meet the approval of Phelan, who said that it was not in accord with the wishes of President Roosevelt.

"Oh, I'll fix that, all right," glibly remarked Harriman. "I have a private wire from New York to the White House."

Of course the implication was that Harriman controlled Roosevelt. But Phelan did not believe it at the time and acted accordingly, and his course was approved by Roosevelt.

During the summer Secretary Root made his trip to South America. It was at the Rio de Janerio Pan-American Conference that he uttered the words which declared the position of the United States in the matter of the Southern Republics, saying:

"We wish for no victories except those of peace. We wish for no territory except our own, and no sovereignty except over ourselves."

Before he left for South America I had a conversation with Secretary Root regarding the status of Cuba, which was giving a great deal of concern and might require intervention by the United States under the terms of the Platt Amendment.

"It is to be hoped that no such action will be necessary," said Mr. Root, "or if we do intervene that it will be only for a short time. There should be no permanent occupation. We do not want to participate in their affairs and, what is more important, we do not want them participating in ours. If we should acquire Cuba the time would come when there would be several states seeking admission to our Union, with Senators and Representatives voting on questions which we have regarded as purely domestic. We do not want to govern Cuba and we do not want Cubans governing us."

In September Secretary Taft made his famous speech at Bath, Maine, which was taken to mean that tariff revision was soon to come. "Speaking my individual opinion and for no one else," said the Secretary, in the course of his remarks, "I believe that since the passage of the Dingley bill there has been a change in the business conditions of the country making it wise and just to revise the schedules of the existing tariff."

Even if it was an individual opinion, the general belief was that a member of Roosevelt's cabinet, and particularly the man whom it was believed Roosevelt had chosen to be his successor, would not have made such an important declaration without the full knowledge of the President.

That Roosevelt did see Taft's speeches in advance there can be no doubt. I remember an occasion when

I was talking with the President and Mr. Taft came in. He was about to go South and deliver a speech.

"Do you want to look over that speech?" asked the Secretary.

"Oh, no," replied the President.

Just as Taft was passing through the door the President called out:

"Will, just a moment. I guess you had better let me see that speech. I understand you are going to discuss southern questions, and I would like to see what you have to say."

Then turning to me:

"Root has to revise my speeches, but I have to revise Taft's; he's so radical."

And the President laughed heartily at the idea of any one being more radical than himself.

Later in the Fall I learned something about the effect of Taft's speech at Bath. The president of a structural steel insurance company in New York told me that their business had fallen off one-half because there had been a general stagnation in the steel market. Intending purchasers of steel, he said, expected a reduction of the tariff and lower prices for steel. About the same time James J. Hill, the railroad builder, told me that the railroads had stopped buying steel, save only that which was actually necessary.

"We are not building roads," he said, "nor buying steel cars; and yet the country needs more railroads and more cars. The greatest need for a railroad at the

present time is a new trunk line between New York
and Chicago."

"Why don't you build it?" I asked.

"I have been figuring on it," he replied. "I have
been making inquiries as to the cost of a terminal such
as the New York Central is now building in New York.
I found that a terminal in New York will cost as much
as a railroad from New York to Chicago could be
bonded for; and there would be many other expensive
stations, a Chicago terminal and the right of way.   No,
I am not going to build that road, nor any other save
such as are necessary in the country where our roads
are now operating."

The interesting political event of the year was the
New York election.   William Randolph Hearst was
nominated for Governor by the Independence League
and forced the New York Democracy to endorse him.

The Republicans had a most interesting convention.
Governor Higgins refused to be a candidate for a second
term, and all the big and little bosses sat around the
hotel at Saratoga and wondered what they would do.
Finally, "Billy" Cocks, the member of Congress from
Oyster Bay, came from the summer home of the Presi-
dent and told them that Roosevelt wanted Charles
Evans Hughes.   That settled it.

Hughes was elected, but all other candidates on the
Republican ticket were defeated.

A New York City political incident was connected
with the Hughes nomination.   Herbert Parsons had
been selected for chairman of the New York County

Republican committee, and he was at the head of that delegation and for Hughes. Sometime afterwards, in front of the executive offices in Washington, J. Van Vechten Olcott was saying to a few friends that Roosevelt had selected him for the New York chairmanship, but later switched to Parsons.

"That would make an interesting story," said a newspaper man.

"Don't you print it," said Olcott. "I would be put in the Ananias Club immediately."

"By George," remarked J. Adam Bede of Minnesota, "a man ought not go about without his initiation fee in his pocket all the time."

The Brownsville, Texas, shooting developed into personalities and politics. Three companies of the 25th Infantry, a colored regiment, were stationed at Brownsville, Texas. The people of the town were very resentful, because colored troops were sent to that garrison. There was bitter hostility between the citizens and troops and clashes occurred at different times. Finally, one night there was a general shooting up of the town and one man was killed. The general impression was that negro soldiers had done the shooting. Such was the opinion of the military authorities, although not a word came from any one of the 160 soldiers implicating any of their number, and no direct evidence of their participation in the shooting was ever obtained.

Because none of them would confess Roosevelt, ordered the discharge of the entire battalion. This, of course, precipitated a very great row and brought forth many protests from negroes and their friends.

One of the most important and earnest advocates and defenders of the discharged soldiers was Senator Foraker. He made it the subject of a senatorial investigation, and fought long and earnestly for the soldiers, but without avail. The majority of the Committee on Military Affairs agreed with the army officers, and held that certain unknown men of the battalion had been guilty of the shooting.

A very interesting fact in connection with this Brownsville affair was that it showed a characteristic of the negro little understood. Negroes will not tell on each other. The War Department spent thousands of dollars, and employed sleuths of all kinds to mingle with the discharged soldiers, trying to get them to implicate their comrades, but without result. A chief characteristic of the negro is secretiveness regarding himself and his people.

President Roosevelt relied a great deal upon Secretary Root. His messages to Congress and some of his speeches were frequently revised by the Secretary of State. I happened to see them at work upon a message, both enjoying certain passages which had been written by Roosevelt, but which Root cut out with Roosevelt reluctantly assenting.

As a side-light on Roosevelt's character, his willingness to accommodate, an incident of the occasion is worth telling. I wanted to get a picture of the President signing his Thanksgiving proclamation to go with a story about Thanksgiving at the White House. Roosevelt not only delayed signing the paper until I could get the photographer to the White House, but he interrupted the work on his annual message with his Secretary of State while the photographer arranged the camera and the sitting.

There was one revision of that message which was not due to Secretary Root. The President sent the message out in advance. In it was a paragraph saying that he would send a message to Congress later regarding tariff revision. He sent copies to various Congressional leaders, among them Speaker Cannon. The Speaker told him:

"I like the message, all but one paragraph, that relating to the tariff. If you want to send in a tariff message later, do so, but you had better wait until you are ready before saying anything about it."

The reference to the tariff was cut out of the message by telegraph. What is more, Roosevelt never did send in a tariff message.

During the year 1906 I wrote a magazine article on the attitude of the President upon two important policies, an attitude which had not been announced. The editor of the magazine knew Roosevelt very well, but he doubted whether I had correctly stated the President's position. He sent a proof to Oyster Bay, and in due time it was returned with a few minor changes in Roosevelt's own handwriting in blue pencil. The editor had the corrections made and locked the corrected proof in his safe. I did not ask why, but I always thought he wanted to be prepared in case there was a change of the Presidential mind.

Senator Thomas C. Platt of New York obtained more notoriety about this time than is relished by statesmen, though Platt had reached a stage where he did not much care what was said about him. He married a second time late in life, and this brought forth a claim by another woman who had a lot of letters written by the Senator.

These were finally secured by Platt's friends, but later suits were filed, one of them against Secretary Loeb, who was charged with having helped to procure the letters without sufficient compensation to the woman to whom they were written. Some of these letters developed the humorous streak in the aged Senator.

"I am writing on the spur of the moment without my spurs on," he penned one day.

On another occasion he complained of weariness.

"I have spent the morning at the White House. Think, my dear, of my having to spend two hours opposite those grinning teeth."

At that time Platt was apparently on good terms with the President, but he never really liked him.

Probably the last time that Captain Peary and Dr. Cook, both of unsettled Arctic fame, were ever together at a social function was the annual dinner of the National Geographic Society in Washington. It was a dinner in honor of exploration. Peary received a medal for having reached farthest north. Dr. Cook was there to tell about how he ascended Mt. McKinley in Alaska. It was a thrilling tale. He took us up, up, up, through the ever deepening snow. With him we encamped upon the side of the giant mountain far up among the clouds. We were all shivering in his silken tent as he was trying to light his oil stove, when——

There was a commotion at the door, a rush, a whirl, and a shouting and clapping of hands.

President Roosevelt had appeared.

Dr. Cook sank into his chair. President Willis L. Moore of the Society introduced President Roosevelt, who called up Captain Peary and gave him the gold medal, expressing the hope that the courageous captain would some time reach the pole.

As to Dr. Cook, we never got out of that snow drift, nor to the top of Mt. McKinley. But it was something of a compensation in later years, when Peary and Cook were rival pole discoverers, to know that we went as far toward the summit of that highest Alaskan mountain in imagination as did Cook in actual climbing.

No President ever made more Cabinet changes than Theodore Roosevelt. He had three each in the State Department, the Treasury Department, the Department of Justice, the Department of Commerce and Labor; two in the Interior Department; five in the Post Office Department; and six in the Navy Department. Only one man served throughout Roosevelt's term. That was James Wilson, Secretary of Agriculture, an exception to all Cabinet rules.

Senator Arthur P. Gorman died during the summer.

Gorman long cherished an ambition to be President.
In fact, a man who once becomes an aspirant for the
highest place in the nation never quite gets over the
desire. Like many other men, Gorman saw the grand
prize go elsewhere, and himself passed by while men of
less distinction in his party were nominated. Gorman
was a born politician. Had he lived in a state on the
Presidential Highway he might have been President.

Another man of less renown, but of long service,
passed away during that term of Congress. Senator
William B. Bate of Tennessee died at an advanced age.
He served with distinction in two wars, becoming a
major general in the Confederacy. But it was the war
of his youth, the Mexican war, that remained green in
his memory. Although no orator and seldom addressing the Senate, he one day woke that body almost to a
point of enthusiasm. It was concerning a bill to increase pensions to Mexican veterans, and Senator Bate
told some of his experiences back in the 40's; his de-
scription of scaling the Chapultepec mountain side
reached the height of an oratorical outburst, and surprised the Senate and the galleries. It seemed strange
to listen to a man talking of battles in which he had
participated nearly sixty years before.

CHAPTER III

LINING UP FOR 1908

Senate Clashes Over Roosevelt and the Negro—Tillman Suggests Senate Minstrels—Republicans Wanted to Attack the President—Roosevelt Out for Taft—"May Have To Take Hughes"—Bourne and Beveridge—Third Term Work Stopped—The Harriman Fund and the $5,000,000 Conspiracy.

THE discharge of the negro soldiers continued to be the most exciting and interesting subject during the last months of the Fifty-ninth Congress. Senator Foraker had broken so completely with Roosevelt that there was no possibility of their ever becoming friends. Both were relentless in the pursuit of an enemy, and every day the discussion went on the more bitter became the feeling between them. There was a general impression that Foraker had a two-fold purpose in keeping the negro question open. Taft was the Secretary of War who issued the order and Taft was Roosevelt's candidate for President. If Foraker could make enough out of the negro soldier episode to discredit Roosevelt, Taft might go down with him and leave the Ohio field open to Foraker, who was a candidate for the nomination in 1908.

Discussion of the negro in the Senate naturally produced a heated debate over the race question. It could not be otherwise while Senator Tillman retained his vigor. Most of the Democrats and the Republicans, also, were supporting the position of the President. Foraker had only a small following.

Probably there was no more caustic speech made than that by Senator Spooner, who announced the end of his friendship with Tillman on account of the sentiments expressed one day by the South Carolina Senator upon the negro and those people who spoke for the black race. There was a clash between Tillman and the fiery Senator Carmack of Tennessee, which caused the Senate to shut itself up in secret session and expunge Tillman's remarks.

The row began when Tillman for a second time in the Senate read a speech which he had carefully prepared. He based it on a paragraph in the New York *Sun*, which called him "the burnt cork artist of the Senate." Tillman said the *Sun* had not gone far enough. "I am surprised at both its dullness and failure to illustrate the situation," he said, and continued:

"This debate on the Brownsville incident has given evidence of shining minstrel talent in wholly unexpected places. If I am entitled to a position among the artists as 'Pitchfork Ben' at one end of the line, the *Sun* ought not to have ignored the claim of 'Fire Alarm Joe' [Foraker] to occupy the other. We both do the Orlando Furioso act admirably."

He referred to Clay of Georgia, whose hair stood straight up, as the "pompadour Senator." He complimented the oratorical powers of Daniel of Virginia, but said that Senator took himself too seriously, which greatly offended Daniel as he subsequently showed. Carrying the idea still further, Tillman said:

"As the negro preacher and telephone artist in the show, who on occasion gets into communication with the White House over the wire and acts as receiver and repeater, a veritable chameleon in his accuracy of reproducing White House colors, we have a Senator [Lodge] hailing from Massachusetts, the home of the sacred cod, where the Adamses vote for Douglas and Lodge walks with the Almighty.

"Then comes the star of the troupe, 'Gum Shoe Bill' [Stone] from old Missouri. He can dance the Highland fling on top of a ten rail fence and never touch the ground, but his greatest feat is walking on eggs without breaking the shells.

"We have the Lone Star artist [Culberson], who has suddenly ceased to play the rôle of detective and performs a solo on the bones in praise of the President.

"Next we have the dying swan, 'Smiling Tom' [Patterson] of Colorado, the state recently bought at auction by one Guggenheim, and the swan song is a dirge for the dying Democracy of the North.

"Next we have the redoubted Tennesseean [Carmack], who was once a Knight, a very Hotspur in the lists, whose spear has rung true and clear upon the vizor of the usurper at the White House. Now, alas, no longer of any use, he lays it at the feet of the victorious Roosevelt as a peace offering, and joins the minstrels to sing a last song to the victor of Brownsville, who whistles

Democrats to come to the White House and lick the hand that has so often smote them.

"Last, we have the artist from the Badger state [Spooner], an acrobat and juggler of international reputation. He is supple, sly, and foxy, and having once been a lawyer, is noted for his ability to get on either side of any question."

It was a further reference to Carmack and his recent defeat for the Senate that caused the scene of disorder. Carmack's retort was so severe that it burned deep into Tillman. At one time it was supposed that there was going to be a personal encounter between the two men. Recollecting the row between Tillman and McLaurin, Barney Layton, assistant sergeant-at-arms, moved over to the back part of the Senate chamber, and speaking to Senator Warren, who had assisted him in separating Tillman and McLaurin, said:

"Are you going to stand in with me on this?"

But the actual fight did not occur. Tillman was uneasy and restless, but curbed his anger.

When he attempted to reply Senator Teller cut him off by moving a secret session. Behind closed doors the difficulties were patched up. Tillman's offensive remarks were expunged, and when the doors were opened there were mutual apologies, and there the matter ended.

The opposition of Senator Foraker to the President destroyed the Ohio Senator as a public man. It was another evidence of the disaster which overtakes a man in Congress who differs with the President of his party.

It reminds me of two men who wanted to attack Roosevelt about this time. One was Senator Carter of Montana and the other was Frank W. Cushman of Washington, a member of the House. The President's attitude on public land questions, and also in the appointment of Federal officials, had been very displeasing to western men. Besides, there was a general ill-feeling among many Republicans in both Senate and House over the dictatorial manner of the President, which found expression in much grumbling and talk of a revolt. The malcontents in the Senate had selected Carter to lead an assault on the President, and Cushman had been put forward in the House for the same purpose. Both of these men had a splendid command of caustic language and would have done the subject justice.

On the way from the Capitol one day Carter outlined to me what he proposed to say, and asked me what I thought about it.

"If you are getting ready to quit public life, you have selected a sure method," I replied. "Roosevelt will kill you politically, just as he has killed every other Republican who has stood in his way."

Carter did not make the speech.

To Cushman I said very much the same thing, although it was not so easy to dissuade him. Cushman, by vitriolic utterance and sarcastic language against House leaders, had forced recognition in the House, and he thought he could do the same at the White House, but the precedents of failures which I enumerated finally convinced him that he had better pocket his grievances or let others make the attack upon the President.

During the winter Senator Beveridge made his frantic fight to secure the passage of a bill prohibiting interstate shipments of goods made by child labor. One of the amusing features of the effort was the manner in which the constitutional lawyers of the Senate smiled pityingly upon Beveridge and poked fun at him. He was accused of allowing his vivid imagination to run away with his judgment.

"Senator," said Beveridge, to Knox of Pennsylvania, "if you do not want to wreck your future career, you will support my child labor bill."

Knox used to regale the Senate with similar utterances which the versatile and energetic Indiana Senator poured into his ears. Knox was regarded as the greatest constitutional lawyer of the Senate at that time, and it was amusing to have Beveridge give him instructions as to the fundamental law.

One law passed during the session caused a great deal of comment and amusement in Washington. It was known as Roosevelt's anti-smoke law. It prohibited black smoke in Washington and had teeth in it. As long as Roosevelt was President, it was vigorously enforced and several corporations had to pay fines. Ever since Roosevelt left the White House it has been a dead letter, neither public officials nor private individuals making any effort to have the smoke nuisance eliminated.

Senator Spooner of Wisconsin announced his resigna-

tion and retirement from public life in 1907. At that
time Spooner was regarded as the greatest man in the
Senate. He had a place on the three most important
committees. He was considered an authority on all
subjects, and one of the best equipped men in the
Senate.

Spooner retired before he had to face a battle with
La Follette for a seat in the Senate—with possible
defeat. He would not make the effort necessary to
secure an election, and he knew that La Follette would
let nothing stand in the way to defeat him. The contest between them had been long and bitter. They
represented two different schools of thought, and their
personalities were as different as one could imagine.
Spooner was genial, frank, affable, outspoken, and always pleasant. La Follette was severe, rather cold
and austere, with a sneer rather than a smile, suspicious
in manner, and sometimes repellent. Yet La Follette
gained the ascendency. His school of thought had
triumphed. He would probably have defeated Spooner
had the latter attempted to continue as a Senator from
Wisconsin.

Spooner's relations with all the Senators and with
everybody, in fact, were most pleasant. Even Democrats whom he assailed in partisan debates were his
personal friends.

Among the Senators who closed their careers with
that session were Berry of Arkansas and Blackburn of
Kentucky. Joe Blackburn was the better known,
having been one of the first "Confederate brigadiers"

to break into Congress as far back as 1874. Blackburn was a famous raconteur and had a never-ending supply of stories with which he regaled his friends. Berry was also a soldier of the Confederacy and had left a leg on one of the battlefields of the Civil War. He was always a supporter of anything purely democratic, and especially of the election of Senators by direct vote of the people.

"When I began urging this constitutional change," Berry told me after his defeat, "Senator Hoar used to talk with me about it. He said that with our primary system and the proposed method of electing Senators we would cause a deterioration in the character of the men elected to the Senate. I told him the people could be trusted. But I was mistaken. See what they have done in Arkansas, elected Jeff Davis to succeed me. You will see what I mean when you see that man in the Senate."

With the end of that session of Congress we saw for the last time in the Senate John T. Morgan and Edmund W. Pettus of Alabama. Morgan at the age of eighty-seven and Pettus at the age of eighty-six died during the summer. These two were the last of the Mexican war soldiers in Congress. They had been brigadier generals in the Confederacy, and both were of that sterling, indomitable character that has made America great. In the evening of life they sat side by side in the Senate, saying nothing, but content to be near one another. Their contemporaries had passed away; they were alone in the long twilight of life awaiting the end.

I suppose Senator Morgan lives in memory as one of the great statesman, but I do not recall a single thing he ever did to earn that distinction except to talk. As I remember he was on the losing side of every issue, save when occasionally he supported a Republican President's foreign policy. His speeches were historically accurate, delivered in perfect English, and always showed profound learning and deep research, but they never were convincing. He was a philosopher, a dreamer of great achievements, one of the kind of men that constitute the necessary balance in a big country.

Years before Morgan died and when he was famed for long distance talking, it was remarked of him that "he could set his mouth talking in the morning and come back at night and find it still going."

"How long can you really talk?" the Alabama Senator was once asked, when he was still a vigorous man.

"It depends upon the subject," replied Morgan. "If it is upon a subject which I thoroughly understand and know all about, I suppose I could talk on it for two days. If it was a subject of which I knew nothing I could talk about it for a week."

President Roosevelt came out openly for William H. Taft as his successor, early in March, 1907. At the same time Theodore Burton was picked as Foraker's successor in the Senate. The activity of Roosevelt in these matters greatly angered Foraker, who fiercely denounced the President for going into different states and interfering in the politics of those states.

Mr. Taft was very much undecided up to the time of

the positive announcement by Roosevelt. He wanted to be a Supreme Court Justice. He didn't know what to do when there were apparently two ways open for him. His family finally decided for him, and concluded that they would rather have a President than a Supreme Court Justice on their genealogical tree.

Roosevelt considered other men. At one time his personal preference was Secretary Root. Root also had a high appreciation of Roosevelt. "He will be known," he once told me, "as the great awakener; the man who aroused the people to the great interest they have in the Government." I asked the President why he did not choose Root instead of Taft.

"Root would be the better man," he said, "but I am afraid he could not be elected. There would be serious objection to his corporation record."

He referred to Root's former law practice. Curious, isn't it, that this same "corporation record" has so often been used against Elihu Root?

While it was well understood by any one with a knowledge of politics that Roosevelt would control the next Republican convention and name his successor, it did not prevent other men from being mentioned, and long before the summer was over we had as avowed Presidential aspirants Fairbanks in Indiana, Foraker in Ohio, Knox in Pennsylvania, and Cannon in Illinois, while there was talk of Hughes in New York.

The Hughes candidacy—if such it could be called, and strictly speaking, I suppose, he never was an actual candidate for anything—was one of the peculiarities of the politics of that time. Without solicitation on Hughes' part Roosevelt had nominated him for Governor. Roosevelt used all the power of his Administration to elect Hughes, but the Governor never seemed to be very appreciative. During the spring of 1907 Roosevelt removed Archie Sanders, a Wadsworth man, as collector in western New York, and named another man. A White House statement said it was done at the request of Hughes and for the purpose of strengthening the Governor. Hughes when asked about it said he did not know Sanders; that it was a Federal matter and had nothing to do with the affairs of the State of New York.

We can imagine how well pleased Roosevelt was with that statement. Soon a rumor was published by the White House papers that the whole Sanders-Hughes matter was a mistake of Loeb. "Blame it on Loeb," became quite a favorite expression in those days.

Not long after this incident, and after I had made a trip to Albany, I was at the White House and had a short talk with Roosevelt.

"I have just returned from Albany," I began.

"Yes?" said the President, and after a pause, "What do you think of him?"

"He is Presidential size," I replied.

"Do you think so?" asked Roosevelt, and without waiting for an answer, he snapped out: "Well, we may have to take him. If these labor decisions by Taft become too prominent and promise to lose us a large number of labor votes, we may have to take Hughes."

As if to add a little comedy to the Republican presidential situation, we had Senator Jonathan Bourne of Oregon with his "second-elective-term" proposition, vociferously supporting Roosevelt for another term. A part of the game was Bourne's constant attendance at the White House. He was there more frequently than Senator Beveridge, and Beveridge was there daily. Roosevelt seemed to enjoy the joke as much as anybody.

At one time it looked as if there might be something in the Roosevelt candidacy. I talked with Frank H. Hitchcock, then First Assistant Postmaster General, and found he was lining up the southern men and encouraging everybody to get in line for Roosevelt. This he continued to do until Roosevelt called a halt, and published a general letter to Federal office holders telling them they must stop working for him as a candidate. I asked Roosevelt why he didn't let them go ahead and nominate him, as no one wanted Taft.

"No," he said, "it would not do. There is a very widespread objection to a third term, and no one would accept Bourne's second-elective-term idea seriously. People have come to believe that no one should have what Washington refused and Grant could not get. While I may be very popular, it is a serious question as to whether I could be elected. In seven years a man makes many enemies who would take that opportunity to get even. I will not consider another term."

A great many things happened during this year be-

Lining Up for 1908   41

fore the quadrennial election.   A letter of E. H. Harriman was published, in which Harriman said that Roosevelt had asked him to raise $250,000 for the campaign of 1904.   Roosevelt promptly denounced Harriman as a liar, and, when the facts came out, said the money Harriman raised was for the election of Governor Higgins in New York.

But this little $250,000 was soon smothered in the smoke of the great $5,000,000 conspiracy.   This was another place where Jonathan Bourne came into the lime light.

The Oregon Senator gave a dinner to a number of his fellow Republicans, and when wit and wine flowed freely they joked him about his second-elective-term theory.   They told him that Roosevelt could not win, and one Senator, supposed to be Penrose of Pennsylvania, went so far as to say, "We've got $5,000,000 already pledged by the big corporations to defeat Roosevelt."

Bourne ran over to the White House the next morning with the story.   Roosevelt and Loeb saw the value of it.   The newspaper correspondents were called in and given an outline of the "five-million-dollar conspiracy" to defeat Roosevelt.   This has always been somewhat hazy, for Roosevelt was not a candidate, but a twist was given to it which meant that the Roosevelt policies for trust regulation and the selection of a man to carry out those policies were to be defeated by this gigantic fund.

What chance had that little $250,000 Harriman

story with this one, when there was twenty times the amount of money involved, and to be used against Roosevelt instead of for him?

Roosevelt had no objection to the use of money in political campaigns so long as it was used for a good purpose, such as electing himself or his friends. Large expenditures he seemed to think necessary. But he never believed that a dollar was ever wrongfully used in his behalf.

As to the campaign of 1904, the trusts and corporations contributed, but not so liberally as they did in the two previous campaigns, and only one check was returned. Afterwards, when the Administration was vigorously fighting the beef trust by securing meat inspection legislation, also the Standard Oil Company in the courts, there were murmurs from both that they were not getting a square deal; that when they contributed to the campaign fund they expected fair treatment.

When these reports were taken to Roosevelt he did not know whether to be angry or pleased. He was inclined to be angry because those people thought they could escape by campaign contributions, but he was happy to think that they had been fooled.

Many of the most earnest admirers of Theodore Roosevelt were unable to approve of his action in allowing the consolidation of the Tennessee Fuel and Iron Co. with the United States Steel Corporation. It has been explained by saying that the men interested went to the White House and told the President that the only way a great financial panic could be averted was by allowing the consolidation, or rather the absorption of the Tennessee Company by the Steel Corporation.

"It always seemed to me," said Senator Hansbrough of North Dakota, who had been a warm friend and admirer of Roosevelt, "that the President missed the greatest opportunity of his life when those steel magnates threatened him with a money panic.

"I wish he had said: 'Excuse me a moment, gentlemen, I desire to send for the United States Marshal to place you under arrest. I will direct the Attorney General to take steps to have you indicted for conspiracy against this nation.'

"If Theodore Roosevelt had taken some such action as that when those money kings threatened a money panic, he would have become a still greater popular hero, and the plaudits of the people would have rung from one end of the country to the other."

Senator Beveridge was very active in those days, and he never concealed his knowledge on great public questions. Strolling along the Avenue with him one day, and discussing the Presidential situation, I remarked:

"Senator, you are the logical successor of Theodore Roosevelt."

"I don't want to succeed Roosevelt," responded Beveridge. "The man who succeeds Roosevelt will have too much to contend with and is doomed to unpopularity. If he follows in Roosevelt's footsteps people will say, 'he's aping Teddy'; if he does not do just as Roosevelt has been doing, he will be accused of 'throwing down Roosevelt's policies.'"

What a true prediction the brilliant young Senator from Indiana made!

There never had been cordial terms between Fairbanks and Beveridge. They did not appreciate each other's abilities, and although Beveridge said he did not want to succeed Roosevelt, he thought that he, rather than Fairbanks, should be considered Indiana's favorite son.

Not long after the conversation above related I was taking with Beveridge again.

"Albert," I said, "do you know what I expect to be the greatest speech of your life?"

"When I present the facts about the condition in——"

But I broke in on him:

"No, when you stand up in the 'Republican national convention of 1908 and present the name of Charles Warren Fairbanks for President."

I am afraid my little joke didn't take with Beveridge. It was too serious a matter with him to be a subject for jest.

Roosevelt could do things which would have cost many a man his popularity. Once in handling a case at the government printing office he restored a non-union worker, who had been discharged because he was not a union man. In 1907 when the men were on trial in Idaho for the murder of Governor Stuenenberg, Roosevelt characterized them in a public speech as "undesirable citizens." Certain labor men started to make a point against him, but without success. He seemed to know what to say and what to do so as to strike the popular chord. During the summer he denounced Rev. William J. Long as a "nature faker," and that, also, seemed to win popular approval.

In that splendid book by Rudyard Kipling, *Captains Courageous*, he explains the success of the cod fisherman, Disko Troop, by saying that when Disko was out after cod "he reasoned as a cod." I have often thought that Theodore Roosevelt applied the same principle to men when he was among the people. He seemed to sense what they wanted or were going to want, and became a leader and promoter of what was maturing in their minds.

CHAPTER IV

"IF I AM THE CANDIDATE?"

Bryan, Apparently Undecided, Expresses His Views—Startles and Dismays a Group of Southern Democrats—What Governor Johnson Would Do—Third Term Talk Revived—"I Work With Such Tools as Come to My Hand"—The Fairbanks Cocktail—The Fleet Goes Around the World—Popular Characteristics of the President

"IF I am the candidate——"

It was William J. Bryan speaking in the year 1907. The "if" was unnecessary. Everybody knew he was "the candidate." In order to find out definitely whether there was any use of any other man seeking the Democratic nomination—a man who might have Bryan's support—a committee of Democrats went to see Bryan and asked him about nearly every man in the party who could by any means be considered a possibility. First one and then another man was named, and to each of them Bryan raised an objection which he said was fatal. Finally, one of the committee said:

"Mr. Bryan, we have suggested every man that we could think of, hoping to find a man you would support. Will you tell us frankly if there is any man whom you would support?"

"How would Ollie James do?" asked Bryan.

Then the committee, and every man to whom they

told the story, knew that Bryan must be the nominee.

Following Bryan's return from his trip abroad he had a way of happening into a city or state just when plans were being formulated to elect delegates antagonistic to him. In most cases he was able to frustrate all such attempts and put his opponents to flight or on the defensive. To oppose Bryan in those days was almost Democratic treason.

It was while Bryan was on one of these missions in a southern state that I heard him use the expression:

"If I am the candidate."

I knew he was the candidate at the time, which made his remarks all the more interesting.

It happened at one of those social functions which occasionally develop into a political discussion. All but one of the twenty-four men present were southerners and Democrats.

"If I am the candidate, it will not be necessary to make a declaration in favor of government ownership," Bryan was saying. "It is not opportune now to put that in the platform."

"But why did you say anything about it?" asked Senator Daniel of Virginia. "You are the candidate, why did you want to make a declaration which was so obnoxious to the people of the South?"

"I just said, 'If I am the candidate,'" said Bryan. "I do not know yet whether I shall be the candidate, but if I am the candidate, my position is too well known for me to dodge. When John Sharp Williams came to

see me in London he urged me to avoid all reference to
government ownership in any speeches I made. When
I made my Madison Square Garden speech I said I was
for government ownership. If I had followed Williams's suggestion and if I were the candidate, I would
be asked on every stump if I had changed my opinion,
and I would be forced to declare for government ownership and unnecessarily make it an issue in the
campaign."

There followed quite an extensive discussion of government ownership, in which governors of several states
participated.

"You of the South," declared Bryan, "are opposed
to government ownership because you are afraid your
Jim Crow laws against the negroes will be abolished by
the general government. As if," he scornfully continued, "your personal objections to riding with negroes
should interfere with a great national reform. But I
tell you that government ownership should not be an
issue now. We must wait to see how government
regulation works out.

"You people also complain because I have declared
for the initiative and referendum. That ought to be
an issue," asserted Bryan. "I will drive every man out
of the Democratic party who does not support it."

"Mr. Bryan," almost wailed ex-Senator Berry of
Arkansas, "I want to live long enough to see another
Democratic President, but I am afraid you are making
it impossible. Why can't you leave these impossible
issues and stick to those upon which you can win?"

"Win! Win!" exclaimed Bryan. "That's it! You want to win! You would sacrifice principle for success. I would not. I would not desire to be elected if the principles I stand for were not incorporated in the platform. I am not sure that defeat is not better than victory, if victory comes with the sacrifice of principles. What an empty thing victory would have been in 1904 when so many of the principles of the party had been sacrificed. I intend, if I am the candidate, that the principles shall be preserved."

"But some of the things you have stood for in the past have proved to be wrong," said Senator Daniel, "and you may be wrong again."

"I have always been right," asserted Bryan.

Well, there was a lot more discussion, with Bryan against all the others. And though they agreed with him on scarcely anything, they knew he would be nominated in 1908, and that he would have the delegates from the states of the South.

"What's the use?" afterwards asked Governor Swanson of Virginia, one of the shrewdest politicians in the group. "Bryan is sure to be nominated, and sure to be defeated. Let us hope that will end him and that we can then elect another man four years later."

Sometime later I was telling James K. Jones, who managed two Bryan campaigns, of the occurrence just related, and he said:

"That is just like Bryan. He was a very difficult man to work with in a campaign. He was wayward and dictatorial, and 'always right,' just as you heard him declare."

Not long afterwards I met Judge Alton B. Parker on a train, and in stating that Bryan would be the candidate of the Democratic party for the third time, I mentioned the rather remarkable fact that in seven Presidential campaigns the Democrats had had but three candidates; that Cleveland was three times the nominee and Bryan would have the same distinction. Then Judge Parker quoted a statement made by Cleveland a short time before, when speaking of Bryan:

"It is not because Bryan stings and stings me like a gnat or a fly at every opportunity that I dislike the man," Cleveland said. "That is only a personal annoyance. But Bryan is a constant menace to the country. His perpetual candidacy will prevent the Democrats from winning an election, and the country suffers from long continued control by the Republicans."

An amusing incident of the preliminary campaign happened at one of the many Bryan dinners in a southern state. One of those voluble, enthusiastic individuals, with a gift for *mal à propos* remarks, glibly advised Bryan to ask the next Democratic convention to nominate Theodore Roosevelt for President. In reply Bryan rather grimly remarked:

"As at present advised I will not ask the Democratic national convention to name Roosevelt for President."

While the nomination of Bryan seemed a foregone conclusion, there was at times an effort made by Demo-

crats who did not want him to secure another candidate.
Judge George Gray of Delaware was brought forward,
but he was open to the charge of disloyalty to Bryan
in 1896, besides coming from a small eastern state.   In
other sections where efforts were made to pave the way
for anti-Bryan delegates, they were frustrated by Bryan
appearing in the community for the purpose of deliver-
ing a lecture or an address.   Before he left the in-
cipient anti-Bryan movement was snuffed out.

The most formidable candidate appearing in the
arena was Governor John A. Johnson of Minnesota.   He
had supported Bryan twice, had been elected Governor
twice in a Republican state, and was equipped with
every attribute of a vote getter.   He was a Scandinavian,
and Republican Scandinavians elected him Governor.
It was figured out that there were enough Scandinavian votes in the northern states to make his election
probable.

Soon after Johnson's name had been mentioned he
became very prominent.   Then from Bryan's friends
came the charge that he was "Jim Hill's candidate."
This was soon repudiated, but it became evident that
Bryan would not consent to Johnson's nomination.

"John," I said to him one day, for we had long been
close personal friends, "if you are nominated, Bryan
won't let you win the election.   He will defeat you just
as he defeated Parker."

"If I am nominated, I'll run a different campaign
than that of Parker in 1904," replied Johnson.   "I
won't take nine baths a day in the Hudson and say the

party is clean, and let it go at that. If I am nominated, I'll take Bryan into the campaign with me and
he'll have to show his hand in every state."

Johnson's remark about "baths in the Hudson" had
reference to the daily report from Esopus, N. Y., during the summer of 1904, that Judge Parker was taking
a swim in the Hudson River.

Judge George Gray of Delaware consented to the use
of his name as a candidate on the Democratic ticket.
Like Governor Johnson the Judge was not frightened by
the fact that any man who dared to oppose Bryan was
likely to be charged with being a "tool of the interests,"
"Wall Street's man," or branded in similar terms as
unfit to be the Democratic nominee.

There was another interesting phase of the preliminary Democratic campaign, besides that of Bryan's
sudden appearances in communities where opposition
to him was developing. When a Democrat who was a
Senator or Representative showed a tendency to oppose
Bryan, or countenanced a movement for the election of
delegates opposed to Bryan, he would soon find that a
candidate had entered his field who was shouting
loyalty to the Nebraskan; and the new man would make
such headway that the man in office was forced to declare for Bryan as a matter of self-preservation. To be
suspected of disloyalty to Bryan in those days was almost like buying a ticket to private life. Bryan was as
popular with the masses of Democrats as Roosevelt
was with the masses of Republicans.

Bryan allowed the discussion of candidates to go on

until the middle of November in 1907, when he made a public statement to the effect that, while he would make no effort to obtain the nomination, if the party wanted him he was willing to accept the nomination.

There was no wild enthusiasm for Taft as the Republican candidate, yet everybody was well aware that no other candidate could be named so long as Roosevelt was supporting Taft and efforts were renewed from time to time to make Roosevelt the candidate.

"We would rather have four years more of Roosevelt than a man whom Roosevelt would boss for four years. Besides, we know Roosevelt and we don't know Taft."

That was to a great extent the idea of standpatters. They knew what Taft had said in his speech at Bath, Maine, and feared that Taft meant a radical reduction of the tariff. They knew that, although Roosevelt had in talk threatened tariff revision, he never sent in a message on that subject.

Owing to the renewed talk of a third term Roosevelt republished and reiterated his statement, made on the night of the election in 1904, that under no circumstances would he again be a candidate or accept a nomination, for President.

Much of the third term talk was kept up by the "fair-haired boys." These were a group of journalistic admirers of Roosevelt, who frequented the White House and wrote articles in praise of the President.

The "fair-haired boys" must be differentiated from the "tennis cabinet." The latter were the President's "second line of advice," ranking below Cabinet officers, but officeholders ever ready to be on hand when the President wanted to play tennis, take a long ramble, or in any other way sought entertainment. The principal members of the "tennis cabinet" were Gifford Pinchot, James R. Garfield, and Lawrence Murray. Tennis was the popular game at the White House while Roosevelt was President. The French Ambassador was frequently one of the players.

Here is one of the best of the "tennis cabinet" stories:

Lou Payn went to Washington one day and visited the White House. Now, Lou Payn was an elderly gentleman, dapper and small, always dressed to the minute with gloves, tie, socks, walking stick, blending and harmonizing like a fashion plate. But he was a "bad man." He was one of the small bosses up-state in New York, and so bad a small boss that Roosevelt when Governor removed him from the office of Insurance Commissioner, notwithstanding the protests of Tom Platt, Ben Odell, Bill Barnes, and other members of the New York political machine.

Great was the surprise then, when Lou Payn called at the White House; not only called, but had a long talk with the President. It was quite a sensation.

Later in the day M. Jusserand telephoned to inquire if the President desired to play tennis that afternoon.

"Tell the Ambassador I cannot play to-day," said Roosevelt to the secretary who brought the message, and then turning to the man with whom he was talking, he said:

"I spent an hour or two with Lou Payn to-day, and to assure Pinchot that I have not suffered any contamination I must go and have a long walk with him."

The ultra reformers, the truly good, who were so averse to politicians that they could not tolerate them, who never thought public positions were honestly administered unless they, the reformers, held the offices, were often pained on account of Roosevelt's association with Tom Platt, Bill Barnes, Boies Penrose, and many other purely political politicians, who did not even pretend to be good. They feared that the President would become contaminated. And they will never know that Roosevelt was a better politician than any of the bosses.

"I work with such tools as come to my hand," the President once told me, when this subject was mentioned. "I am not going to quarrel with Platt or any other man. I am going as far as I can in working with the big and little bosses in every state. All I ask of them is that they recommend to me honest men, and I will appoint such men to office when I can."

These politicians seldom recommended the truly good for positions, those men who always bolted the party when they were dissatisfied, consequently a large number of this class feared that Roosevelt was often in dangerous company, and subject to a great deal of bad advice on account of his associations.

A sort of adjunct to those who were voluntarily assisting Roosevelt to be President was developed in a so-called "People's Lobby." This organization carried many distinguished names among its officers and directors. Its announced object was to "lobby for the people," to tell the Congress what legislation ought to be passed and what should be defeated.

Just think of it! Here was an organization, composed of men who had no experience in legislation, living for the most part quiet and retired lives among their books, which assumed to tell Congress, composed of Senators and Representatives from every section of the country, what the people wanted.

It was used by the officeholders, just as any other organization would be used by shrewd men. The "People's Lobby" boosted most of the Administration policies and helped to kill off opponents of the Administration who were becoming obnoxious.

During the summer Vice President Fairbanks became a victim of one of the fool-friends that afflict men in high station. President Roosevelt was passing through Indiana on one of his many trips, and stopped at Indianapolis where he was entertained at luncheon by the Vice President. The fool-friend of Fairbanks thought that the luncheon was incomplete without cocktails and ordered them sent from one of the saloons, and there on the Vice President's table when the guests assembled were the cocktails. President Roosevelt drank the one in front of him, as did other guests who were so inclined.

The capriciousness of the public was shown in the fact that there was no general condemnation of Roosevelt for drinking the cocktail, but the temperance societies severely condemned Vice President Fairbanks for having cocktails on his table. More than that, the Methodist Church refused to send Fairbanks, who never took a drink of anything spirituous, to the Methodist council, but did send Senator Beveridge.

It is almost a tragedy, the way Fairbanks got the worst end of little things. He was cartooned as an icicle, and paragraphists devoted much space to quips about his secretive and reticent manner. As in the cocktail incident, he suffered for much without reason while others went scot free.

"Speak softly and carry a big stick," was one of the phrases that President Roosevelt made famous—a phrase coined when urging greater naval preparation. Thereafter the "Big Stick" became a part of the Roosevelt collection of uniques. Probably no other object has figured so much in the cartoons as this Roosevelt weapon.

No doubt the President had something like the "Big Stick" in mind when he sent the fleet of sixteen battleships around the world. Previous to the sailing of the fleet Japan had expressed dissatisfaction with our objection to Japanese laborers in this country and the efforts of California to deny Japanese the privileges of the public schools. It was asserted by the Administration in the most emphatic terms that the fleet was going on a purely friendly mission, but it was well understood that the real object was to give the Japanese and the rest of the world an opportunity to see that the United States really had a Navy, and that it could be sent abroad if occasion required.

About the time that the fleet was sent around the world President Roosevelt introduced an innovation which stirred the Navy deeply and caused the retirement of Admiral Brownson as Chief of the Bureau of Navigation. The President ordered a surgeon of the Navy to take command of a hospital ship, whereupon line officers made a vigorous protest against the assignment of any staff officer to a position of command at sea. It was a warm controversy while it lasted, but of course the President had his way as Commander-in-Chief of the Army and Navy.

There was one other matter in regard to the Navy in which he did not have his way. He ordered the Marines off the ships, but was overruled by Congress. A provision was inserted in an appropriation bill, which Roosevelt had to sign, restoring the Marines to the ships. The Marines had friends in Congress, in fact they are stronger with the legislative branch of the government than either the Army or the Navy. In every measure designed to increase the personnel and efficiency of the Navy the Marines always secure more advancement than the larger arm of the sea-fighting force.

Roosevelt endeared himself to the young men of the country by the interest he took in sports and everything that pertained to young men. "Don't foul! don't flinch! Hit the line hard," he once told a group of young men. His contempt for "mollycoddles" aroused the unbounded enthusiasm of every virile young man or boy.

Taking such an interest in football as to have the committee on the rules of the game meet with him at the White House was very characteristic of the President. His delight in a good boxing match, and all contests involving strength, skill and courage endeared him to the younger element in the nation. And so, when he summoned the celebrated Japanese wrestler to the White House and had a wrestling match in the East Room of that historic edifice, the youth of the land met every criticism by echoing the President's own "bully!" uttered so frequently when he was well pleased.

CHAPTER V

PRESIDENT DIFFERS WITH CONGRESS

Relations between Executive and Legislative Branches Strained—
Rejection of the Four-Battleship Plan—Rhode Island Senator the
Leader of the Senate—"Third House" Composed of Governors a
Failure.

LEGISLATION and politics were freely mixed in the session in December, 1907. There was the usual demand for tariff revision, but announcements were made by the Republicans that tariff revision would be postponed until after the Presidential election. This did not stop the agitation for immediate action for free pulp and newsprint paper which had been so forcefully urged by the newspapers of the country. In fact the demand for free pulp and paper had more to do with forcing a promise of tariff revision than anything else. James R. Mann, as chairman of a special committee, made an exhaustive inquiry and report on the subject, and thus formed the basis of a stronger demand for a great reduction of duty, if not free trade in pulp and paper.

When the clamor for tariff revision was at its height Speaker Cannon put an end to the speculation by saying that no action would be taken during that Congress, and Uncle Joe was then at the summit of his power in the House.

It was a session of many messages. The President outlined enough work for Congress to keep it busy for ten years, and before one message was fully digested he would send in another. Some of these messages showed that he was fighting hard for his policies, and occasionally he would take a shot at his critics.

In some way there was a belief among the Democrats that Roosevelt was really playing for a third term. To forestall anything of the kind an effort was made to pass an anti-third-term resolution in the House. Henry D. Clayton of Alabama had the resolution in charge and worked industriously to bring it to a vote, but the Republicans would not permit it to reach that stage.

Roosevelt was frequently the subject of bitter attacks in Congress, particularly in the Senate. Democratic Senators who had stood by him in the Brownsville affair, and had been severely criticized for so doing, seemed to be trying to equalize the situation by vitriolic assaults upon the occupant of the White House. Incidentally there were many Republicans who thoroughly enjoyed the attacks upon the President. Senator Bailey of Texas in one of the discussions of Roosevelt said:

"If he were a better man, he would be a Democrat. . . . He is a mixture of good and bad. He may be brave, but he is as rash as he is brave. He is said to be honest, but he is as arbitrary as he is honest. . . . He has done more to change the character and structure of the government than all of his predecessors combined."

Among other severe critics of Roosevelt were Senator

Rayner of Maryland, Senator Culberson of Texas, and Senator Tillman, of course. Rayner often spoke of "presidential usurpation" and "executive dictation." His frequent attacks on Roosevelt indicated personal as well as political antipathy.

Senator Simmons of North Carolina was another vigorous critic of "rule from the White House, which was so apparent in Congress."

Roosevelt did not remain silent under these criticisms, and sometimes hit back in messages or in letters to personal friends which were made public.

It was during his last year in the White House that Roosevelt made his great fight for a naval program of four battleships a year. He sent a special message to Congress pointing out the necessity for such increased construction in order that the country might be adequately prepared. He wanted a large navy to insure peace. Not to provide it was "mischievous folly." The answer of the House of Representatives came the next day when two battleships were voted, while the four-battleship plan was overwhelmingly defeated. The Republican leaders who opposed the President were Cannon, Tawney, Burton, Foss, Payne, Dalzell and Bartholdt, all men of long service and recognized leaders. Tawney, in fighting the program, made the assertion that seventy-two per cent of the revenues of government were used to pay for wars past or in preparation for war.

Roosevelt carried the fight for four battleships to the Senate. His champion in that body was Senator Beveridge. The Indiana Senator was earnest, alert, and constantly in the debate, but his manner, and his unpopularity among his fellow Senators, did more harm than his championship did good. Lodge and other personal friends of the President could not be followers of Beveridge.

Opposition to the four-battleship plan was lead by Aldrich, Allison and Hale, and it was defeated by more than two to one in the Senate.

Senator Aldrich's power in the Senate, despite his antagonism to Roosevelt's policies, or most of them, was surprising. Aldrich had been a leader for years, not only on account of his ability, but because of his close attention to everything pertaining to the Senate. He was always in the Senate or near at hand, and he always knew what was going on, either by personal observation or through the activities of a number of lieutenants who were glad to help him.

Aldrich early in his senatorial career secured a place on the Finance Committee, which gave him prominence, particularly when the membership of that powerful committee was limited to eleven members. He was Chairman of the Committee on Rules for many years. While this committee is not important in one sense, it is in another, because the chairman is brought in close touch with each individual Senator, having the assignment of all rooms and supervision of the Senate wing.

Aldrich made it a point to see many Senators each day. He rarely remained in his own seat, but was forever on the move, oftentimes on the Democratic side.

"He is using his chloroform bottle," once remarked Senator Hansbrough of North Dakota, when Aldrich was moving from one Senator to another. "When Aldrich wants to put something over, either to pass or defeat a bill, he goes about with what I call his chloroform bottle. It is invisible, but I am confident that he carries it in his pocket all the time. He sits down beside a Senator and the first thing that Senator knows he has been chloroformed, and is completely under the Aldrich influence."

What Hansbrough meant to convey was that the charming personality of the Rhode Island Senator was such that he completely captivated men when he wanted to secure their support for any purpose. He was so suave and plausible that a man found himself compelled to agree with him, or promised support before he realized what he was doing.

Roosevelt had occasion to be very much displeased with Congress because it would not provide for the continuation of the Waterways Commission which he had created. Jim Tawney again incurred the President's displeasure by shutting off the appropriation for the Commission.

"If Congress will not perpetuate the Waterways Commission," said the President, in his usual emphatic manner, "I will find a way."

And he did, but Tawney was able to block him again, and this developed a very interesting episode at the close of the Roosevelt administration.

President Roosevelt, among many other experiments,

attempted to organize a "Third House," consisting of the governors of the different states. I suppose the idea he had in mind was that the governors, living among the people, would know better what the people wanted than the Senators and Representatives, also that they would be more independent, and, finally, that when these governors made recommendations Congress would be bound to obey them.

The first conference of governors was called to meet at the White House, and was a very interesting gathering. Then Roosevelt discovered a strange condition. These governors were not of one mind. For the most part they agreed with their delegations in Congress upon the fundamental questions affecting the country and local conditions affecting their states. Some of them were even more outspoken in opposition to the Roosevelt policies than the men in Congress.

I believe the governors did hold subsequent sessions, but one was enough to show that in the matter of legislation the Senate and House must be considered, and the only effective outside influence must come from the White House.

It was during the conference of governors that Roosevelt and Bryan had a sharp difference. Bryan, and a few others in public and business life, had been invited to attend the conference. The differences between the two men, who had been so prominent for so many years, were mainly on the old party lines, Bryan for a time showing concern for states' rights, and Roosevelt protesting against the "twilight zone" between the states and the Federal government, which afforded a refuge for the bad corporations.

President Roosevelt also had a disagreement with Andrew Carnegie in regard to military preparation. It occurred at the laying of the corner-stone of the new building for the Bureau of American Republics. As Carnegie had contributed the money to erect the building, he felt free to express his opinions on disarmament and peace. Roosevelt would not stand for that without making a reply, and took issue with Carnegie, thus providing quite an interesting diversion.

On account of what subsequently happened in politics the commendation of Elihu Root by Theodore Roosevelt on that same occasion is well worth repeating. He said:

"I believe that history will say that, though we have had other great Secretaries of State—and I wish you to remember that I am accustomed to speaking with historical accuracy—we have had none greater than Elihu Root."

CHAPTER VI

ROOSEVELT ELECTS TAFT

Exhibition of Loyalty to "Theodore" by "Will"—Futile Efforts of the "Allies"—Independence of Hughes—Woodrow Wilson Hits Two Popular Favorites—Dinners and Politics—Roosevelt Stampede Fails—Effort to Reduce Southern Representation—"Sage of Fairview" Receives Pilgrims—Demonstrations at Denver—Lack of Political Interest until Roosevelt Injects Ginger into the Campaign—Hughes Again Named for Governor of New York.

WITH his high estimate of Root's ability and his confidence in Root's integrity, it would have seemed logical for Roosevelt to have made his Secretary of State instead of his Secretary of War his successor in the White House. But linked with his belief that Root's corporation connections might be a handicap he evidently feared that Bryan would defeat Root, although he was not usually the victim of fear of any kind. Of course there is another idea, more than a suspicion, that Roosevelt really doubted whether he could control Root after he elected him. Of Taft he was sure. Taft had been a veritable pack horse for the Administration. Roosevelt loaded tons of work upon his Secretary of War, and the harder he was pushed the better work he did.

Taft did little without consulting Roosevelt. They were together a great deal at the White House. I have seen them sit on a sofa, each with a leg curled up and facing each other, earnestly discussing politics and administration affairs.   At such times it was "Theodore" and "Will."

Having decided to make Taft his successor, Roosevelt went about it in his usual aggressive manner. Frank Hitchcock resigned as First Assistant Postmaster General, and began to gather in southern delegates, adopting the methods which Mark Hanna used so successfully in 1896.   This started the story that Roosevelt was using the Federal offices to elect delegates for Taft.   Roosevelt denied the stories in a letter to Wm. Dudley Foulke in which he said:

"The statement that I have used the offices in an effort to nominate any Presidential candidate is both false and malicious."

Of course he didn't use them.   Officeholders didn't need to be told what to do.   They knew that Roosevelt, as a "citizen," was doing all he could to nominate Taft.   They felt that, as "citizens," they had a perfect right to do the same.   And it is my recollection that no Federal officeholder was called to account for supporting the President's choice.

Taft's loyalty to Roosevelt was unquestioned.   He would not allow any one to say anything detrimental about Roosevelt.   On one occasion Simeon Ford, a humorist, was one of the speakers at a Boston banquet when Taft was present.   Ford poked fun at the Chief Executive.   He called him "Theodore the First," and said that he was "a blue pill which the nation had

WILLIAM H. TAFT

to take." His present attitude, said Ford, "makes a noise like a third term."

Taft resented the remarks, and was soon on his feet, saying:

"When I love a chief, and when I admire him from top to toe, I cannot be silent and permit such insinuations, although they may be hidden in a jest."

There was really not much to the preliminary canvass. There was an organization called the "allies," a combination of all other candidates against Taft. The supporters of Fairbanks, Cannon, Knox, Foraker, and others flocked together, for each of these men had so little support that their adherents were lonesome by themselves. I omit Hughes from among the "allies," and for reasons soon to be stated.

In states where there were favorite sons the Taft men made no effort to capture delegates, but they would not have had any such scruples had it been necessary, and such delegates could have been obtained. In other states the Taft, or rather Roosevelt, men gathered up the delegates as fast as the conventions were held.

Massachusetts furnished an interesting incident. Senator Crane, who was at heart for Knox, wanted an uninstructed delegation. In this he was opposed by Congressman Gardner. "I am not in favor of sending a delegation with a 'to whom it may concern' tag on them, and to be delivered at the proper time to some candidate," remarked Gardner.

And that delegation, like many others, was instructed for Taft. At one time when the "allies" seemed to be

making progress, and showed a disposition to contest
many states, Roosevelt confidentially told some sixty
or seventy newspaper men at the White House a little
secret, anent this activity of certain people to defeat
Taft:

"If they don't take Taft, they'll get me."

These joyful tidings went all over the country, and
were followed by such a revival of third term talk as to
call forth an explanation that Roosevelt meant that, if
the opponents of Taft should combine and defeat him,
nothing could prevent a majority of delegates from
nominating the President again, which was the fact.

The candidacy of Governor Hughes, if such it could
be called, was one of the interesting features of the ante-
convention campaign.   He had no campaign manager;
no banners; no boosters; no press agents; in fact, nothing
that usually surrounds the candidate seeking a nomination for the Presidency.   For a long time he ignored
all talk of his candidacy, and it was asserted that one
reason why he was brought out by New York politicians was because Roosevelt wanted another man.

When Hughes consented to the use of his name, he
took the same position he assumed with respect to the
nomination for Governor in 1906.   He would not seek
or solicit support, but was grateful for the confidence
shown in his fitness for the position.

But in spite of this attitude of the Governor, nearly
the entire delegation was for him. Bill Barnes and
a dozen others voted for Taft, but the rest were for
Hughes. Barnes said he was opposed to Hughes,

Roosevelt Elects Taft 71

"because he has no deep concern for the party that created him."

Hughes demonstrated, both in 1908 and 1916 his belief in that oft-quoted phrase, "the office should seek the man."

Early in 1908 Woodrow Wilson delivered an address in Chicago which attracted some attention at the time, though, strange as it may seem, little has been said of it since. His remarks were evidently aimed at the two people who occupied the center of the stage and attracted all the lime light, and because of that, caused more than passing comment. Mr. Wilson criticized "the country's passion for regulative legislation," and "government by commission," adding: "Advocates of government regulation talk of it as a necessary safeguard against socialistic programs of reform, but it seems to me to be itself socialistic in principle. . . . Such methods of regulation, it may be safely predicted, will soon be completely discredited by experience."

There was no doubt that the words were directed at Roosevelt and Bryan, who were then the foremost advocates of government regulation.

As the time for the national conventions approached, it became evident that Taft and Bryan would be the candidates pitted against each other. Not only did these men fight each other at long range in public speeches, but sometimes they clashed in the same gathering. The Gridiron Club enjoyed one such encounter at one of its famous dinners early in 1908, when Taft and Bryan were afforded an opportunity to exchange compliments. It proved a most interesting feature, and everybody who heard them felt sure that they were to be rivals in the great quadrennial contest.

There were Democrats who thought it unwise to nominate Bryan again, and at one time it was proposed that a delegation of the most influential men in the party should go to him and ask him to step aside. When this story was taken to Bryan, he said:

"Men who come to me to speak for the Democratic party must show their credentials."

He knew that only those who had opposed him theretofore would be bold enough to ask him to step aside. He was assured that none of his real supporters would ask him to retire.   A curious idea prevailed in the minds of Democrats who supported Bryan, which was that the oftener a man was defeated the more reason why he should be nominated again.   "We would rather go down to defeat with Bryan than win with another man," said the Bryan followers.

The Republican national convention was held in Chicago in June, and, aside from the shrieks of those who represented the "allies" when Hitchcock's steam roller was at work throwing out the anti-Taft delegates, there was not much real interest in the preliminaries. Taft was to be nominated; the question accordingly was centered on the Vice Presidency, and a contest for Vice President does not afford much genuine convention excitement.

A great many men were suggested for second place,

among them Senator Dolliver of Iowa. Two objections
were raised against Dolliver. One came through Congressman Dick Bartholdt of Missouri, who said that
Dolliver's record in favor of prohibition would cost two
million votes controlled by the liquor interests. This
was not very important, because the threat was not
taken seriously. The really important objection came
from Iowa. It was voiced by Congressman John F.
Lacey, who said:

"We have just concluded a fight within our party in
Iowa and with Allison we defeated Cummins. If
Dolliver is taken out of the Senate, it will mean the
renewal of that fight, for Cummins will be a candidate,
and some one representing our faction will enter the race
against him. Another Cummins and anti-Cummins
fight will disrupt the Republican party of Iowa."

That practically settled the question. Besides, Dolliver was not anxious to be shelved by a Vice Presidential
nomination.

New York's position was peculiar. As often is the
case, New York went to the convention with a Presidential candidate, but really anxious to nominate
another man for second place on the ticket. Their
man was James S. Sherman, then a member of the
House. On June 13th, a week before the nomination,
I published a story that Sherman would be the nominee
with Taft. It was inevitable, as it always had been,
that New York would be allowed to name the tail
of the ticket, with a western man for President.

As the delegation had been elected for Hughes and

was under instructions for him, it was in an amusing
plight.   Finally, Herbert Parsons, he who had been the
Hughes leader two years before, was selected to "bell
the cat."   He sent a long telegram to Governor Hughes
explaining that the New York delegation was embarrassed; that as long as it supported him for President
it could not make a fight for Vice President, which
the delegates desired to do in the face of the fact that
Taft was sure to be nominated for President.   The
reply of Hughes was of the kind that made him still
more unpopular with the New York leaders.   He said
he had not been a candidate, had not sought the nomination nor urged the election of delegates in his behalf,
and that he would not take any steps to influence those
delegates.   They were free to act as they desired.   Not
having asked their support, he would not presume to
decline it at that time.

So there was nothing for the New Yorkers to do but
to go forward and vote for Hughes for President, supporting him openly, but secretly planning the nomination of Sherman on the ticket with Taft.

The high light in the convention was a sentence
uttered by Senator Lodge when he made his speech as
permanent chairman.   Detailing the achievements of
Roosevelt, he said:

"The result is that the President is the best abused
and the most popular man in the United States to-day."

The convention went wild and for nearly an hour the
cheers and roars of applause were continued.   After
the first ten minutes the demonstration was one of the

"manufactured" kind, carried on by interested shouters. The supporters of the "allies" were the chief instigators. They had reached an anti-Taft frenzy, which led them to desire the renomination of Roosevelt in preference to Taft.

Lodge let the demonstration continue and enjoyed it, for Roosevelt was his friend. He never was an enthusiastic Taft man. As I saw him sitting there, it occurred to me that Lodge might well have been wondering why he, the most intimate friend of the powerful President, could not have been made his heir.

But Lodge had another reason for enjoying the situation. He was even then ready to pour a cold douche over the "allies," for when he resumed his speech, he said:

"The President retires, by his own determination, from his high office on the fourth of March next. His refusal of a renomination, dictated by the loftiest motives and by a noble loyalty to American traditions, is final and irrevocable."

One other interesting feature of the convention was the almost successful movement to reduce southern representation in Republican national conventions. It was led by James Francis Burke of Pennsylvania, and only the most earnest work by the Roosevelt men prevented the adoption of the minority report. It seems to have been the irony of fate that the failure of that movement had far-reaching effects four years later. But for the full representation of southern states Roosevelt would have been nominated in 1912.

One of the most active men against the Burke minority report was Frank B. Kellogg of Minnesota, whose reward is a bit of interesting aftermath. The Minnesota delegation liked the Burke proposition and decided unanimously to support it, but the influence of Kellogg was sufficient to win half of them to the other side.

One of the Minnesota delegates was Walter W. Heffelfinger, the giant Yale football player.

"Why not support this minority report?" he asked in the Minnesota caucus. "It's a good thing; it's right; let's put it over."

"You can't run a national convention as you would a football game," remarked William Henry Eustis, another delegate. "This is a political game."

The Burke amendment was defeated by only thirty five majority, with such states as Colorado, Connecticut, Illinois, Indiana, Maine, Massachusetts, New Jersey, New York, Pennsylvania, South Dakota, Utah, Vermont and West Virginia, voting solidly for it. The solid vote of the South and the states dominated entirely by the Roosevelt influence defeated the Burke amendment. It so happened that California, Idaho, Kansas, Minnesota, and scattering votes from other states so intensely for Roosevelt in 1912, voted for the continuation of a condition which made Taft's second nomination possible.

There was an underlying influence which had great weight in determining the question favorably to the South. There was much dissatisfaction among the negroes on account of the dismissal of the battalion of the 25th infantry as a result of the shooting up of Brownsville. It was feared that to add another cause of dissatisfaction might alienate the negroes in a number of states necessary to Republican success and endanger the national ticket. Threats of negro revolts in Illinois, Indiana, Ohio, West Virginia and Delaware were freely made. The same fear of alienating the negroes in these states and giving them to the Democrats controlled as in the previous conventions.

Lincoln, Nebraska, in the summer of 1908 had an opportunity to entertain nearly as many distinguished Democrats as Denver, Colorado. Lincoln was almost on the direct route to Denver for most of the delegates, and a great many stopped to consult the "Sage of Fairview" before going on to Denver to nominate him a third time for President.

Those pilgrims, if they were inclined to be observing and analytical, must have learned something about William J. Bryan, even if they learned very little from him. They should have learned that Bryan was the most secretive man who had ever been prominent in public affairs. Men who had been intimately associated with Bryan from the time of his first campaign saw him and talked with him, and they found out as much about what Bryan intended to do as he wanted them to know—and no more. I spent several days at Lincoln, more for the purpose of writing the personal side of the candidate than to obtain his political views, but of course I tried to get a line on what the platform would be, and also his choice for Vice President. I

learned just as much as did his intimate associates, for
in talking with them when they reached Denver I
found they had been told just as much as I, which was
nothing. Bryan did not let the platform get into any
one's possession until after the committee was appointed, and then the important features were given
over the long distance telephone.

Bryan never took any one into his confidence, and to
my knowledge never discussed politics or public questions in that intimate, personal way so characteristic
of all other public men.   I have never known any man
who thought he could speak for Bryan, or could give a
hint as to what Bryan was going to do.   Anticipating,
I may say this was equally true during the time he was
with the Wilson administration, as it was in politics
before he held an official position.

One thing Bryan told everybody; he said he was going
to be elected.   It was after this statement to me that I
said that he would have to give up a very beautiful
home, but that the White House was also considered
a very comfortable residence.

"It is my chief regret," replied Bryan, "that I must
give up my home for four years, but I must make the
sacrifice."

There was nothing in the Denver convention save
two Bryan demonstrations, one when the blind Senator
from Oklahoma, Gore, mentioned Bryan's name.   It
being near midnight and with nothing to do the crowd
spent an hour cheering and marching about the hall.
The second time was when Bryan was placed in nomina-

tion. Then the demonstration was even longer, although the convention had a lot to do, and it was also in the middle of the night.

The Bryanites were impatient over the speeches nominating Governor Johnson and Judge Gray, and the orators were almost howled off the platform.

The nomination of John W. Kern for Vice President ended the convention, which was as tame as the Democratic convention of 1888, and as all conventions are when dominated by one man.

There was just one little side-light at the convention. Mrs. Nicholas Longworth, daughter of President Roosevelt, and Mrs. Ruth Bryan Leavitt, daughter of Mr. Bryan, were both in Denver. They were in the receiving line at one of the receptions given to entertain the wives of prominent men, and the toady *par excellence* passed by, shaking hands.

To Mrs. Longworth he said: "I have voted twice for your father and I hope to vote for him again."

Then to Mrs. Leavitt: "I have voted twice for your father and I hope to vote for him again."

But the acute ears of Mrs. Longworth heard him.

"Oh, the fraud!" she cried, addressing Mrs. Leavitt, "he just said the same thing to me."

Owing to the fact that Bryan was making a third race and that Roosevelt was running a man of his choice as his successor, there was very little interest in the campaign. The West was the center of greatest activity, as the big fight was being made in that section. The Democratic headquarters was a very busy place,

full of life and confidence. The Republican headquarters was a cave of gloom, "the morgue," it was
called by the newspaper men.

Frank H. Hitchcock, who had been selected after a
spirited contest as chairman of the national committee,
was on the go most of the time. It was said that he
found "the morgue" so depressing that he would immediately take a train for New York. In New York
the gloom was so thick that he would at once leave for
Chicago. Roosevelt was running the Republican campaign, and there never was any interest at either the
headquarters in New York or Chicago.

An incident was a newspaper controversy between
Roosevelt and Bryan. It grew out of the Hearst-
Foraker-Archbold letters, which I mention only to say
that they contributed to the plan of Roosevelt to retire
Foraker to private life. However, there was a clash
between Prince Hal and Hotspur—on paper—and it was
a fierce battle while it lasted. Finally, Bryan began to
hit below the belt—at least he was getting under the
skin—and every devotee of the prize ring is aware that
a rigid referee would allow a claim of foul under such
circumstances. And so Roosevelt, in a statement from
the White House, said that Bryan had turned the discussion into personalities and he (Roosevelt) would not
continue it further.

Roosevelt could give Bryan cards and spades and
big casino in the game of politics, and then cut circles
around him. The metaphor is a little mixed, but to
express it more plainly, let me say that, in this political

game, Bryan was an infant—an over confident infant
—matched with a trained gladiator.

A short time after the Roosevelt-Bryan controversy
I was passing through Washington and called at the
White House. Roosevelt was in particularly fine
fettle. I mentioned the correspondence and suggested
that he showed wisdom in stopping at the right time.

A broad grin overspread his countenance.

"I thought there ought to be some ginger injected
into the campaign," he said.

During the summer the New York Republican situation became very acute. The Republican bosses were
antagonistic to Governor Hughes and did not want him
renominated. President Roosevelt was not fond of
Hughes and would have thrown him overboard, save
for one thing. There were times when Roosevelt became uneasy politically. Just as in 1904, when he
appealed to Harriman, in 1908 he was afraid of the consequences if Hughes should be dumped at the behest of
political bosses. Hughes had never shown the least
gratitude towards Roosevelt for the nomination of 1906,
and had gone his way independently.

When it came to a point where Roosevelt had to
decide, a press dispatch from Oyster Bay stated:

"President Roosevelt has ordered the renomination
of Governor Hughes."

Of course that settled it. The machine Republicans
of New York had been accustomed to taking orders
from their boss, and they never had a more imperious
boss than Roosevelt.

Soon after Hughes was nominated he made a tour of
the country. In his speeches are found the only genuine
and intelligent discussion of the campaign issues. It
was that series of speeches which made Hughes a
Presidential possibility in after years.

Mr. Taft had the powerful support of many influential
Catholics. His negotiations with the Vatican in regard to the friar lands and his treatment of the Catholics
in the Philippines made him many friends. It is true
that after his nomination his religion became an issue,
and many strong orthodox Protestant churchmen asserted that Taft, being a Unitarian, was no more than
a heretic. But that did not affect him with the Catholics. The vote showed what an important factor the
Catholics were in the election. Again Tammany was
unable to hold a great body of its voters, and the big
city, so potential in deciding Presidential elections, for a
second time gave a majority against Bryan.

A number of interesting things outside of politics happened during the Summer. One of them was
the ninety-mile test ride which Roosevelt prescribed for
army officers. They criticized it, but they had to ride
thirty miles a day on three different days. Roosevelt
had made the distance in one day, and he thought the
officers ought to be able to ride the distance in three
days. Roosevelt was accompanied on his ninety-mile
ride by Dr. Cary T. Grayson, a young surgeon in the
medical corps of the Navy.

On one occasion late in the Fall Roosevelt invited
about forty army officers stationed in Washington to

meet him at the White House. He proposed a ramble
in the woods, which all accepted. An invitation from
the President to an army or navy officer is the same
as a command, because the President is commander-in-
chief.

And so they set out, Roosevelt and Wood in the lead
and the others trailing along. The President led them
out through Rock Creek Park. When he came to a
place where the water was deepest he plunged in up to
his neck and scrambled up the opposite bank. Some
of the officers balked, one voicing the sentiment of
several others when he said: "I'm not going to
make a damn fool of myself."

But others felt they ought to be as game as the commander-in-chief, and so they followed through the
stream, and wet and bedraggled they climbed steep
hill sides and tore through underbrush. Those who
remained to the finish were a sorry looking lot when
they trailed back to town shivering and disgusted.

Senator Allison of Iowa died that summer, closing
the longest continuous service ever known in the Senate. He was one of the most likable men in the Senate
and the least positive. He never expressed an
opinion, if there was any way of side-stepping and
avoiding directness. Scores of jokes have been told
about this trait of Allison, some of which were invented.
He was one of the perpetual and unsuccessful candidates for President. He was offered cabinet places
several times by Republican Presidents, but declined
because he thought the Senate a better field.

For nearly thirty years in the Senate Allison was one of the "Big Six," the group of half a dozen Senators who managed the Senate. His vigor and long service gave him a dominance that few men ever attained. Had he lived, it is quite possible that the Payne-Aldrich tariff law might have been a different measure. It might have been more liberal, more western, and not so much a measure for that region east of the Alleghany mountains.

CHAPTER VII

Taft Makes a Discovery: "The King is Dead; Long Live the King"—Last Days of Roosevelt in the White House—Bitter Contest with Congress—Secret Service and the National Legislators—Final Clash with Tillman—Had a "Bully Time" as President.

SOMETHING very strange happened in the life of William H. Taft almost immediately after election. He made a discovery. Men who had been coming to him with statements to the effect that President Roosevelt says "do this" or "do that," began to approach him with an almost fawning manner. Taft had been bossed so long, had been under direct orders of superiors for so many years, that the change was something wonderful. He was free, and he began to feel his freedom and exercise it, as a young bird does its wings when it first begins to fly. He did not break with Roosevelt; he still felt profound gratitude to the President for all that had been done for him, but he began to realize that Taft, as President-elect with four years before him in the White House, was a bigger man than Roosevelt with only four months to serve in that historic edifice.

Taft's gratitude to Roosevelt was shown in a note to the President in which he wrote:

"Next to my brother I owe more to you than to any
one man for my election."

"He puts money above brains," was Roosevelt's
sarcastic comment.

Charles P. Taft had financed the Taft campaign, but
it was Roosevelt who had really made Taft the nominee
and elected him.

Taft continued to make the White House his home
when in Washington. Elsewhere he found himself
surrounded and sought after by men who wanted something done; who wanted positions for themselves and
friends. He began to realize that he was the big man
of affairs; that he was the man of power and influence.

While this idea was sinking into the mind of the
President-elect a certain group—those who had assumed to shape Presidential politics—gave it out that
Speaker Cannon was not a sincere friend of tariff revision and ought to be replaced by another man. Taft
announced that "tariff revision should be honest and
thorough."

Encouraged by this announcement the fight against
Cannon was made with redoubled efforts. Then came
a change. The Cannon men, the standpatters, the Old
Guard, if you please, served notice on Taft that if he
wanted a fight in the party at the beginning of his Administration he could get it at once. This defiance
had the expected effect. There were many conferences
between himself and the Republican leaders in Congress, and very soon it was stated that there was perfect harmony between the President-elect and the

Speaker; that Mr. Cannon would have no opposition from the new Administration.

But the curious thing about the whole affair was that it had all the appearance of a victory for Cannon and the standpatters. Had Roosevelt been in Taft's place, no matter how the affair was arranged, it would have appeared before the public as a Roosevelt victory.

Roosevelt had many disagreements with Speaker Cannon during their long association. Cannon did not always strike his colors to the impetuous President, and Roosevelt knew that Cannon could not be crowded into a corner without making a fight.

On one occasion a group of men were urging a certain measure, and the opposition of Speaker Cannon was put forward as the only obstacle.

"Mr. President," said one of them, earnestly, "you must lay down on Uncle Joe."

"It will be a good deal like laying down on a hedgehog," retorted the President.

The last three months of Roosevelt's term were stormy in the extreme. The disagreements he had with Congress became intensified, as men who had long bowed to his will began to show a spirit of revolt.

"Roosevelt's star has set; he is no longer a power," Senator John Kean of New Jersey said to me. His remark was not important, save that he voiced the opinion of Aldrich, Hale, Crane, and other Senate leaders who were antagonistic to Roosevelt.

In the House the opposition to Roosevelt centered around James A. Tawney of Minnesota, Chairman of the Committee on Appropriations. Associated with Tawney were Walter I. Smith of Iowa and John J. Fitzgerald of New York, all members of the Appropriations Committee. Smith was an able representative, but belonged to that wing of Iowa Republicanism which opposed the ideas of Cummins and others who were known as progressives. For party reasons, if for no other, Fitzgerald, a Democrat, was opposed to Roosevelt.

One of the first outbreaks in the short session came when the committee began consideration of an appropriation bill, and mention was made of the old Pennsylvania railroad station. This structure stood upon a government reservation. Tawney and other economists saw an opportunity to use it for offices or storage. But during the recess of Congress Roosevelt had ordered it removed.

"We have no money for that purpose," explained the superintendent of public buildings and grounds.

"I have found a man who will remove it for the material," replied Roosevelt. "Set him to work at once."

And when the members of the committee came back to Washington they found the old station site bare. They called the superintendent before them, intending to thrash Roosevelt over his shoulders, but he told a straight story, and Roosevelt was chuckling with glee at the other end of the Avenue. Six years later the site of that old station became fine tennis courts. In the summer of 1918 these gave place, as well as many fine trees in the adjacent park, to adobe-looking structures which sheltered the largely increased clerical force engaged in war work.

But that was just a beginning. Congress, under the leadership of Tawney, had struck at the secret service, not only curtailing the activities of the bureau which goes by that name, and which is only a small part of the system, but severely criticizing the sleuths in all departments. Tawney had said that from nine to ten million dollars annually were expended for the spy system, various departments having special agents, inspectors, etc., but all doing detective work.

Roosevelt took an opportunity in his first message to hit his enemies and stand up for the secret service. His message gave an intimation that one reason why Congressmen wanted the activities of the secret service curtailed was because they, themselves, feared investigations, and he referred to cases in which special agents of the Interior Department and inspectors of the Post-office Department had secured the conviction of two Senators.

Then went up a wild rumor that Roosevelt had secret service men trailing Senators and Representatives, and great indignation was expressed.

Roosevelt let the idea circulate through his well-organized press service that reports of secret service men on Congressmen would prove interesting reading if sent in as a special message.

Then there was consternation. No man would care to have all his movements shadowed and a public report made upon them. Both House and Senate showed their indignation in resolutions. The House went so far as to refuse to refer the message to various committees, a time-honored custom, and laid the secret service message on the table as a rebuke, about equal in effect to a small boy making faces at the sister of another boy who had thrashed him.

The Senate took other means of showing its resentment. Roosevelt was severely criticized for his refusal to restore the negro soldiers dismissed on account of the Brownsville affair, and also for permitting the consolidation of the Tennessee Fuel and Iron Company with the Steel Corporation.   The Senate passed a resolution calling upon the Attorney General for the papers in the case. Roosevelt directed the Attorney General to deliver the papers to him at the White House. He locked them up in a safe, and in a letter to the Senate told that body politely, but in terms that stung, that the action taken was none of its business.

Senator Tillman was the most violent and vitriolic in denouncing Roosevelt. The Prince Henry dinner incident rankled, while everything said and done by Roosevelt seemed to anger the South Carolinian.

Early in January, 1909, the President sent to Senator Hale, acting Chairman of the Committee on Appropriations, a copy of a document, prepared for the Senate and the press, and sent out to be released when Hale received it.   This document contained an investigation by the special agents of the government into land questions in Oregon, and showed that Senator Tillman had been trying to secure lands which would become valuable in the future. It was an unpleasant kind of notoriety for a Senator because the lands were a part of the government domain.

Tillman made an explanation, but it was not up to his standard. It was of the kind to excite sympathy. Before that time Tillman's speeches were such as to excite admiration or anger, but never pity. I recollect that in the gallery was the wife of a southern Governor, then visiting in Washington, and as she left the Senate she remarked:

"Poor old man, I felt very sorry for him."

That night there was a reception at the residence of Vice President Fairbanks. The Governor's wife who had spoken of Tillman was there. She was well known to the President, as he had been a guest at the home of the Governor. It so happened that the lady and myself came face to face with the President as he was passing through one of the rooms accompanied by his military aides.

His greetings were cordial, and pleasantries regarding his visit in the South were exchanged, but he was bubbling over with excitement. Turning from the lady and addressing me, he said:

"Did you see! I got the goods on old Ben Tillman!"

It was almost an explosion of boastfulness.

I drew the lady away. Her face was flushed and I did not know what she might say.

"Well," she exclaimed, when we had moved a short distance, "it's well you looked out for your friend. I was on the point of slapping his face."

In one of his counter-attacks upon the President,
Tillman charged that his mail was being tampered with
and his letters opened. That might have been true.
Senator Foraker told me, when he was having his difficulties with Roosevelt, that his letters were opened in
transit. A man I knew, who had a great deal of difficulty with the Postoffice Department, resorted to every
method to keep the contents of his letters from the
department officials, using sealing wax and other pro-
tective measures, but it was no use. One of the officials
told him to save his time as the inspectors had the art
down fine, and could open any letter and reseal it so
that nothing could be actually proved.

President Roosevelt had a very interesting and exciting winter. He knew that many men in his own party
thought he was a "dead one" and rejoiced thereat.
He intended to make them understand that he was
President up to the last moment. This he did by sending frequent messages to Congress, and by other means
which kept him before the public.

Through the Department of Justice he had two newspaper editors indicted for criminal libel because of
something they had published concerning him and the
Panama canal. Nearly eighteen months later a Federal
judge dismissed one of the indictments, and Roosevelt's
comments were in his usual vigorous style and were
really the beginning of his attacks upon the courts.

Congress was thoroughly aroused and antagonistic
towards the President. The House, under the leadership of Tawney, put into the sundry civil appropriation

bill amendments which were particularly distasteful to Roosevelt. One of them still further curtailed the activities of the secret service, and another made it impossible to continue the various commissions which the President had appointed.

One was the famous "Homes Commission." The ridicule heaped upon this commission, which toured the country in an effort to uplift the farmer, caused Roosevelt more irritation than anything that had happened during his term in the White House. The commission was pictured in high hats and frock coats, going among the farmers and telling them how to live. Its usefulness was destroyed by laughter. Five years later, one of the commissioners became Ambassador to Great Britain.

Roosevelt did not veto the bill which contained the obnoxious provisions, but in signing it he attached a memorandum severely arraigning the men who were responsible, saying that the action in regard to the secret service would "only help the criminal classes."

A year later President Taft appointed Walter I. Smith, one of the men responsible for the legislation, a judge of the Federal court. Two years later, when Roosevelt's influence in the First Minnesota district defeated James A. Tawney, Taft named Tawney for a fat job on a Federal commission which had been created for "lame ducks."

Before he retired President Roosevelt had the pleasure of welcoming the fleet from its wonderful trip around the world. The sixteen battleships steamed

majestically between the Virginia Capes, whence they
had sailed more than a year before, and each boomed
a salute of twenty-one guns as they passed the May-
flower, with the President on board. It had been a
magnificent cruise and one which had served well its
purpose, that of convincing the powers of the world
that the United States had a Navy.

Roosevelt was always proud of the Navy and gave
a great deal of attention to it. He thought it an excellent service. A girl once called to see him concerning a brother in the Navy. He was very much
interested until she told him that since her brother's
enlistment he found he did not like it and she wanted
to get him out.

"He ought to be man enough to stand his term,"
replied Roosevelt with some fire, and when the girl
seemed to be scared, he added with more kindness:
"You would be sorry if you should get him out. You
will see what I mean when he comes home after having
done his duty as a man should do it."

Roosevelt as President had his own way—most of the
time. Unlike some men he would not persist when he
saw that he could not win. He would take another
course and become the leader of something that could
win.

Roosevelt exacted obedience from those close to him.
Men might differ with his views, but they were not
allowed to put their views in operation. The person
who flattered Roosevelt and always agreed with him
could become his parasite—and he had many such

about him, as well as others who were his sincere supporters and admirers.

Roosevelt knew what was going on all the time. He had the best information bureau of any man I ever knew. He not only believed in the secret service system, but the army of Federal detectives believed in him as a friend and tried their best to serve him. Besides these he had a vast number of volunteer detectives among those who always had been his devoted friends. They belonged to all classes, clerks, printers, typewriters, telegraph operators, stenographers, and men in other walks of life. Information concerning what people were doing and what they were saying, particularly as it affected Roosevelt, was constantly being conveyed to him direct, or into channels which would reach him. He knew the attitude of nearly every man of any influence in the country towards himself.

No man was ever more prolific with messages to Congress than Roosevelt. It suited his idea of authority to tell Congress what it ought to do. During the seven and one-half years he was President he sent 421 messages to Congress treating of public affairs. More than 100 of these were sent in during the last two years of his service.

A short time before the close of his term I saw him at an official reception. He seemed to want everybody to understand that he was not leaving with regrets, for he was in a livelier mood than I had seen him for many days. In the course of his progress through the crowded rooms we met. His greeting was more than cordial.

"This man has been with me from the beginning," he cried. "You remember back when I was Civil Service Commissioner, when we made Tom Reed Speaker?"

There was a good deal more of reminiscence, and then I asked him if he had any regrets about leaving the Presidency.

"Yes and no," he replied. "I have had a bully time and I have done something worth doing. I won't say that I like giving up all that I must give up, but it is right for me to go and I am going without vain regrets, well satisfied with the work I have done and the enjoyment it has given me."

And he played the game right up to the last moment. He rode to the Capitol with Mr. Taft, remained throughout the inauguration ceremonies, and when they were over he rode away in a covered carriage, to which clung several secret service men as it ploughed through the snow and slush of an awful storm towards the railroad station.

CHAPTER VIII

A MARKED CHANGE

Striking Difference Between the Roosevelt and Taft Administrations—
The Old Crowd Not Recognized, While Standpatters Are Re-
ceived—Tariff Revision and Its Train of Troubles—Dolliver-
Aldrich Row—"Traded for Borah and Were Cheated"—The
President on a Vacation and Western Tour.

PRESIDENT-ELECT TAFT devoted a good portion of his time during the winter of 1908–1909 to
selecting his Cabinet.   He had considerable difficulty,
as there were various interests to consider.   The recommendations of Roosevelt were embarrassing.   It was
well understood that Roosevelt would have been
pleased to have Frank B. Kellogg of Minnesota made
Attorney General, but Taft chose George W. Wicker-
sham of New York for that position.

He chose Philander C. Knox of Pennsylvania for
Secretary of State.   Everybody thought it was a most
excellent appointment, but the surprising feature was
that none of the great constitutional lawyers around
Taft or in the Senate knew that Knox was con-
stitutionally ineligible, because the salary of the office
to which he was appointed had been increased during
the term for which Knox had been elected to the Senate.
It was a newspaper man who made the discovery.

Congress attempted to remedy this defect by reducing the salary of the Secretary of State. And so Knox became the premier.

There was considerable discussion concerning the Treasury portfolio, and finally the office was bestowed upon Franklin MacVeagh of Chicago. The next highest position, Secretary of War, also went to a Chicago man, Jacob M. Dickinson, which caused a prominent Republican of that city to remark:

"Taft has selected two men from my ward for the Cabinet—both of them Democrats."

Roosevelt wanted Truman H. Newberry retained as Secretary of the Navy, but Taft could not do this, as he had to transfer George von L. Meyer from the Post-office Department to the Navy in order to make a place for Frank H. Hitchcock, who had been the campaign manager. To return Meyer to private life at that time would have disturbed a settled condition in the Republican politics of Massachusetts.

Mr. Taft found opportunity to travel during the winter. He spent several weeks in Georgia, and played golf with politicians who followed him to that southern clime. Then he went to Panama to inspect the canal work.

While in the South during the winter Mr. Taft made a number of speeches, in one of which he said that the Republican party in the southern states was "no longer to be run for convention votes." This was something of a surprise, for the collection of southern delegates by the old Hanna methods had greatly assisted Taft's nomination. And, to anticipate a few years, it was found that the Republican party in the South, "run for convention votes," was absolutely necessary to secure Taft's second nomination in 1912.

It was unofficially known that President Taft would call Congress in extra session to revise the tariff, consequently the Ways and Means Committee held hearings during the winter. These hearings for the most part ran along as usual. Men came before the committee and told the same stories. There were some enlivening occasions when Champ Clark would cross-examine advocates of high protection, and occasionally there were exchanges of repartee that were interesting.

One witness created a mild sensation. When he appeared Chairman Payne asked him whom he represented.

"The people," he said with some embarrassment, explaining that the people were interested in free lumber.

That caused smiles, some of derision, and guffaws. As a consequence there were some stirring stories written about the occurrence. The country was regaled with indignant and pathetic tales about the man who was almost laughed out of the room because he dared to say that he represented "the people."

As a matter of fact, he represented a number of wealthy American citizens who had bought immense timber tracts in British Columbia, and were trying to remove the duty on lumber. It would have been somewhat embarrassing for this Minnesota man to have

named the several Minnesota lumber barons he was
really representing.

One feature of those hearings which is worth record-
ing was the creation by Henry S. Boutell of Illinois of a
new character in tariff talk. This was the "Ultimate
Consumer." Every witness was questioned by Boutell
as to what result a change of duty would have upon the
ultimate consumer, and so the "Ultimate Consumer"
became a fixture in the tariff.

The tariff was also discussed casually by the President-elect and Senator Aldrich, Chairman of the Senate
Finance Committee. One of these conferences took
place when Taft was paying a flying visit to the
White House. Other leaders also saw him when he
visited Washington and they, as well as those who
visited him in the South, began to speak of him as a
"man of judicial temperament," while others went
farther and talked about a "reign of reason in the
White House." It was also observed that the group
of men who were known as "the allies" and their
supporters before Taft was nominated at Chicago, were
getting to be quite friendly with the President-elect.
It began to percolate through the minds of a few observers that Taft, Roosevelt's radical cabinet officer,
would not be such an out-and-out radical as had been
anticipated when Roosevelt selected him for President.

Finally, the awful March 4, 1909, arrived. The
worst storm ever experienced in Washington at that
time of year greeted the hundreds of thousands who
came to Washington to see the new President inau-

gurated. I called on Mr. Taft the night before, and as we listened to the downpour of rain—the snow and sleet had not begun—he remarked that the outlook for the inauguration was not very promising.

"But you know Willis Moore has staked his reputation as a weather prophet that to-morrow will bring fair weather," I said.

"Well," and there was a merry "ha, ha," that has been heard in all parts of the world, "you know Willis hasn't much reputation—as a weather prophet—to lose."

If there had been superstition lurking in the minds of Republicans, the weather might well have made them fear dire political calamities—and they would have had their fears confirmed.

Soon after the inauguration President Taft issued the call for the extra session which assembled March 15th. Before that date everybody who had any business at the White House realized that there had been a marvelous change.

Those who first experienced a jolt were the "fair-haired boys." They went to the White House as before, but were not wanted; they did not get an opportunity to retail all of the tittle-tattle, offer advice, and come away with a load of alleged Presidential secrets. They did not get anywhere. They neither saw the President nor did they get a word from Carpenter.

The successor of Wm. Loeb was as unlike that most successful secretary as a man could be. Carpenter was a self-effacing, patient, painstaking little man. He had been with Taft for many years, and had learned that the most pleasing service he could render his chief was to keep people away from him. This service Carpenter carried out with fidelity and without the least discrimination. He had no conception of the relative importance of White House callers, but as for that—neither had the President.

The former "Kitchen Cabinet" received no more consideration than the "fair-haired boys." They were not asked to call, nor were they received. Their latch-keys were no longer good. But that was not the worst of it. At the White House it was found that Aldrich, Hale, Cannon, Payne, Dalzell, Tawney, and a lot of other ungodly standpatters had access to the President.

Here was a pretty kettle of fish. The friends of Roosevelt, friends of the man who had elected Taft, were shut out, while the enemies, old and new, of Roosevelt were admitted. Worse than that, Senators Bailey and Tillman, Democrats who had been most vituperative in their abuse and denunciation of Roosevelt, and who had become conservative after many years in the Senate, called at the White House and were received by the President.

Thus shock upon shock followed. In an obscure, sporadic sort of way the "Back from Elba Club" began to form at that time.

But there were people who began to comment in a favorable way upon the change that had taken place. Members of the Old Guard were often quoted as expressing their gratification that an era of peace had come to the country, and that "judicial poise had succeeded erratic temperament at the White House."

It is quite difficult to understand Taft's early days in the Presidency, unless one considers the circumstances of his political career. He had been pushed by his friends into every position he ever held. He left one position for another with regret. From the time he left the circuit bench until he became President he had been bossed and overworked. As President it was the first time in ten years that he could do as he pleased and was responsible to no one but himself.

He was a man who did not like to be bothered. Why should people come to him? Why should he be asked to settle disputes about patronage? The man who went to Taft with a request was under suspicion. If he was not trying to get something he was not entitled to, why should he come bothering around? If he was all right, the thing he sought would come to him in the natural course of events. That is the way everything had happened for Taft, and why were not others content to get what they were entitled to without bothering him about it?

This estimate of his probable attitude is reached after close observation and talking with many men who had relations with Mr. Taft. It is the only explanation I can give of his treatment of friends and Republican leaders during the four years he was President. He acted very much as if he were afraid of being biased by personal influence. As one man expressed it, "he stands up so straight he leans backwards."

It is difficult to write of President Taft's four years
in the White House without seeming to be severely
critical. He did so many things which made him unpopular, and which must be recorded, that I want to
say at the outset, that it was a great pity a splendid
jurist was not allowed to carry out the ambition of his
life, but was taken from the bench and thrown into the
complexities of politics.

Personally, William H. Taft was a lovable character.
It was a pleasure to meet him and hear his cheery laugh.
In many ways his occupancy of the White House was
ideal, and too much cannot be said in praise of the First
Lady of the Land, Mrs. Taft, who did much to make
the social side of the Taft administration a great success.

Had Mr. Taft succeeded a man like President Arthur,
President Harrison, or President Cleveland, his Administration might have been a success. But he was
handicapped by succeeding the most marvelous man
of the age. He was much in the same position as that
of a man who is handed a red-hot stove. He had to do
the best he could under the circumstances. It was his
misfortune that he was not fitted for the conditions and
responsibilities which came with the office.

Revising the tariff is a dangerous political pastime.
No one ever heard of Theodore Roosevelt fooling with
that kind of dynamite during his seven and one-half
years as President. It was Mr. Taft's burden. He had
assumed the responsibility in a speech at Bath, Maine,
in 1906, when he advocated tariff revision. It has been
a political axiom that the party revising a tariff will

meet defeat at the ensuing election. The exception is only in case of war, which saved the Republicans after the revision of 1897, and the Democrats after 1913.

When Congress met, the President stated the object of the session in a message of 324 words. That was startling, for the Roosevelt messages were always long. The brief message was received with loud applause in the House, where everybody seemed relieved to get from under the rule of Roosevelt. In the Senate the smiling countenances of Aldrich and Hale, and those who acted with them, gave ample proof that the change was highly appreciated.

With more or less tribulation Chairman Sereno E. Payne steered his tariff bill through the House, where there were men who claimed that the rates fixed were inadequate and where Republican tariff reformers— the embryo insurgents—claimed that the reductions were insufficient and the revision a sham.

In the Senate the tariff fight was more bitter. The Republican insurgents by joining the Democrats could not muster a majority, but they conducted a long debate. Jonathan P. Dolliver of Iowa was the leader of the insurgents, with such followers as Nelson and Clapp of Minnesota, La Follette of Wisconsin, Cummins of Iowa, and Bristow of Kansas.

Dolliver viciously attacked the bill reported from the Finance Committee, particularly the woolen and cotton schedules. It was while talking of the woolen schedule that he referred to the "wedding of the weavers and shepherds" nearly forty years before, when the manu-

facturers and sheep raisers had agreed upon the famous
Schedule K.   It was also about this time that Dolliver,
speaking of President Taft, said:

"The President is a good man surrounded by men
who know exactly what they want."

Dolliver was particularly severe upon Senator
Aldrich, and at one time Aldrich remarked that he knew
the exact cause of Dolliver's irritation.   Nearly everybody knew what Aldrich meant, but the reference was
the nearest public statement that was made regarding
the personal differences between the Rhode Island and
Iowa Senators.   It antedated the death of Senator Allison, when Dolliver showed a disposition to "get off the
reservation."   When Senator Allison died, Dolliver,
by all precedents, should have been made a member of
the Finance Committee.   But Aldrich would not allow
him to be chosen.   With five vacancies on the committee, the selections were so arranged as to keep Dolliver from getting the desirable place.   Cullom of Illinois
was lifted off the Appropriations Committee by main
force and placed on Finance in order to give that state
representation.   McCumber of North Dakota was
given Hansbrough's place, while Reed Smoot of Utah
and Frank Flint of California, men serving their first
terms, were given positions.   It was a blow in the face
for Dolliver, a slight that he deeply felt.   Aldrich did
not like the insurgent tendencies of Dolliver.   Aldrich,
like other Republican leaders of that time, punished
independence with severity.   Dolliver did not forget.
On more than one occasion he drove Aldrich from the

floor of the Senate by his bitter invective and cutting
ridicule.

It was during the consideration of the tariff bill that
Aldrich side-tracked an amendment for an income tax.
One of the interesting features of the proposed income
tax was the discovery of insurgent tendencies in Senator
William E. Borah of Idaho.

Borah retired from all corporation law practice when
elected to the Senate. When the Senate committees
were organized, at the beginning of Taft's administration, Borah sought a place on the Judiciary Committee,
which at times handles very important measures. At
the White House one night the subject of assigning
the new Senators to committee places was under consideration, and a question was raised about Borah; he
was a comparatively new man and it might be taking a
risk to place him on such an important committee as
the Judiciary.

"Oh, he's all right," said Senator Aldrich; "I have
had him looked up. He is the attorney for seven
different corporations."

So Borah went on the Judiciary Committee. And
very soon it was found that Borah was not "all right."
Senator Hale remarked to a select gathering, which was
taking stock of the situation in the Senate, that "we
traded for Borah and got cheated."

Borah not only earnestly supported the income tax,
but also the constitutional amendment for the election
of Senators by direct vote of the people. His position
on the Judiciary Committee resulted in a favorable

report of that amendment. Truly, could the "elder
statesmen" of the Senate declare that Borah was not
"all right" and claim that they had been "cheated."

About that time Senator Borah received from Idaho
a score of telegrams from men connected with the
eastern corporations he had represented before his
election to the Senate, asking him to oppose the income
tax and not to press the constitutional amendment for
the election of Senators by direct vote of the people.
Borah did some telegraphing on his own account
and investigated those telegrams, and a few days
later he met the Rhode Island Senator, and said to
him:

"Aldrich, why didn't you come to me direct about
the income tax proposition instead of first wiring to
New York, having New York wire to Idaho, and Idaho
wire to me?"

"I thought my plan was the better way," replied
Aldrich, with the shrewd twinkle in his eye that was so
pleasing, and the good humor that he never allowed to
wane.

"To save you the trouble hereafter," said Borah, "I
will tell you that I severed all relations with corporation
law practice when I was elected to the Senate."

"That was a pity," was the comment of Aldrich,
but he knew then, positively, that Hale was right when
he said "we traded for Borah and got cheated."

The tariff bill was finally passed, but the Republican
party had been split, and everybody was more or less
dissatisfied. The high protectionists did not get all

they wanted, while the advocates of tariff revision felt that they had been buncoed.

When the final vote was taken twenty Republicans in the House voted against the conference report. Among them was James R. Mann, who asserted that the duty on pulp and print paper was too high. That had a great effect subsequently and was used by newspapers in criticizing the bill.

It happens sometimes that men from the same state represent the two houses on a conference. That happened in 1909, when Lodge and McCall, both from Massachusetts, were on the conference committee. When the bill was agreed to I met McCall and noticed his smiling face. I asked him about the bill, and he said it was a splendid tariff.

A few moments later I met Asher C. Hinds, a member from Maine, who knew the members and the business of Congress well, and I spoke of McCall's pleasure and commendation of the bill.

"I do not wonder," responded Hinds, "for Massachusetts never went away from Congress carrying more in her craw than she's got in that tariff bill."

When it was all over Taft gave what was called a "tariff feast on the terrace," a dinner to the Republican members of the Finance Committee and Ways and and Means Committee, on the terrace at the White House.

Then in midsummer he went away to Beverly for his vacation.

Again the contrast between the former and new

Administration was pronounced and, unfortunately, to Taft's disadvantage. Roosevelt always kept doing things that gave the newspaper men something to write about. Even his recreations showed versatility.

After the larger questions of national or international importance in the daily dispatches there might be a few lines about a game of tennis, a horseback ride, a row on the bay, chopping down a tree, pitching a load of hay, romping with the children, etc.

From Beverly the national news was meager, while there was a daily story about golf. "The President played golf" with this or that man; "the President made the round of the links"; "the President's golf score," etc. In a land where this game was confined to a comparatively few persons, and they were supposed to belong to the leisure class, this frequent connecting of the name of the President with a golf game, whether on his vacation, traveling, or in Washington, proved to be one of several unpopular features of his Administration.

My experience with the President at Beverly was somewhat peculiar. I had a close acquaintance and friendship of twenty years with Mr. Taft. Representing publications having a very large number of readers, I thought it would be a good thing to write a series of articles about Mr. Taft's first six months in the White House. I hied me to the North Shore and went to see Secretary Carpenter and unfolded my plan.

"The President sees the newspaper men on Wednesdays; you can see him then," was all I could get out of

Carpenter. So on Wednesday I wandered out to the Presidential cottage, and found there a number of distinguished journalists. The Washington correspondents of several important papers published in large cities were there.

There was a heavy downpour of rain and we tried to get shelter under the trees, and when the deluge increased we huddled under the eaves of a garage. Secret service men saw to it that newspaper men did not approach the cottage.

Captain Archie Butt saw us and beckoned us over to the cottage, where we found shelter on the generous porch. Patiently we all waited. I think it must have been two hours from the time we began flitting about under the trees until we saw a southern politician going away down the pathway.

Then Carpenter disappeared around the corner of the cottage.

"Must I see those men again! Didn't I see them just the other day!"

It was a snarl, but it was Taft's voice. There was a murmur for a moment and then Carpenter reappeared, motioning us to go forward, and we passed around the corner to be greeted with "the smile that wouldn't come off," and after a quip or two, a merry "ha! ha!" the routine questions were asked and answered. A Boston newspaper man asked the President what he thought of Dr. Cook's discovery of the North Pole, and showed him a paper with a bulletin to that effect.

"Very interesting, if true," was the comment of the President.

That was the last time I saw Mr. Taft at the Beverly cottage. And that series of articles was never published.

One incident of the year 1909 worth recalling, because of what happened three years later, was a speech made by Prof. Woodrow Wilson during the summer, in which he criticized business magnates and labor union methods, saying that "no one is suffered to do more than the least skilful of his fellows can do."

President Taft made an extended Western tour during the Fall months. He made a number of speeches at different points, and preached a lay sermon one Sunday in the Mormon Tabernacle at Salt Lake City, Utah. While it might have been the natural thing for a man to do, it caused fierce denunciation by several leaders of other churches.

But by far the most important utterance of the tour was the Winona speech, a speech that made history. Mr. Taft defended the Payne-Aldrich bill in general, but said that the woolen schedule was indefensible. As Winona was the home of Representative James A. Tawney, Mr. Taft took occasion to commend him highly, although Tawney had been assailed more bitterly by Roosevelt than any other man in the House. In later years that Winona speech figured very prominently in politics.

On his way home from the Southwest Mr. Taft stopped at El Paso, Texas. President Diaz of Mexico was at Juarez across the Rio Grande. The heads of the two Republics exchanged calls, each crossing the border. At one time it would have caused more than ordinary discussion, for there had been a tradition that no President of the United States had ever gone outside of United States territory. But Roosevelt had shattered that tradition by going to Panama, and was several times outside of United States territory.

Some of the incidents of 1909, no larger than a man's hand at the time, grew into black clouds at a later date. One of these was the dismissal of a clerk named Glavis from the land office. This man became an ally of Gifford Pinchot, and together they worked up the charges against Secretary Ballinger of the Interior Department.

Another was the recall of Charles Crane, appointed Minister to China, but stopped at San Francisco as he was about to sail for his post. Crane became an implacable foe to the Taft administration and a supporter of the Progressive movement.

President Taft also had to reverse his predecessor on the question of "What is whiskey?" In doing so he decided against Dr. Harvey W. Wiley and former Attorney General Bonaparte. The whiskey decision was only one of a number of cases involving the pure food law in which Dr. Wiley was the stormy petrel of vigorous controversies, which finally resulted in his leaving his position.

Reading men out of the Republican party was also a feature of the year 1909. It began during the consideration of the tariff bill and was carried out when Speaker Cannon announced the committees at the close of the session. The Republican insurgents were demoted from leading places on committees or left off entirely. Men who had shown independence were punished by being deprived of the power which a good committee assignment gives them. About a dozen or fifteen leading insurgents felt the heavy hand of the Speaker for having opposed the House machine. More than that, the Speaker in a speech in a western state mentioned the Republican insurgents of the House and seven Republican senators who voted against the tariff bill, and said:

"If they are Republicans, I am not."

Great advances in aviation had been made, and the Wrights, following the principle evolved by Prof. Langley, had demonstrated the feasibility of the airplane. They received a medal presented by President Taft in the East Room of the White House. The President could always do these things gracefully. After commending the Wrights, he predicted great developments in aërial navigation.

"I presume," he said, "my predecessor being venturesome and energetic, would go up in your machine. For myself," he added, "well, I think I will forego the sensation. I am not built along aviation lines and I do not believe I was intended for an aviator."

Before President Taft had been ten months in office he became a prophet, saying in one of his public speeches:

"In four years I shall step down and out."

CHAPTER IX

DEMOCRATIC VICTORY OF 1910

Factions of the Dominant Party Continue to Fight Each Other Bitterly
—Insurgents Not Regarded Within the Party—Roosevelt Returns
from Europe and Enters New York Politics—Crushing Defeat for
the Republicans.

GRADUALLY there were arrayed against the Republican party the forces which presaged defeat in the Congressional elections of 1910, and the fulfillment of Taft's prophecy that he would step down and out at the end of four years. The beginning was in the tariff law, which was followed by a chain of other events tending toward dissatisfaction. There was much criticism of the tariff law in the newspapers and magazines. They had brought about tariff revision in the first place, the newspapers by their demand for free pulp and newsprint paper, and the magazines because their writers were generally free traders. The newspapers were not benefited in the least by the reductions made, and many of them joined the magazines in denouncing the Payne-Aldrich law as a sham revision.

The year 1910 had not far advanced when President Taft took cognizance of these criticisms, and in a speech said:

"Perhaps the newspapers don't carry in their pockets all of public opinion, and perhaps the American people are able to see something of the hypercriticism, something of hysteria, and something of hypocrisy, and to have a real sympathy for the man, who, under considerable responsibility, is doing the best he can."

Early in the year 1910 war was declared on the Republican insurgents who had opposed the Taft program, or rather the tariff bill in Congress. The leaders in Congress skilfully intertwined their program with the President's program, so that opponents of the leaders were made opponents of the President. It was stated that Postmaster General Hitchcock had cut off the postoffice patronage from insurgents, and that other departments had cut off big places, and the Treasury Department the smaller positions in the internal revenue service.

It was also stated that the Republican congressional campaign committee would give no assistance to insurgents in the coming election.

About this time Speaker Cannon met his first defeat since he had become the second great power in the nation. President Taft removed Gifford Pinchot as Chief Forester. Pinchot had serious differences with Secretary Ballinger of the Interior Department. The imbroglio arose over conservation and resulted in a Congressional investigation. In the selection of the members of the committee in the House the insurgents joined the Democrats and supported a motion that the committee should be elected by the House instead of being appointed by the Speaker. That motion was adopted.

In March George W. Norris of Nebraska offered an amendment to the House rules enlarging the Committee on Rules and making the Speaker ineligible as a member. Up to that time the Committee on Rules was all powerful. With the Speaker as chairman, and two of his closest friends as majority members, the committee could do almost as it pleased in the House. It virtually made the Speaker absolute, particularly as he had the power of recognition of members to make motions, and the still greater power of naming members of all the committees. There was no getting around his dictatorship.

Assisting Norris were Cooper and Lenroot of Wisconsin, Gardner of Massachusetts, Murdock of Kansas, Fowler of New Jersey, Poindexter of Washington, and Davis of Minnesota, and others to the number of forty-three, theretofore affiliated with the Republican party.

During the contest Speaker Cannon gave out a statement defending his action in demoting men who had not acted in harmony with the party. President Taft about the same time was making speeches urging party loyalty. But the insurgents were determined, and were supported by nearly all the Democrats, Fitzgerald of New York, with a few followers from Tammany and members from Louisiana, voting with the Speaker.

But the large proportion of the Democrats, under the leadership of Champ Clark and Oscar W. Underwood, with the Republican insurgents, constituted a majority which took the first step toward shearing the Speaker of his great power.

Fitzgerald labored hard with Clark to prevent him from supporting the movement to cut down the power of the Speaker.

"You are very likely to be the Speaker in the next House," said Fitzgerald, "and you will want this power. You are simply destroying your coming heritage."

But Champ would not take the advice. "I have been in the minority so long," he said, "that I have seen the advantage and power of the Speaker. The minority leader is pitted against the Speaker as a leader of the majority, and the Speaker has all the advantage which his power over members gives him. If I am Speaker I do not want that power. Let it be a fair fight between the leaders of the two parties on the floor of the House, and the Speaker be the umpire instead of majority leader and umpire as well."

Did Champ Clark at that time take the position which helped to defeat him for the Democratic nomination? I think so; as I shall later show.

There were other troubles for the Republican party. The "Back from Elba Club" was more than a vision. It began to be a reality.

Colonel Roosevelt on leaving for Africa had been given a parting salute by his friends, one of whom asserted that it was the prayer of the plutocrats and many others that "the lions of Africa would do their duty."

But the Colonel returned safe and sound from the dark Continent, and after stopping long enough in Egypt to tell the English that they were not governing the country properly, he went on to Italy.   At Rome he had an unfortunate affair with the Vatican, and by refusing to comply with a request not to speak to the Methodist colony in Rome, he was debarred from an audience with the Pope.   It was not realized until several months later that this action was to injure seriously Roosevelt's popularity with the Catholics, but it was felt in subsequent political campaigns.

One of the most significant utterances, also showing a fine vein of humor, in view of the hunting trip which had just ended, was that of the Papal Secretary, Cardinal Merry del Val, who explained the attitude of the Vatican by saying that "the Pope did not propose to be put into Mr. Roosevelt's game bag."

Soon after Roosevelt emerged from the African jungle Gifford Pinchot dashed off to Europe to meet and acquaint him with conditions in the United States. Other members of the "tennis cabinet" and a number of the "fair-haired boys" did the same, but no one was able to get a word from Roosevelt as to affairs in this country.

When Colonel Roosevelt reached England he reiterated the statement made in Egypt, and told the gasping Britishers that if they could not rule Egypt they ought to get out; that Egypt was no place for sentimentality, but for vigorous measures.   Some of the British papers said he was right.

The next day William Randolph Hearst published a statement in a London paper saying that Roosevelt was a "tin soldier, a toy Colonel, who refused to submit to discipline for the short time he was in the Army, and does not represent the United States in what he says."

The first mention of a new party was made at a banquet given to Gifford Pinchot at St. Paul, Minnesota, June 11, 1910. It was then suggested that Roosevelt, Pinchot and Garfield should be the leaders. The man who made the suggestion was more of a prophet than he realized.

One of the first severe jolts the Republicans received was at a special election in a Massachusetts district. Eugene Foss, then a Democrat and running on a low tariff platform, was elected by an overwhelming majority in a district which had given a very large Republican majority in 1908.

Two Republicans, evidently men who could see a real political storm on the horizon, decided to retire from the Senate. Eugene Hale of Maine and Nelson W. Aldrich announced that they would not be candidates again, each having thirty years of service.

For a long time they had been dominant figures and ruled the body. While I have spoken of the Senate being managed by a "Big Six" of the inner circle, in later years it narrowed down to two men, Hale and Aldrich.

Hale was the most senatorial Senator I ever knew. His life was centered in the body. He spent more time in the chamber than any other man. He was the best manager of appropriation bills I have ever seen. He was strictly honest and incapable of double-dealing.

It is true that his speeches were rather dismal and his utterances full of gloom, but that was when he lectured the Senate for delaying public business, or talked about extravagance.

Aldrich was a different type of man, but they worked together, and up to the time they quit public life they were masters of the Senate.

"What will be done with the Republican leadership in the Senate?" I asked Senator Dolliver when the announcement was made that Hale and Aldrich were to retire.

"I think it will be put in commission," replied the Iowa Senator, using a term which means in England that the office will not be filled.

And Dolliver was right. Since that time there has been no "inner circle," no "Big Six" giving orders and exacting obedience. Maybe the situation is no better, but dominance of the Senate by a clique no longer exists.

Senator Dolliver continued his criticism of the Payne-Aldrich law, and included President Taft in his strictures. On one occasion he said, referring to a speech by Cannon in New York, that he "could scarcely agree with the venerable Speaker that some of those men calling themselves Republicans were traitors who ought to be hanged."

He said that the patronage club was being used to force recalcitrant Republicans into line, but he did not believe that Republicanism was to be measured by doling out offices.

Turning to the tariff, with one of those humorous flashes which made him such an entertaining speaker, he said:

"The past year witnessed two events of unusual interest—the discovery of the North Pole by Dr. Cook and the revision of the tariff downward by the Senator from Rhode Island—each in its way a unique hoax, and both promptly presented to the favorable notice of the people by the highest official congratulations."

The last part of the statement referred to President Taft.

It was in this speech that Dolliver had a most interesting colloquy with Elkins of West Virginia. Elkins never liked Aldrich, and, like Dolliver, had been kept off the Finance Committee by the Rhode Island Senator. He took occasion to make unfavorable remarks about the tariff, and when asked by Dolliver why he was silent when the bill was under consideration, Elkins explained:

"I was on the reservation and had to accept the dictation of the Senator from Rhode Island in order to save certain things in the tariff bill affecting my state."

Elkins was not the only Senator who had been "kept on the reservation" by the shrewd tactics of Aldrich, who thus saved his bill, and prevented reductions in many rates. By giving certain Senators what they wanted for their states he was able to pledge them for a whole line of tariff schedules.

Developments such as these, showing that the tariff was a log-rolling measure, much as a river and harbor bill or a public building bill is, caused renewed criticism of the tariff-making system.   During the summer President Taft met this by declaring for revision schedule by schedule after a report on each industry or schedule by a tariff commission.

In the midst of the political turmoil of the year 1910 Theodore Roosevelt returned from abroad and was warmly and officially welcomed by the American people.

Oyster Bay became the Mecca for the disappointed men in the Republican party.   All the discontented elements went there to tell Roosevelt that his policies were being abandoned and that his enemies had triumphed.

At that time the Ballinger-Pinchot row over the Alaskan claims and the handling of western lands was at its height.   Roosevelt naturally sided with Pinchot, and the opponents of Ballinger seemed always welcome.

At one time it looked as if President Taft was going to yield to the criticism and throw Ballinger overboard.   W. Murray Crane went west to meet Ballinger as the Secretary was coming east.   It was well understood that Crane was "the bearer of the poisoned cup," but the Cabinet officer refused to drink.

All summer long the regulars and insurgents were at each others' throats, cutting and slashing.   Speaker Cannon stormed at the magazines and muckrakers.

Roosevelt went west, and in several speeches announced the policy of "new nationalism."   He began to use the word "progressive." While he was making a speech in Kansas a man in the audience tried to class him as an insurgent. "Don't get the bridle off," he admonished the man, using an old cowboy term. On another occasion he exclaimed, "No lion in Africa did its duty!"

On his way home the Colonel created an explosion at Chicago by canceling an engagement to dine with the Hamilton Club if Billy Lorimer was to be present. Lorimer was then undergoing an investigation as to whether he had bought his seat in the Senate.

It was both asserted and denied, with seeming authority, that Roosevelt would be a candidate in 1912. Meanwhile it was also stated that President Taft had said that one term was enough for him.

In April of 1910 President Taft had named Governor Hughes for the Supreme bench.

Hughes did not immediately relinquish his position as Governor. He had certain matters of legislation to put through which were opposed by the Old Guard. Roosevelt became interested in these reform measures and earnestly supported them.

In the Fall of the year Roosevelt entered upon one of those contests which meant nothing if he won save a little personal gratification. A suggestion was made that he should be chosen temporary chairman of the state convention. Roosevelt said that if he were selected he would say just what he thought in his speech and it might not be satisfactory to the leaders. They thought so, too, and the state committee chose Vice President

Sherman as temporary chairman, although some one presented Roosevelt's name.

The defeat in the committee aroused the fighting blood of the Colonel, and he went out for that chairmanship. Strange to say, he had not only the support of Hughes, but also that of the national administration. This was a severe blow to Sherman and the Old Guard.

Roosevelt won, dominated the convention, named Henry L. Stimson for Governor, and fought hard for him, but saw his man go down to defeat, as did many other Republicans that year.

"Why do you get into this fight?" I asked the Colonel, before the convention; "I don't see anything in it, win or lose."

"I have been forced in," he replied. "They made the fight on me, and I have got to vindicate myself."

"It doesn't seem to me that a man who has been President needs any such vindication," I said, "but what practical result can you accomplish?"

"I can prevent them from nominating one of their crowd for Governor," he replied.

"Yes, and if you win, you must name the candidate for Governor, and he is sure to go down to defeat. This is a Democratic year."

"I think you're right," was the reply. "But we might pull through with a progressive candidate."

Confidence in his strength with the people was ever a characteristic of Colonel Roosevelt.

Long before the election of 1910 it was evident that the Republicans were doomed to defeat. The divisions were very pronounced. Dissatisfaction was everywhere apparent. But the strange feature of it all was the attitude of the regulars or standpatters. They believed that the insurgents had no following, and that they had broken away for personal reasons. The standpatters did not realize that men in Congress do not break away from their own administration unless they have backing at home.

Into the campaign had been injected that intense issue, the high cost of living. Twenty years before, after the enactment of the McKinley tariff, there was an increase of prices and the party which passed the tariff law was swept out of power. In 1910 there was a similar situation, intensified by the criticisms of the Administration by so many insurgent Republicans, and the retaliation by the Administration in words and the withholding of patronage.

The first blow was the election in Maine. The Democrats made a wonderful sweep, the first in thirty years, but what was more surprising they carried the legislature and would send a Democrat to the Senate for the first time in sixty years. And Maine was a state which was given everything she could ask in the tariff bill.

The next day an amazing thing happened. Secretary Norton—he had succeeded Carpenter as Secretary to the President—made public a letter to an insurgent which stated that the policy of withholding patronage from insurgents had been abandoned; although the President had felt it a duty to pursue that course with those who had not supported Republican policies.

James A. Tawney was defeated in the primary in the first Congressional district of Minnesota. This, despite the endorsement of Taft in his Winona speech. Tawney was defeated by Roosevelt. Roosevelt's henchmen flooded the district with literature that showed an intense and bitter feeling. Tawney paid the penalty of opposing Roosevelt in the House. He was classed as an undesirable. Roosevelt when President had a way of disposing of men who opposed him by saying, "he's a crook," or "he belongs to the interests." That was sufficient to condemn a man, and if followed up in a political campaign usually caused the defeat of the man denounced.

It was a landslide all right, that election of 1910. The only wonder is that the defeat was not even greater. The Democrats secured a majority of sixty-three in the House, made a gain of eight seats in the Senate, and elected governors in several hitherto Republican states.

The party which had elected its candidate in 1908 by a plurality of 1,269,804 votes, carrying twenty-nine states with 321 electoral votes to 162 for the Democratic opponent, was a total wreck in two short years. Not only was it a complete rout, but it meant a Democratic victory in the Presidential election two years later.

One of the incidents of the election of 1910 was the resignation on October 15th of Woodrow Wilson as President of Princeton College in order to make his campaign for Governor of New Jersey. After Wilson had been elected there was a spirited controversy over the senatorship. Former Senator James Smith, Jr., had been largely responsible for the nomination of Wilson for Governor. Smith wanted to be sent back to the Senate, but Wilson insisted that the preference primary, which had by a meager vote given a majority for James E. Martine, should govern in the legislature, and he had his way. One of the side-lights of that controversy was a criticism of Governor Wilson by Speaker Cannon for interfering in the selection of a United States Senator.

There were a number of interesting events during the year 1910, not wholly political. One of them happened in the East Room of the White House when, to the tune of a lively jig, President Taft and Speaker Cannon danced an old-fashioned "hoe-down," much to the amusement of the assembled guests.

The Senate of the United States enjoyed one of the most remarkable treats in its existence when it listened to the farewell speech of Colonel James Gordon of Mississippi. Colonel Gordon had been appointed to fill a short term in the Senate. He was one of the old southern plantation gentlemen. He told the Senate that he had been a millionaire, but that he had lost all in the great civil strife of the 60's. He had had a wonderful career as a soldier; many adventures such as come to a brave and active officer. He was never known in public life until that short term in the Senate. His farewell speech was humorous and pathetic, and betrayed much common sense, at times rising to sublime heights in patriotic fervor, pleas for national unity, and expressions of hope for the future of the Republic.

Former President Roosevelt paid a visit to President

Taft at Beverly during the summer.   It was expected
to be political, but was only social, a bit dramatic.

"Mr. President," "Theodore," and the two men had
their hands on each other's shoulders.

"It used to be 'Mr. President' and 'Will,'" remarked
the Colonel, turning to the others in the group.

His face looked to be entirely smile and teeth.   Mr.
Taft's characteristic "ha! ha!" tended to relieve the
situation.   Then they sat down and talked until Roosevelt went away with Senator Lodge, while President Taft
went to the golf links.

During the summer the somewhat celebrated suits
instituted by Colonel Roosevelt against two editors,
alleging libel in regard to the Panama canal, were dismissed by a judge in the Federal court.   Colonel Roosevelt expressed his opinion of the judge in perfectly plain
terms, but the judge did not desire to make a contempt
case of the matter.

It was about this time that Colonel Roosevelt gave his
opinions freely regarding the Supreme Court and some
of its decisions, paving the way for his later endorsement
of the recall of judges.

Just as a part of the game of keeping in the public
eye, Colonel Roosevelt went up in an aeroplane while
in St. Louis.   He had been down in a submarine.   In
fact, he had done about everything a man could
do.

Jonathan P. Dolliver died in the fall of 1910.   It was
an untimely end, for he was at the zenith of his career.
The future of a man like Dolliver would have been very

interesting. He was on the up grade in power and influence when he died. His death revived the story that
he narrowly missed being President, and did so by declining the Vice Presidential nomination in 1900. That
never was true. Dolliver did not decline the nomination. It was not offered to him, and he could not have
been nominated. In a previous chapter I have told the
facts about that nomination.

Dolliver's remarkable gift was in coupling the most
bitter denunciation with sparkling humor. He entertained while he drove home his arguments. All his
life he saw the humorous side of things. He knew his
own ability, but he never took himself seriously enough
to think that he was the superior of all mankind. He
was a deep student and had the ability to absorb information quickly. He had no equal as a debater
during his last years in the Senate.

After the election of 1910 I was one of a number attending a luncheon that was a regular feature of the
days that Colonel Roosevelt spent in New York. The
magazine with which he was connected seemed to control the gatherings, which were held in a private room
of one of the literary clubs. Not only guests of the
magazine, but also personal guests of the Colonel, made
up quite large parties on these occasions.

"Those luncheons," remarked Senator Elihu Root,
after having been a guest, "seem to have a purpose—
or at least they are very useful. The members of the
staff of the magazine are always present. There is a
free discussion of many subjects, and I have observed

that the ideas and views which have been expressed
find their way into the editorials of the magazine."

At this particular luncheon Henry L. Stimson was a
guest, and Colonel Roosevelt allowed his sense of humor
to bubble over in commenting upon Stimson's running
abilities. Never for a moment did he give the impression that Stimson had been his selection and that it
was in a measure a Roosevelt defeat.

A little later at a personal conference the political
situation and developments of the past two years were
reviewed by Colonel Roosevelt. I then learned of his
bitterness towards President Taft. It appeared that a
number of things—left overs of the Roosevelt administration—had not been carried out according to what
Roosevelt regarded as promises.

After that interview, however, I was convinced that
Roosevelt would not oppose Taft, but would give him
at least a perfunctory support in 1912. But at that
time Roosevelt did not know that Taft was about to
shoulder additional burdens and to make himself still
more unpopular.

In December, 1910, President Taft gave the country
a great surprise. He nominated Associate Justice
White as Chief Justice of the United States Supreme
Court. The surprise was not because Justice White
was unfitted for the place, but because he was a Democrat, a Confederate soldier, and a Catholic. It was
believed that political pressure by the dignitaries of the
Catholic Church had much to do in securing the appointment, but Mr. Taft, during his entire public

career, had been on the most friendly terms with the
Catholics. His services in the Philippines and negotiations with the Vatican had made him many friends
among the churchmen. More than that he was frequently a prominent figure at Catholic celebrations,
particularly when Cardinal Gibbons was honored.
These associations worked both in his favor and to his
detriment in the campaign of 1912. Members of the
other churches became somewhat antagonistic on
account of the close relations which had been maintained between him and leading Catholics.

There was another consideration in the selection of
the Chief Justice that caused a deep feeling. On the
bench at that time was John M. Harlan, a veteran of
the Union army, a man who had been a Republican in
Kentucky when it tried men's souls to keep the party
faith. In the selection of an Associate Justice of the
court for Chief Justice, and the establishment thereby
of a precedent, it was thought by many that Justice
Harlan should have been accorded that honor.

I am aware that it will be said that Justice Harlan
was not disappointed and that his death was not hastened by that disappointment. Perhaps not, but that
he felt it deeply was evident from a remark which he
made to one of his intimate friends after the Chief Justice had taken the oath of office.

"As the senior member of the court," said Justice
Harlan, "it became my duty to administer the oath of
office. On that day I wore my Grand Army and Loyal
Legion buttons, so that they were plainly visible as I

faced him; and I never more profoundly nor more solemnly pronounced the words of that oath than upon that occasion."

After more than fifty years there was still in the heart of the famous jurist a feeling that had been engendered and fostered by four years of war.

The President also had an opportunity to name another Associate Justice for Chief Justice, and had he done so, while it would have made no difference in regard to the campaign of 1912, it would have materially changed the situation in 1916.

When President Taft offered Governor Hughes a position on the Supreme bench he told him that, if the Chief Justiceship were vacant, he would appoint him to the place, but he did not want that statement to be understood as a promise that such a tender would be made if at a later time a vacancy occurred.

No doubt Hughes, and such friends as knew the circumstance, wondered what had happened between the time that the New York Governor was tendered the place on the bench and the following autumn, that caused the President to name a Democratic Associate Justice, particularly when he had expressed the opinion that Hughes was at one time his choice for the more desirable position.

If Charles E. Hughes had been Chief Justice he never would have accepted a nomination for the Presidency.

CHAPTER X

CANADIAN RECIPROCITY

An Unpopular Agreement Which Wrecked Two Party Governments—
Spilt the Republicans in the United States and Defeated the
Liberals in Canada—Democrats in Control of the House for the
First Time in Sixteen Years—Speaker Shorn of Power.

FOR several months there had been rumors that the
President, through the State Department, had
been negotiating a reciprocity treaty with Canada.
Considerable uneasiness had developed among Republicans on this account; more especially was this
apparent in delegations from states on the northern
border, as the people feared an influx of Canadian farm
products. Soon after the short session of the Sixty-
first Congress commenced the President sent in a message with the reciprocity agreement. The uneasiness
among Republicans became consternation when they
saw the terms of this agreement.

Then began a fight which still further divided the
party. Samuel W. McCall of Massachusetts was
chosen by the President to manage the reciprocity bill
in the House. The Democrats, with few exceptions,
were all for the agreement. It was not difficult to
bring it to a vote, and it was passed with seventy-
eight Republicans voting for it and eighty-seven against,

while one hundred and forty-three Democrats voted for the measure and only five against it.

While the bill was pending there were many protests filed against it. The National Grange and other farm organizations made a vigorous protest. The fishing interests of New England were also much alarmed. One of the large farming delegations which went to the White House and made a protest was told by the President that they were "seeing ghosts." At another time in a public speech the President said, "Insistence on too much protection will arouse an opposition in the country that will know no moderation."

Although the reciprocity bill passed the House, it went against a stone wall in the Senate. Down deep in their minds the Republicans were almost unitedly opposed to the Canadian reciprocity measure, but many felt obliged to support the Administration and they, with the Democrats, constituted a majority in the Senate. But the Republicans who were opposing the reciprocity bill served notice that it could not pass during the short session, although there was a threat from the White House that there would be an extra session unless there was a vote on the measure.

While Canadian reciprocity was causing dissensions among Republicans and raising a revolt against the President, the Administration indulged in another contention which caused very much criticism and had a great influence upon the politics of the future. This was an effort to increase the rates of postage on periodicals.

It was the demand of the newspapers and magazines for a reduction of the duty on pulp and paper which finally forced the tariff revision of 1909. When that revision was accomplished, it was found that the reductions on pulp and paper had not changed the price of paper. Not only that, but there was an increase in the price of all commodities, particularly in the articles that entered the household, the necessaries of life. Hence the clamor about the high cost of living.

Many newspapers and most of the magazines asserted that the Payne-Aldrich bill was a sham revision. Utterances of men like Dolliver and other insurgent Republicans gave color to those assertions, and a general impression prevailed that the tariff had been revised upward instead of downward. That idea was fostered in the opposition press and in the magazines, although the regular Republicans asserted time after time that there had been a downward revision.

The first intimation that an attack was to be made on the publishers came from Harry Loudenslager, secretary of the Republican congressional campaign committee, and in charge of the headquarters in New York. Some time before the election we were going over the situation, and both of us realized that the Republicans were going down to a severe defeat in the congressional elections of 1910.

"We'll get even with the fellows who have done this to us," said Loudenslager. "The newspapers and magazines have been lying about us and the tariff for more than a year now, but we'll get even with them this winter. We'll increase their rate of postage; that's what we'll do."

I had almost forgotten what the New Jersey Representative told me until a short time after election, when it was rumored that the Administration, working through Postmaster General Frank H. Hitchcock, had evolved a plan which would hit the periodicals hard, but would not affect the newspapers, it having become a foregone conclusion that the postage rate on newspapers could not be raised. Senator Carter of Montana had just returned after a losing fight in that state, and had reason for being sore. Carter had given much time to postal matters.

"Yes," he said, in answer to my inquiry, "they (the magazines) have been responsible for bringing defeat to the Republican party and disaster to the country. We will give 'em an increase of postage and see how they like it. They have been enjoying a good thing too long."

And then began a fight which lasted until the post-office appropriation bill was passed. The Hitchcock plan proposed quadrupling the rate on sheets in periodicals on which advertising was printed, the Postmaster General having the authority to say what should be considered a periodical and what a newspaper. This discrimination could be exercised in dealing with weekly publications, as many of them were on the border line between newspapers and periodicals.

The publishers made a very strong fight against the proposition, and before it was over a feeling of bitter hostility towards the Administration had been created. The periodical publishers felt that a most unfair attack had been made upon them.   The postage rate had been in existence since 1889, and all publishing business had been adjusted on that basis.   Then the periodicals felt that it was unfair to take them as a class, for the newspapers had been equally critical of the Administration.

The Hitchcock proposition failed, but the damage had been done.   The periodical publishers had been arrayed against the Administration and the Republican party as then organized.   The defenders of the periodicals on the Republican side were mostly of that band of insurgents and progressives who were more than ever in open hostility to the regular Republicans.

It was during this short session of Congress that Jonathan Bourne became the head of a new party, the Progressive Republican party.   This stormy petrel of the political waters is said to have the distinction of having been chairman of several different political parties in Oregon, and was made chairman of this new party which was sloughing from the Republican organization.

Bourne had been a golf companion of President Taft day after day, although he had been a second-elective term man supporting Roosevelt when Taft was a candidate.   But in two years the warm friendship was severed, and Bourne was at the head of an organization antagonistic to Taft.   While Bourne was often treated as a joke when a member of the Senate, his prominence as an organizer against the regular Republican party at the most critical time in its history brought him into notice. He opened a correspondence with Governor Woodrow Wilson in which he discussed progressive politics. Those who read Bourne's screeds against Wilson after he had been President three years could not but be struck with the fact that it takes only a few years to alter political views.

Senator Owen of Oklahoma conducted a successful filibuster against the bill admitting New Mexico as a state because Arizona was not included. Arizona had been dropped out because she had provided for the recall of judges in her constitution. The House Republicans would not permit Arizona to be made a state with the recall, and Owen would not allow New Mexico to become a state unless Arizona was granted the same right, and with her progressive constitution.

The votes and debates over this bill were what caused Senator Bailey's first resignation, the one he subsequently withdrew. Bailey found himself the only Democrat voting against admitting Arizona with that recall provision.

"I am without a party," he told me, after he had been persuaded to withdraw his resignation. "If they are right, I am not a Democrat. If what they are voting for is Democracy, then I don't want to be a Democrat. And the worst feature of it is that they do not believe in this as Democracy. In the cloak rooms and private conversation they tell me I am right, but in the Senate they will not vote with me."

Speaker Cannon closed his eight years as Speaker in a stormy session.

Subject to many denunciations and severe criticisms during much of his career as Speaker, it was not until the closing day that Mr. Cannon was actually threatened with physical violence while in the chair. A spare man, seventy-four years of age, was threatened by a six-foot Kentucky congressman in the prime of life. And in that moment Uncle Joe became the man of the hour, for he defied his would-be assailant with courage, and maintained his dignity.

Early in the year 1911 Stephen B. Elkins died. He was one of the most remarkable men of his time. Born in Ohio, a resident of Missouri, and soldier of the Civil War, he went to New Mexico when the war was over. He had made money and he made a great deal more in the western Territory. Twice he represented the Territory as a Delegate, and came very near having New Mexico admitted as a state, in which event he would have been one of its Senators. Despairing of political preferment in a territory, he located in West Virginia and added millions to his fortune. He was Secretary of War in Harrison's cabinet and three times elected to the Senate.

He absolutely wore himself out and died as a result of overstrain upon his nervous energy. He would do the work of three men every day. As a Senator he was not wholly a success, because he would not give time to the business of the Senate. He would sit in his committee room attending to his vast business concerns, and one of his clerks would watch the Senate from the gallery. If anything came up in which the Senator was interested, the clerk reported to Elkins and the Senator would hustle down and look after it and then return to his committee room. He was always getting ready to give up business and look after his Senate duties exclusively, but he never did. He died in harness.

"The trouble with the Senate," he once told me, "is its method. Why, half a dozen men will sit around a table at a directors' meeting and dispose of more business in an hour than the Senate can do in a week."

Elkins recognized the big power wielded by the money interests. He would have extended what was known as the Elkins road to the seaboard if he could. "You see," he told me, "I can't do it; and if I tried they would shut me up. I can build only such spur connections as they are willing shall be built. I want to run a road away over here or there, but they won't let me.

"They won't let me have the money," he went on to explain. "They won't let anybody have the money to build any more railroads unless they are built where they want them built. Oh, we understand each other; I know them and they know me. It is a mighty sight easier to work with them than to buck them."

"They," referred to by Elkins in this talk, were the big financiers, the men who controlled the money of the country, and who could finance a new system of railroad, or prevent the construction of a railroad.

Elkins' activities and adventures gave rise to many good stories. I heard some tales of adventure in the West that were far more thrilling than the ordinary "hair-raisers." He was once a captive of Quantrell's band of guerillas and was saved by Cole Younger, whom he had known in days before the war. He had narrow escapes from the Indians, and a full share of close calls in other ways.

Henry Gassaway Davis was Elkins' father-in-law and business partner. They were also very warm personal friends. One summer they traveled extensively in West Virginia, buying coal lands. All members of the party soon found that Elkins had the good fortune or faculty of getting the best bed in all the little country hotels. Davis made up his mind to beat Elkins in the selection one day, and arranged to have his son-in-law detained while he went up to the room and made a choice. Davis found four beds in the room assigned to their party, and after a careful examination found one with good springs and a soft mattress. He placed his hand bag upon the bed and went down well satisfied.

In a little while Elkins went up and soon found that the good bed had been pre-empted. He said nothing, but selected another bed and put his grip on it. A little later he gave the chambermaid a dollar and told her to change the springs and mattress, but to be sure to replace the hand bags.

Davis went up to the room with a smirk. Elkins, a little more active, was in bed first. The older man threw himself on his bed and struck a mattress that was hard and supported by slats that did not give. He knew at once what had happened.

"Oh, Elkins, you've robbed me!" he groaned.

Speaking of a Senator who was opposing something he wanted, Elkins once remarked: "I must have a horse-shed talk with him."

"A real horse-shed talk," he explained, "generally happens outside a country church where a meeting is going on. You will see two old fellows get together in a horse-shed, one sitting on a wagon tongue, the other with a foot on the hub of a wheel, both whittling and arguing. They are making a trade and each is trying to get the better of the other. Some mighty fine trades are made in a good horse-shed talk."

"Don't scratch up more snakes than you can kill," was one of his mottoes. He used to say that to the Republican leaders when they were inclined to go beyond what he thought was good politics.

Elkins never could be one of the "inner circle" in the Senate. He was too often an insurgent. He had lived in the West and was generally for the West; particularly was he in favor of the admission of the territories as states, and in this respect was not in harmony with the leaders of his own party.

Elkins was a Blaine leader for years. He was a Blaine man until after 1888.

He often wondered why certain men did not make themselves President. "If I lived in New York, Pennsylvania, Ohio or Illinois, I would make myself Presi-

dent," he once told me.   "But what can a man do with
only twelve delegates back of him from his own state?"

Elkins wanted the nomination for Vice President on
the ticket with McKinley in 1900, but he had no power
against the forces then operating in the Republican
party. He may have had an idea that McKinley
might not live out his term, and that by succession he
would attain the grand prize.

The Governor of West Virginia appointed Davis
Elkins as the successor of his father. This selection
created an interesting and unusual circumstance which
up to that time never had been equaled. Three
generations of one family represented the same state in
the United States Senate. Mrs. Elkins attained a distinction which no other woman had gained. She had
a father, a husband, and a son in the Senate of the
United States, and lived to see all of them attain the
honor.

No one in Congress, not even the Democrats who
came into control of the House, desired an extra session
of the Sixty-second Congress which President Taft
called in April, 1911, for the special purpose of enacting
the Canadian reciprocity agreement into law—a tariff
law which largely reduced the rate of duty on goods
coming into the United States from Canada. It was a
tariff bill drawn by the executive, and was not even
amended by the tariff-making body, the Congress.

Most of the Republicans were opposed to the reciprocity measure. Men of insurgent tendencies from
northwestern states thought it was aimed at them,

while real standpatters on the tariff were as bitterly opposed to the agreement as were the opponents of President Taft.

Many regulars, such as Gallinger of New Hampshire, Warren and Clark of Wyoming, McCumber of North Dakota, and others, who had stood squarely for the Administration from the beginning, were intensely opposed to the Canadian agreement.

It did not take the Democratic House long to pass the legislation. With the Republicans divided and their own large majority they gave the bill an overwhelming vote. In the Senate the success of the measure was assured. Although the Republicans were in the majority, they were divided and an almost united Democratic minority, after a long debate, made the reciprocity agreement a law on the part of this country.

But it was still to be ratified by Canada.

Canadian reciprocity wrecked two political governments, one in Canada and the other in the United States. It is quite likely that the Taft administration could not have been re-elected even without the burden of Canadian reciprocity, but that measure made defeat a certainty. In Canada the opposition was such that the Liberal party, with the popular Sir Wilfrid Laurier at its head, went down to defeat.

The defeat in Canada can be attributed to the opposition of the Catholics. It was Catholic influence that kept Canada from joining the American colonies in 1776, and this same influence defeated a French-Canadian Catholic premier in 1911. The cause of this

opposition was the fear of annexation. The French
Catholics in the eastern provinces of Canada long ago
secured concessions regarding schools and the distribu-
tion of public funds which would not be permitted
under our government. These concessions make them
intensely loyal to Great Britain and antagonistic to
annexation to the United States.

The fear of annexation had been greatly enhanced by
the utterance of the two most prominent men in public life in this country, or at least those who held the
two most powerful positions. In advocating the Canadian reciprocity agreement President Taft said that
it would lead to a closer relationship mutually advantageous to both countries. The President was quoted in
Canada as having said:

"Before Canada is irrevocably fixed in a policy leading to consolidation and strengthening of the British
empire we must turn her from her course."

Speaker Champ Clark in the House, when the
Canadian bill was first pending, had gone much further,
and said:

"I look forward to the time when the American flag
will fly over every square foot of British North America
up to the North Pole."

These utterances of the President and the Speaker so
alarmed the people of Canada who opposed annexation
that they defeated the government which had negotiated the reciprocity agreement.

Politically the damage was as great on this side of
the border as on the other. The seed of distrust had

been planted and it could not be uprooted in one year.

The House of Representatives, called in extra session to pass the fateful Canadian reciprocity measure, was the first which the Democrats had controlled in sixteen years. Although the Democrats had been denouncing the methods by which the Republicans governed the House, and in the previous session had, with the aid of insurgents, shorn Speaker Cannon of a part of his power, they really followed in the footsteps of their political antagonists. They made changes, but the result was only a transfer of power from one position to another. The greatest loser in this transaction was Champ Clark, yet he was the most insistent advocate of the change.

During the winter of 1911, when the Democrats were getting ready for their control of the House, it became apparent that they would go much farther and would not only continue to have the Committee on Rules separated from the Speakership, but would also deprive the Speaker of the power to appoint the committees which gave him such control over the House. Members of the House know that good places on committees are the most important part of their congressional career, and they are under obligations to the man who has the power to name the committees.

The Democrats proclaimed that, in liberalizing the rules and depriving the Speaker of power, they would transfer that power to those to whom it belonged, the members of the House; the House should elect its own committees! That was to be a real, a great, a wonderful reform!

Of course, in order to facilitate matters, the leaders on the Democratic side conferred and discussed, and canvassed somewhat, and finally it was announced that in view of the probability of an extra session the Democrats would hold a caucus and make arrangements for the selection of committees. The new members-elect were invited to participate. Everybody was to have equal treatment.

It was suggested that the Committee on Rules should select the committees. This was quickly abandoned as conferring too much power on a committee that had been so severely criticized in the past. It was then decided—by these leaders—that a regular legislative committee of the House should prepare the list of committees to be presented to the caucus. It was only natural that, as the Ways and Means Committee must be selected early so as to go to work on the tariff, it should also be designated to nominate the committees.

Before the caucus assembled it was known that Champ Clark would be nominated for Speaker; that Oscar W. Underwood of Alabama was to be Chairman of the Committee on Ways and Means, and the name of every other member of that committee had been designated. When the caucus met the slate went through without a protest.

The power in the House of Representatives had been transferred from the Speaker to the Chairman of the Ways and Means Committee.

When Congress assembled the Democratic caucus ratified all that the Ways and Means Committee had done in selecting the committees. If certain men were sore, they had to swallow their grievances. To attempt to overturn the action of the committee would have been futile.

For the most part, the Ways and Means Committee had followed seniority, just as Speakers generally had done. The ranking man secured the chairmanship. Speakers sometimes upset this precedent, but it cannot be done when the body elects. It is rarely ever done in the Senate. In only one instance was there a deviation from the rule of seniority by the House.

William Sulzer of New York did not succeed to the chairmanship of Military Affairs, of which he was the ranking Democratic member. James Hay, one of the main wheels in the Virginia political machine, wanted to be chairman of the military committee. So there was a shifting about. Henry D. Flood was derricked from the head of the Foreign Affairs Committee and made Chairman of Territories, in order to make a place for Sulzer, for the New Yorker was willing to give up the military for the foreign committee. It was not the only time that Hal Flood was sacrificed to meet the necessities of the Virginia machine. When Senator Daniel died, Wm. Hodges Mann was Governor of Virginia, and he wanted to appoint his personal friend and favorite, Hal Flood, as Daniel's successor. But he wasn't allowed to do it. He had to appoint Claude A. Swanson, for the latter had been training for this place, just as Hay had been training for the military committee, and as both were Flood's senior (in the machine) they secured advancement.

Right at this point it might be well to pursue the selection of Sulzer a little further. As chairman of the committee he was instrumental in securing the adoption of a resolution which abrogated our treaty with Russia. This was done because Russia mistreated the Jews in her dominions. Going still further, we might point out that the abrogation of the treaty did not help the Jews one iota; that it greatly injured our trade with Russia, and the net result was the election of Sulzer as Governor of New York.

An attempt was made to punish Fitzgerald for his previous espousal of the Cannon rules. He was the ranking Democrat on the Appropriations Committee. Albert S. Burleson of Texas was next in line and wanted the chairmanship. Probably a majority of the Democrats would have voted for Burleson, but Fizgerald showed fight.

"Go ahead if you want to start something," he told them. "Of all the chairmanships in the House only three are given to northern Democrats, and one of these is the unimportant chairmanship of Invalid Pensions. You have deposed one northern Democrat, Sulzer, from his rights in order to give place to a southerner. Now, if you want to, go ahead and take the only important chairmanship that goes to a northern Democrat and give it to a southerner. You won't get away with it without a fight in caucus and another on the floor of the House. And I'm not sure that you'll be able to organize the House after the fight is made."

That ended the attempt to depose Fitzgerald. There were too many men who realized what such a fight as he would make might mean to the party. Furthermore, there were many Democrats who knew that Fitzgerald had been right in the rules fight, and it was scarcely just to punish a man for being right, even if he had to desert his party in order to vote his convictions.

The effect of the fight on Speaker Cannon, in which Clark and Underwood stood together, the changing of the rules, and the shifting of the power from the Speaker to the Chairman of the Ways and Means Committee, had even more far-reaching results than the incidents described.

Champ Clark lost the Presidency on account of that combination of circumstances.

The power and prestige which Oscar W. Underwood secured by the change made him a Presidential candidate. Had Clark retained the power of former Speakers, he would have had the delegations from a number of southern states which were carried by the Alabama man on account of the prominent place he attained in the House. With those delegates Clark could have been nominated, notwithstanding the combination which brought about his defeat.

The Republicans did not nominate Mr. Cannon for Speaker, thus making him minority leader. Instead they chose James R. Mann of Illinois, who, although a regular, had not been so obnoxious to the insurgent wing of the party. But even Mann could not command the entire strength of the minority. Several members showed their independence by voting for other men. When one new man cast his vote for Cooper, former Speaker Cannon asked:

"Who is that pinhead?"

Minority Leader Mann was authorized to select the Republican members of the committees, and he made such good use of his power as to increase his prestige in the House, and also to win back would-be insurgents who were inclined to remain aloof from the regular organization.

CHAPTER XI

PLAYING POLITICS—MEXICO

Democrats Make the Most of the Extra Session and Pass "Pop-gun" Tariff Bills—Long Public Career of Senator Frye—"Gag" Order Revived—Trouble Breaks Loose in Mexico and Troops Are Sent to the Border—A Policy Inaugurated Which Continued Through Two Administrations—Enlarging the Monroe Doctrine.

WHEN President Taft called the Sixty-second Congress in extra session he specified that it was for the purpose of passing the Canadian reciprocity agreement. There was no need of other legislation.

"But," argued a number of Republicans, even those who had promised to vote for reciprocity, "once the Democratic House is in session it will not adjourn until it pleases; until it has passed a number of tariff bills, and perhaps other legislation which may be embarrassing."

The usual hearty laughter of Mr. Taft greeted this remonstrance. He expressed the opinion that these men were unduly alarmed, making mountains out of mole hills and "seeing too many lions in their path," and, besides, why should a Republican Senate fear a Democratic House.

It was futile to explain that the Republicans had lost eight Senate seats in the last election, and that there

were a dozen insurgent Republicans who might vote
for the tariff bills. So the extra session was called.

After passing the Canadian bill the House began by
passing an enlarged free list bill, for which twenty-four
western Republicans voted, and the same number
voted for the free wool bill which followed. This bill
also reduced the duties on manufactured woolen goods.
In the Senate seventeen Republicans voted for the free
list bill and thirteen for the wool bill. Soon after the
cotton bill, largely reducing duties, was passed by the
House and was brought before the Senate.

Consideration of the cotton bill in the Senate afforded
Senator Penrose of Pennsylvania an opportunity to
play an amusing game with Senator La Follette of Wisconsin. When the wool bill was taken up in the Senate
La Follette took complete charge. At the head of
thirteen insurgent Republican Senators he held the
balance of power. Voting with the Republicans he
defeated the Democratic measure. Then offering his
own schedule he secured the Democratic votes to pass
it as a substitute for the House bill.

When the cotton bill was reached La Follette had his
substitute all ready to go through the same program.
But on the very first motion made by a Democrat
the Republican regulars did not vote and the Democrats
had full control. They amended and fixed the bill as
they desired, and then passed it with the insurgents
voting in opposition and the regulars leaving the
chamber or refusing to vote.

There was quite a hubbub raised about this turn of

affairs. Penrose gave it out flatly that he did not propose that La Follette should run the Senate in combination with the Democrats; that La Follette had to work
either with the Democrats or with the Republicans,
but there would be no more maneuvers such as that
with the woolen bill.

It was while everybody was playing politics with the
various tariff bills that Underwood made a fierce assault upon William J. Bryan. The majority leader of the
House took exception to what Bryan had said of Underwood and his conduct regarding the iron and steel
schedule. Underwood denounced Bryan as a falsifier,
and with a few exceptions had the entire Democratic
side loudly applauding him.

President Taft vetoed all the tariff bills, as he was
expected to do, after having said that the Payne-Aldrich
bill was one of the best tariff measures ever enacted.
That these bills were simply the footballs of politics
was perfectly evident from the start. The fact that
they were passed schedule by schedule in separate bills
showed what the Democrats intended. They wanted
to "put the Republicans in a hole." Two years later,
when they had full control, they did not try any
schedule by schedule business, but the very same men
passed a tariff bill as a whole. Twenty years before
when the Democrats were putting through similar bills
a member of their party called them "pop-gun tariff
bills."

The bill for the admission of New Mexico and Arizona
was passed during the special session. It contained

the Arizona constitution rejected by the previous congress, including the recall of Judges. President Taft promptly vetoed the bill on this account, and statehood was again delayed.

Attempts to pass the statehood and the tariff bills over his veto failed. The statehood bill, with the objectionable features eliminated, was finally passed, and the last of the territories within the old limits of the United States came into the Union.

At this special session the resolution providing for the election of Senators by direct vote of the people was passed. It was speedily made a part of the Constitution by ratification of three-fourths of the states.

The session was enlivened by a clash between Senator Heyburn of Idaho and John Sharp Williams. It was over a resolution to keep on the pay roll a negro who had once been a body servant of Jefferson Davis, and, I think, it was the last time the animosities of the Civil War were aired in Congress. Heyburn was very bitter in his denunciation of everything pertaining to the Confederacy.

Senator Frye of Maine died during the session, after a long and continuous service in both House and Senate. Frye had been a prominent member of the House when he succeeded Blaine in 1881, Blaine having been appointed Secretary of State.

Frye was a most remarkable man in many respects. For years he was President pro tempore and a very satisfactory presiding officer. Once when he advocated a measure, and the opponents of it intimated that he had been influenced by money, he made a statement which has always seemed to me surprising.

"When my mother put me in my first pair of trousers," he said, "she put a piece of silver in my pocket. From that day to this I have never wanted for a dollar."

Frye was a strong advocate of a ship subsidy bill, and he also was an expansionist, supporting all measures for acquisition of territory.

On one occasion, when he made a speech on the old Nicaragua canal bill, his command of statistics and other facts was little short of marvelous. He spoke of distances, tonnages, depths of water, prices, and everything else connected with shipping, always using figures and hundreds of them, and never once did he refer to a note or hesitate. This mass of statistics rolled out in a flood of oratory.

Senator Frye in consequence of his pronounced views was often termed a jingoist. Two or three times he made a fiery speech about the protection of American citizens, in which he commended in the highest terms, and described in vivid language, the march of a troop of British soldiers through a hostile region and their endurance of many hardships in order to rescue a British subject who had been denied his rights in a foreign country. About the time that Frye died Senator Stone of Missouri was hunting for that speech to quote, in order to show that President Taft was not doing his duty in protecting American citizens in Mexico.

The extra session came to an end in August, the

Democrats having had all the best of it. They had
passed their tariff bills and widened the split in the
Republican party. The Republicans were more hopelessly divided than ever before. In the House twenty-
five Republicans refused to work with the regulars and
most of them voted for Democratic tariff bills. In the
Senate there were thirteen insurgents, most of whom
voted with the Democrats on several tariff bills. The
feeling in the Senate was so intense that Senator Gallinger, the senior in service, was refused an election as
President pro tempore by the action of half a dozen
insurgents who would not vote for him.

Quite a sensation was made over President Taft's
"gag-order," which was an order that no one in any of
the departments should give out any news or information save the heads of the departments. Much was
made of it until it was found that Taft had simply
reissued an order first made by Roosevelt.

Years ago newspaper men in Washington could
browse around the various departments and through
friendly officials pick up many interesting items of
news. Then, also, men who were persecuted by those
higher up could get their side of the story to the public.
Oftentimes the publication of facts about what public
officials were doing for the public proved very annoying, hence the "gag-order." It is utterly impossible for
any head of a department, to know all that is going on in
that department and much of the news about the
government at Washington has been suppressed.

But the department heads like the order, and not

only was it continued by Taft but also by his successor.

One development occurred during the year which had a bearing on events of 1898. General Bixby, Chief of Engineers of the United States Army, went to Havana and made an examination of the wreck of the old *Maine*. He reported that it was evident the ship had been destroyed by an internal explosion. It was because our people believed that Spain had destroyed our ship that the war feeling in this country was fanned into a flame. Had it been known that the ship was blown up as the result of an accident, the Spanish war might have been averted.

Mexico began to figure in our politics before half of Taft's administration had passed into history. The disintegration of the Diaz government brought about a condition in Mexico from which that country suffered for many years. There was almost a parallel between what happened under the two administrations of Taft and Wilson, save that under Taft the United States forces did not fight on Mexican soil.

Early in the year 1911, 20,000 American troops were ordered to the Mexican border and were kept there a long time. They were a menace to Mexico, and there were many people on both sides of the border who thought it meant an invasion of Mexico.

There were constant stories of murders and riots in Mexico and destruction of American property. President Taft issued warnings to the Mexican leaders, telling them the lives of American citizens and their property

must not be destroyed. Then there were raids across
the border, and the Mexicans fighting on their side
fired shots into American territory. American citizens
were wounded and killed. Senator Stone of Missouri
grew fiercely indignant, and in a speech in the Senate
breathed war in no unmistakable terms. Notes were
sent to Mexico from the State Department declaring
that the killing of American citizens must cease. Later
a dispatch was sent to our Ambassador in which Americans were told to get out of Mexico. Replying to one
of the notes, the government then in power in Mexico
said that the United States had no business interfering
in Mexico's internal affairs.

This brief review of the striking events, and the
policy in regard to Mexico, during the last two years of
the Taft administration shows that a change of parties
did not change the methods.

As showing a further parallel, a story was afloat, in
1911 as I recall, that Theodore Roosevelt was going
to raise a division of volunteers for Mexican service,
obtain a major general's commission, and enter upon a
soldier's career. In 1916 the same story was circulated
again.

It may be interesting to note that the situation in
Mexico did not enter into the campaign of 1912. It
is true that President Taft was criticized by some Democrats for not protecting Americans and their property,
but there was no more desire for a war with Mexico
in 1912 than there was in 1916.

The last lottery we shall see in the United States

Senate for many years occurred early in the regular session of Congress when the Senators from New Mexico and Arizona were sworn in and drew lots to see who should have the long and who the short terms. There are three classes in the Senate, and the length of terms of Senators from new states is determined by the luck they have in drawing.

At this writing it is difficult to say what will be the next state or when it will be admitted. Probably Alaska, although both Hawaii and Porto Rico will in time make claims for statehood.

The Senators who took their seats at that time were Catron and Fall of New Mexico, and Ashurst and Smith of Arizona. Catron had been a Delegate from New Mexico. Fall became a thorn in the side of the Taft administration on account of his criticism of the lack of a Mexican policy. Ashurst was soon known as one of the flowery talkers of the Senate. On one occasion, when different Senators had been describing the scenic grandeur of their respective states, Ashurst turned loose his flow of language about Arizona, and his adjectives, superlatives, and flowery rhetoric out-distanced every man in the Senate.

The speech recalled an incident of the campaign in Arizona. Ashurst was known to be an advocate of all the progressive, "crazy" ideas as they were often called, and it was suggested that one of the elder statesmen, such as Senator Lodge, should campaign in Arizona and engage this young man of wild ideas in joint debate. Members of the committee found

Ashurst willing, and some one began to tell him what he
ought to say.

"That's all right, gentlemen," he interrupted, "you
get the man here and I will furnish the stage setting and
the scenery."

In view of what happened a few years later, one of the
important measures passed during the summer was that
providing that American coastwise ships could pass
through the Panama canal free of tolls.   It was a subject that caused a great deal of debate.   European
nations, and particularly Great Britain, protested vigorously against the proposed law.   It was adopted by
a large majority in both houses, the Senate passing the
bill after the Democratic national convention had
adopted its platform, one of the planks containing a
declaration for free tolls.

Billy Lorimer had to stand a second trial for his
seat as a Senator from Illinois, and was ousted after a
very sensational exposure of the methods by which
Senators were elected in that state.   One of the interesting incidents of the Lorimer trial was the strong speech
of Senator Bailey in favor of the right of Lorimer to re-
tain his seat.   Sitting near the Texas Senator was
Tillman, feeble in health and stricken by the passing
years.   At times he wept like a child.   He voted for
Lorimer, largely because he then believed, as he had
for a long time, in the mental and personal integrity of
Bailey.

It was so well understood that President Taft was
using the power of his office to influence votes in the

Lorimer case that the Senate passed a resolution rebuking Presidential influence in matters wholly within the jurisdiction of the Senate.

Only a few years before President Roosevelt had used his influence openly in the case of Senator Smoot of Utah, when an effort was made to unseat Smoot because he was a Mormon Apostle, but no rebuking resolution was then passed.

An extension of the Monroe Doctrine, so far as a vote of the Senate could extend that sacred, but somewhat nebulous dictum, was provided in a resolution introduced by Senator Lodge, and passed by the Senate without opposition. For several months there had been rumors that a concern, under the guise of obtaining fishing rights, was securing privileges in Magdalena Bay, Lower California, but that the real intent was to transfer the concession to Japan for a coaling station. The Lodge resolution made it quite plain that such an acquisition would be regarded as an unfriendly act. About the same time information was conveyed to Mexico that the United States could not permit Japan to obtain a concession on the Pacific which might mean a coaling station or a naval base.

The unpleasant duty of vetoing a bill restricting immigration was put upon President Taft. Cleveland had to veto such a bill, but McKinley and Roosevelt escaped. McKinley escaped by having bills held in committees, and because the agitators were not so insistent as in later years. During Roosevelt's administration Speaker Cannon prevented action on the immigration bill at the earnest wish of the President.

Years after Augustus P. Gardner, the most intense advocate of immigration restriction, learned of Roosevelt's attitude.   He saw a copy of a letter which Roosevelt had written to Cannon.   When he had read it Gardner remarked:

"Ah! Father-in-law [Lodge] as well as myself was deceived.   I suspected he [Roosevelt] was lying to me, when he said he was in favor of restriction, but the Senator said no.   Uncle Joe has his side in writing while we have only his word."

Even so, there came a time when Gardner supported Roosevelt for a third term, and "Father-in-Law" voted for Roosevelt on the second ballot at Chicago in 1916.

Senator La Follette was much in the limelight during the session, and took keen delight in attacking both Taft and Roosevelt and the standpat Republican Senators.

"There are only fourteen Republicans listening to me now," he remarked one day.   "I wonder if that is a prophecy of what is to come?"

He reminded them that when he came to the Senate he stood alone, and then promised that if he did not have a following before his service closed there would be many Republican seats vacated.   Subsequently, in recalling this matter he referred to the fact that there had been thirty Senate changes since he made his first prediction.

La Follette charged the Administration with rifling his mail. This was denied, although the Wisconsin Senator showed letters to the Senate which had been opened, and said he could produce hundreds of others. It is curious that such denials are made when every public man or big business man who is marked by an administration suffers from interference with his mail in transit through the postoffice.

In assailing Roosevelt Senator La Follette said that he was a trust President, and showed how the trusts had multiplied and thriven during Roosevelt's administration despite the Sherman law then on the statute books. La Follette said that Roosevelt was destroying the progressive movement; that he cared nothing about a man's politics or his ideas on the great subjects before the country, but that Roosevelt's sole question was "How do you stand on me?"

CHAPTER XII

CHICAGO 1912

The Republican Split Complete—Taft Supported by the Conservatives—
La Follette the Candidate of the Progressives—The Colonel's "Hat
in the Ring"—Bitter Contest for Delegates—Old Guard "Goes
Down the Line"—Feeling Runs High and Riot Feared—The
Roosevelt Bolt and Birth of the Progressive Party.

A S the time approached for the Presidential election
of 1912 everything pointed towards Democratic
success. The management of affairs in the House had
been such as to keep the party together, while the
minority continued to be divided. Not only had the
Republicans divided on Canadian reciprocity, but also
on various tariff schedules. Republican insurgents
were not getting any nearer the White House and no
effort was made to bring them over. It was a conflict
between two contending factions which could not be
harmonized.

President Taft threw additional fuel on the flames
by negotiating and submitting a number of arbitration
treaties, and pressing them with a great deal of vigor.
Many Senators thought these treaties surrendered
cherished rights of the American people, including the
Monroe Doctrine. They were finally emasculated by
amendments and sent back to the President. Not

only insurgents, but also regulars opposed the arbitration treaties.

One of the interesting incidents in connection with the arbitration treaties was a propaganda financed by Andrew Carnegie, and continued with great vigor until the Administration began suits against the Steel Trust, when the canny ex-ironmaster at once ceased his financial efforts to promote peace on lines that would bring credit to Mr. Taft.

Progressive Republicans began a campaign to control the next Republican convention and nominate a man of their own. As chairman of the Progressive party Jonathan Bourne announced that La Follette was to be the man. Senator Cummins of Iowa also became a candidate, but the Progressives turned to La Follette, who seemed to be the favorite, although no one really believed he could wrest the nomination from Taft.

The idea of La Follette and his loyal supporters was that Taft with his machinery would capture the convention, be nominated and defeated. His principal competitor, supposedly La Follette, would have the nucleus of an organization and the prestige as a Progressive which would give him the nomination in 1916. In October, 1911, La Follette was proclaimed the Progressive candidate by two hundred Progressive Republicans assembled at Chicago.

From various utterances of Taft it was evident that he never entertained any real hope that he would be elected a second time. Early in his Administration he had spoken of himself as a one-term President, and

on other occasions he had given evidence that one term
was all he expected.   One evening at the White House,
when Speaker Clark was the guest of honor, President
Taft said to him:

"Champ, as you are going to succeed me, I think I
will show you over this place."

And he did so.   It was known then that the Speaker
was a candidate for the nomination in 1912.

In the Fall of 1911, when Taft was making one of
his periodic swings about the country, an enthusiastic
man at Salt Lake City, introducing the President to an
audience, predicted Taft's election in 1912.   Taft
remarked that "the young man is a better Republican
than a prophet."   Within a month, at Chicago,
Taft in a speech indicated that the Republicans were
going to lose, and his remarks caused a great deal of
adverse comment by members of the party.

From the time Roosevelt retired from the Presidency
there was a strong, determined, and ever active, though
not entirely cohesive, organization working to bring
him back to the White House.   It wanted him for a
third term and wanted him as the successor of Taft and,
four years later, as the successor of Wilson.

Just when and where the determination was reached
to make Roosevelt the candidate in 1912 is difficult to
establish.   An attempt has been made to show that it
was Roosevelt's jealousy of La Follette's growing
prominence as a Progressive leader that caused him to
become a candidate himself.   That is not the fact.   The
men who were supporting La Follette had no idea that

the Wisconsin Senator could defeat Taft for the nomination, and yet they believed that a Progressive Republican could win in 1912. Men with those ideas were responsible for Roosevelt's candidacy.

During the year 1911 a number of men who thought they could speak for the Colonel found themselves mistaken. Early in April one of them felt at liberty to quote Roosevelt in a widely read publication as saying: "I am not a candidate for the Presidency, and my friends will do me a cruel injustice if they seek to make me such."

In June Roosevelt denied a published statement that he was pledged to support Taft. A month later there was a sharp difference between Taft and Roosevelt over the arbitration treaties. Taft said that the war with Spain might have been avoided by such a treaty. To this statement Roosevelt, as one of the chief instigators of the war, took exception, claiming that the United States could never submit the question involved in the controversy with Spain in 1898 to any tribunal.

In the *Review of Reviews* appeared this statement: "Aug. 21. Colonel Roosevelt announces that under no circumstances will he consent to the use of his name for the Presidential nomination of 1912." In November one of Roosevelt's alleged spokesman said he would keep out of the campaign entirely. In December Roosevelt's name went on the Nebraska ballot in the primary contest.

And yet the year closed without much definite knowledge as to whether Roosevelt would be a candidate.

A few friends had been informed that they might go as far as they liked; that "the bridle was off." One of the men to whom this information was imparted through a mutual friend, and who at that time became a strong supporter of Roosevelt, was Senator Borah of Idaho.

Before the campaign actually began the friends of Taft saw trouble ahead. Senator Borah as a member of the national committee, which met in December, 1911, tried to have the primary system adopted for the election of delegates. This was regarded as an anti-Taft, progressive move and was voted down.

Then also began active work in various sections for Roosevelt. Men who saw him carried the word far and wide. The understanding seemed to be very complete.

At that time came forward the "Eight Little Governors," as they were humorously referred to, who made a demand upon Roosevelt that he become a candidate. They were Stubbs of Kansas, Johnson of California, Osborn of Michigan, Glasscock of West Virginia, Hadley of Missouri, Bass of New Hampshire, Aldrich of Nevada, and Vessey of South Dakota.

Before Roosevelt replied to the governors he was to make a speech in Ohio, when it was expected he would announce his principles. In discussing the situation before the speech he told me that he would be a candidate for the nomination, but that the announcement was to be withheld until after his speech. At that time I pointed out to him the absolute certainty that he could not be nominated because the national committee would see to it that enough delegates were seated to prevent his success. Strange to say, he agreed with me, but said he was going in nevertheless. A few days later came the stirring phrase:

"My hat is in the ring!"

Of the preliminary canvass it may only be said that it was so conducted as to insure defeat for the Republican party. The men who were managing the campaign for President Taft and Colonel Roosevelt were not responsible for everything which was said and done, but they helped it along. All the differences which had been created in four years, all the hatred which follows when a house divides against itself, broke forth in a flood of vituperation and vilification, charges and counter-charges, until the whole country was amazed.

And why shouldn't there be amazement at such a spectacle? An ex-President and a President were contending for the great office. The men who had been friends were fighting each other. Roosevelt who had made Taft President was fighting to be his successor. The man who said that under no circumstances would he be a candidate for or accept another nomination was fighting for the nomination. A President was compelled to use all the power of his great office to secure a renomination. It was a spectacle, but a humiliating spectacle.

The fight in the Republican party had reached a stage at which the factions preferred the success of the Democracy to the success of their rivals. There was constant talk of a third ticket, particularly when any trick was turned by which Taft delegates were elected.

The two most memorable conventions in the history of the country, save those of 1860, were held in 1912. The Republican convention was not unlike the Democratic convention in 1860, which was so divided by factional strife as to insure the election of a Republican, though by a minority of the popular vote.

At Chicago the national committee sat for eight days and made up the temporary roll of delegates; in fact determined who should be delegates. In 1896 the national committee controlled by Hanna seated the McKinley delegates. In 1908 the national committee controlled by Roosevelt seated the Taft delegates. In 1912 the national committee seated the Taft delegates.

The committee in 1912 at Chicago went about its work like men who had determined to carry out a preconceived plan. There were thirty men who said they would "go down the line," as they called it, and carry out their program. There were among them one or two wavering men, men with scruples, who occasionally handed their proxies to men like Gerrit J. Diekema of Michigan and James A. Tawney of Minnesota, when there was some particularly disagreeable job in the way of voting out Roosevelt delegates to do, but necessary if the Taft men were to control the convention.

For eight days I sat in that committee room and "watched the wheels go round." Oftentimes the Roosevelt men on the committee voted for delegates who had no right to seats, and frequently there were loud complaints from the Roosevelt people over the action taken by the majority of the national committee, complaints that were not justified. Unfortunately for the Roosevelt men, they instituted hundreds of contests in which they had no valid claim, and this gave color to an assertion, which one of the over-enthusiastic Roosevelt newspaper men made, that many contests had been instituted for effect, so that it would look as if the national committee were doing a wholesale steamroller business in unseating Roosevelt delegates. To this day that shadowy newspaper assertion is given as a reason for justifying the committee in all that it did. "Bogus contests" is what they called the Roosevelt contests.

On most of the votes thirteen or fifteen men would vote on the Roosevelt side, but occasionally they would get five or six others who said the case was "too raw" for them. There were no roll calls, the Taft members of the committee having at the beginning taken the precaution to provide that it should take a demand of twenty members to order a roll call. There never were twenty members to make such a demand.

It is only that I may state the situation accurately that I give my idea of what took place in the committee. A friend of Senator La Follette went over the record and came to the conclusion that fifty delegates had been unjustly deprived of their seats, and La Follette was at no time for Roosevelt. Senator Borah, who attended all sessions of the committee, made the number fifty-two. My own estimate, after hearing all the testimony and reading a stenographic report of the proceedings, is that fifty-one Roosevelt men were deprived of seats to which they were entitled. As a matter of fact there would have been more if necessary. The men who were in control had determined that Roosevelt should not again have the nomination of the Republican party. They were prepared to take such action as to insure his defeat, let the future condition that would follow be what it might.

My, but that was an interesting time! The campaign managers were issuing all sorts of screaming screeds, charging each side with all kinds of political knavery.

William B. McKinley, who was in charge of the Taft campaign, said he had to house and guard carefully the negro delegates from the South to keep agents of George W. Perkins from buying them for Roosevelt. Joseph M. Dixon, the Roosevelt manager, asserted that the national committee was robbing the people of their rights. Colonel Roosevelt from Oyster Bay was charging the committee with being criminals. Francis J. Heney, and others of his ilk, abused the committee members while in session. Heney was particularly vicious in his assaults upon Penrose, Crane and Stevenson of Colorado. "Big Steve," he called the latter in an offensive way. Four years later "Big Steve" was a Roosevelt delegate in the same city.

Senator Borah led the fight in the committee for Roosevelt. Frank B. Kellogg of Minnesota and Cecil Lyon of Texas were his supporters. Subsequently the Old Guard wrung Lyon's neck with a twist which gave him a shock. Lyon and his Texas delegates, who, with him, had been fairly and legally elected, were thrown out of the convention. Half a dozen members of the committee, who had been "going down the line" on other cases, stood up and voted for the Lyon delegates. It was the most flagrant of all cases decided.

"You Taft men have as much interest in doing justice here as we have," Senator Borah on more than one occasion told the committee. "You want to elect your candidate if he is nominated. You do not want him to go out of the convention with a taint upon his title."

But the idea that prevailed there was that Roosevelt should not control that convention and be nominated.

After the clean-up had been made the Taft people had a small majority over all others, the Cummins, La Follette and Roosevelt delegates combined. There are men who still believe that if Roosevelt had not talked bolt, had not in fact gone to the extent of saying that his name should not go before the convention "until the roll was purged," Taft would have been defeated. There are men who say they know where the votes could have been found which would have turned the trick when the time came. I do not believe it. I have seen that machine in operation too often and too long to think that it could be fooled. There were members of it who thought they ought to have made more certain their control; that the entire delegation from California should have been thrown out in order to "make it a cinch," but there were others who figured that "Roosevelt would do something" that would make it safe for them to go ahead with what they had.

Elihu Root was made both temporary and permanent chairman of the convention. The first contest was over the temporary chairmanship. That was the test. On that vote a number of men who had been elected under instructions to vote for Roosevelt would not vote for Roosevelt's choice for temporary chairman. More than that, there had been backing and filling over this choice. Senator Borah was first chosen, and then it was learned that La Follette would put forward a man for the place, and so the Roosevelt men switched to Governor McGovern of Wisconsin. The out-and-out La Follette men would not vote for McGovern, and so the first vote showed a greater Taft strength than would have been shown on a ballot for the nomination.

As soon as Senator Root became chairman he assumed the full responsibility of his position. His rulings were in accord with what was expected. He recognized the temporary roll as the convention, and permitted delegates who had been seated by the national committee, but whose seats were contested, to vote, in spite of the protests by Roosevelt men that they ought not to be allowed to vote.

Soon after he was chosen chairman Senator Root demonstrated the forcefulness that was in him. William Flinn of Pennsylvania was given the opportunity to subside or be ejected by the police. Flinn was at the head of a very strong delegation, and he started to make trouble with vigorous and noisy objections to Root's ruling. Gently but firmly Root told him that he would be orderly or given over to the police. Chief Healy of the Chicago force was standing there with many bluecoats at his back to execute any orders that Root might give.

Roosevelt rushed to Chicago to accomplish by his personal presence what seemed to be slipping away from his lieutenants. To this day many of his followers think he made a great mistake, asserting that he might have been nominated if he had let them manage the campaign.

Roosevelt became suspicious of his lieutenants, Hadley and Borah, as both were talked about as compromise candidates. Borah was withdrawn as the candidate for temporary chairman. Governor Hadley was made the Roosevelt floor leader and given such a demonstration on his first appearance that some of the Roosevelt supporters were seriously concerned. It was to some extent, a Roosevelt demonstration, but a number of the Colonel's satellites, not recognizing this fact, jumped to the conclusion that Hadley had hopes of a nomination for himself.

As a matter of fact, all talk of a compromise candidate was absolutely futile. There was no possibility of agreeing upon a third man. Taft or Roosevelt had to be nominated. If Taft had withdrawn, enough of his delegates would have gone to Roosevelt to have nominated him. If Roosevelt had withdrawn, a large block of his delegates would have gone over to Taft. Neither man could have delivered his delegates to a third man.

There was much talk about Roosevelt going before
the convention and speaking. It would have been a
bold thing for him to do. But there is a very grave
question whether he would have been allowed to speak.
Perhaps the convention might have voted to allow him
to speak, but that is the only way it could have happened. Elihu Root would not have permitted a man
who was not a delegate to address the convention,
unless the convention itself so ordered. Theodore
Roosevelt knew Elihu Root very well. Perhaps he,
also, had a good idea of what Root would do under the
circumstances.

From the beginning of the convention there was talk
of riot, and there were rumors of an attempt on the part
of the Roosevelt men to use "strong-arm" methods.
At every session of the convention there were many
policemen in every aisle, while the routes leading in
from each entrance were crowded with policemen who
were ready to rush in at a signal. When Chairman
Root had his altercation with Bill Flinn, the convention
hall swarmed with policemen ready for action.

After one of the stormy sessions, and a more stormy
period around the Roosevelt headquarters in the evening; after a denunciatory speech by Roosevelt and a
still more fiery speech by Governor Hiram W. Johnson
of California, feeling ran high and there was real danger
in the air.

Later there were secret meetings and closed conferences. The night did not send these men to rest. It
was about 3 o'clock in the morning that I saw Senator

Borah descend one of the several stairways in the Congress hotel. Looking about he saw Jim Tawney and called to him. They had an earnest, but not a very long discussion.

After Borah left I asked Tawney what it was about. "He just told me," said Tawney, "that while he was an earnest supporter of Roosevelt and believed that he was entitled to the nomination on the showing made, he did not think any man's nomination was worth bloodshed and riot. Besides, he thought it was doubtful if any man named could be elected, if there should be bloodshed over the possession of the convention hall. He said that we had possession of the hall and it could not be taken from us without a fight, the consequences of which would be more disastrous to the Republican party than all that has been done. He advised me to see to it at once that a guard be maintained about the convention hall sufficiently strong to preclude any possibility of an attack being made."

Within an hour more policemen were sent to the coliseum, and the first men who reconnoitered in that vicinity in the early morning hours saw about the building a cordon of blue which would have discouraged even the most ardent set of men thirsting for an opportunity to render a service to the man they so much admired.

So far as Roosevelt was concerned he had bolted long before the convention reached a ballot. When the report of the committee on credentials was made and the convention adopted it, confirming what had been done by the national committee, Roosevelt announced that his name should not be presented to the convention. When the ballot was taken many Roosevelt delegations, still retaining their seats, refused to vote. Others voted for Roosevelt, because they did not intend to lose their Republican regularity.

After the convention was over Roosevelt men, delegates and others, met in a mass meeting, nominated Roosevelt, and called themselves "Progressives." It was the "parting of the ways," and a sad parting for many men who had been life-long Republicans.

Late that evening, and I tell the story as it was told to me by Colonel Cecil Lyon, there was a last gathering in the Roosevelt rooms. Some were jubilant and others sad. Some were in deep throes of agitation in trying to decide what to do. Beveridge was crying because he had to leave the Republican party. Others were engaged in earnest talk with their fellows; while still others stood around in a dejected attitude. Colonel Roosevelt entered the room and began "running around in circles," looking first one way and then the other. Finally he asked:

"Has any one seen my Herodotus?"

CHAPTER XIII

THE BALTIMORE CONVENTION

Champ Clark and Woodrow Wilson Lead a Field of Candidates—The
Missourian With a Majority of Delegates for Him Could Not Win—
Bryan's Betrayal of a Life-Long Friend—The Speaker's Bitter
Words of Comment—Why Marshall Was Named—A Famous
Platform.

WOODROW WILSON became a Presidential possibility as soon as he was elected Governor of
New Jersey. Likewise every other Democratic governor of a northern state. Champ Clark, Speaker of
the House, was the most conspicuous figure in the
Democratic party. Clark and Wilson overshadowed
all others, Bryan, of course, excepted.

Governor Wilson was regarded as a progressive candidate by many Democrats. By others he was thought
to be allied with big interests. As he had been brought
forward as a candidate for Governor by Colonel George
Harvey, of New York, and James Smith, Jr., of his
own state, it was supposed he had leanings towards big
business, with which Harvey and Smith had close relations. Even after he broke with Smith he maintained
close relations with Harvey, who was supposed to
be the real connecting link between Wilson politics
and big business. But Wilson repudiated Harvey

at a time when it appeared that Harvey was about to lead him among those men who are so very successful in finance, but unsuccessful in politics.

As the progressive tendencies of Wilson became manifest he received endorsement from an unexpected quarter. Both Governor Wilson and Senator La Follette addressed the Periodical Publishers' Association at a banquet in Philadelphia. In the course of his speech the Wisconsin Senator turned to the Governor and said:

"I hope you will be nominated by your party, Governor Wilson. If my party should not nominate a progressive I hope to see you elected President, Governor Wilson."

In the background, but a more active force in the Democratic party than any other one man, was William J. Bryan. He was not a candidate, but he was apparently for no particular man. Yet he assumed to say what kind of a man should be chosen by the party. In this connection he formulated and put forth thirteen questions to all Democratic aspirants, the answers to which were intended to define their positions and show whether they were proper men to nominate.

Early in 1911 Bryan was on the same platform with Wilson and gave the New Jersey Governor such a strong endorsement as to cause many people to say that Bryan was a Wilson man. On another occasion Bryan said that Wilson was a "Saul of Tarsus." That was about the time that Wilson kicked over the Harvey-Watterson-Ryan combination that seemed ready to take charge of him and his campaign.

WOODROW WILSON

Early in 1912 a professor of an eastern college interested himself in the selection of Woodrow Wilson for the Democratic nomination. He visited a number of men, including former Senator R. F. Pettigrew of South Dakota, whom he had known when he was connected with a western educational institution. In February, 1912, the professor visited William J. Bryan at Lincoln, Neb., and on behalf of Governor Wilson offered Bryan the office of Secretary of State if Governor Wilson should be elected President of the United States.

A mutual friend of the professor and Bryan heard the offer made. He was a supporter of Speaker Clark and informed Clark of the offer.

"Why," replied Clark, frankly, "if I were elected President I would, of course, expect to offer Bryan the position of Secretary of State."

In fact almost every Democrat who was a candidate at that time would have been glad to have secured the support of William J. Bryan by offering him the premiership of the Cabinet, for shrewd politicians were aware that it was in the power of the Nebraska man almost to make, and at least to mar, any man in his party.

Thus matters stood during the preliminary stages of the canvass. One incident occurred which it was thought would disturb the growing political intimacy between Wilson and Bryan. Some one got hold of a letter written by Wilson to Adrian H. Joline, a western railroad President, in which the Governor said: "Would that we could do something, at once dignified and effective, to knock Mr. Bryan once for all into a cocked hat."

That Bryan did not altogether relish the remark of the Governor was shown in an observation he made during the preliminary campaign.

"Governor Wilson is a good man," he said, "one of the big men of the country, but it does seem a little strange that a man who is Governor of a great state, and a prospective nominee for President, should express the wish that a man who has been three times the nominee of his party for President might be knocked into a cocked hat."

Bryan possessed a grim sense of humor himself.

About the time the Joline letter was published a great Democratic love feast was held in Washington, a Jackson Day dinner, which included nearly all the Democrats of national prominence, as the meeting of the Democratic national committee at that time brought them together. Senator O'Gorman of New York was then, and until the nomination, one of the most prominent and active supporters of the New Jersey Governor for President. O'Gorman had been selected to preside over the Jackson Day dinner. Both Wilson and Bryan were to be present and both were to make speeches. O'Gorman was much disturbed about the publication of the Joline letter, as he knew that Bryan probably could nominate, or at least prevent the nomination of, any man at the national convention. O'Gorman conferred with both Wilson and Bryan. Bryan said he thought the Governor owed him an apology or should at least make a statement. O'Gorman agreed with him. Wilson told O'Gorman that he would make a statement and give it to the newspapers. Then O'Gorman had a brilliant idea. He told the Governor that instead of making a statement there would be an opportunity to say something at the Jackson Day dinner which would in a public manner show that he had no feeling against Bryan, but in reality admired him very much, and there need be no reference to the Joline letter in any way whatever. This suggestion of Senator O'Gorman afforded Governor Wilson an opportunity to get out of an embarrassing situation without an apology, without any reference to the letter he had written, and at the same time, salve the wound of Bryan. Wilson made "the effort of his life" at that Jackson Day dinner. His audience consisted of about seven hundred leading Democrats from every part of the country. He had been talking for ten or fifteen minutes when he turned, and as if casually mentioning Bryan, paid the Nebraskan the highest compliment one man can bestow on another. Not in fulsome praise, Wilson was too wise for that, but in well-chosen words and well-rounded sentences he paid a tribute to Bryan as a man and a Democrat, that caused wave upon wave of applause to sweep over the dining room. This great demonstration Bryan took to himself, and nothing could please him more than the roar of a multitude voicing its approbation of the Great Commoner. That ended the Joline letter incident.

Bryan had put the seal of his disapproval on Governor

Harmon and Mr. Underwood, leader of the House.
But both persisted in being candidates, just as Parker
continued to be a candidate in 1904, when Bryan made
the character of Parker's supporters an excuse to express disapproval of him and oppose his nomination.

Bryan had no objection to Underwood because he
was a southern man. He never was sectional. He
sustained cordial relations towards southern men.
About the time that Underwood was making headway
in the South Bryan wrote to Hoke Smith of Georgia saying that there was no reason why a southern man should
not be a candidate for President, and he hoped Smith
would get into the race.

Senator Smith replied and expressed his thanks,
adding that he "was not going to pull anybody's chest-
nuts out of the fire."

Meanwhile Bryan, like a large number of other delegates, had been elected and instructed for Champ
Clark. Before the primary was held Bryan wrote to
Clark and asked him to withdraw as a candidate in the
Nebraska primary, saying that by remaining in the
field Clark would be likely to cause the success of Harmon in that state. Bryan added that he would be one
of the delegates, but did not want to go under instructions for Harmon. Clark replied that he had no doubt
whatever that he would carry Nebraska, and refused to
withdraw. He was right and did have a substantial
endorsement in the primary.

The convention at Baltimore was of the kind that
marks an epoch in the political fortunes of a nation,

and it has already been written into the history of the
country; all save that which went on inside the headquarters and underneath the surface.

The Democratic convention crowded close upon that
at Chicago. Bryan was in Chicago writing for a syndi-
cate of papers, and he saw, what every other man
could not help seeing, that the Republican party was
hopelessly split, and that whoever was nominated at
Baltimore would be elected President.

The preliminaries at Baltimore were under way
while Bryan was still in Chicago, and it so happened
that I interviewed him several times on Democratic
proceedings, particularly when the national committee
decided to make Alton B. Parker the temporary chairman. Bryan considered that a distinct slap in the face
for himself and he determined to resent it.

On the train from Chicago to Baltimore Bryan for
the most part maintained that grim silence for which he
is noted, but he did a great amount of thinking—and the
Presidency was in his mind. He had not been a candidate during the election of delegates, but with a dozen
candidates in the field, and a deadlock almost certain,
anything was possible.

Whatever hopes Bryan may have had, when he
reached Baltimore he received a rude shock when Judge
Parker defeated him for temporary chairman. His
reasoning powers told him that a convention which
refused to give the temporary chairmanship to a man
who had been three times the standard bearer of the
party was not likely to nominate that man for President.

The supporters of Parker gave Bryan and the progressive element in the party an opportunity to make capital by creating an impression that the same forces which controlled in 1904 were in control at Baltimore. Bryan expressed the hope, which was taken as a threat, that a third ticket for progressive principles might not be necessary. There was talk of Roosevelt and Bryan as a ticket in case the Baltimore convention became reactionary.

It was Champ Clark's convention—up to the time his managers began to make fatal blunders. By splitting Clark delegations between Bryan and Parker in the vote on temporary chairman they toyed with both sides, and afforded Bryan the opportunity to sow the idea that Clark was working with the monopolistic element of the party.

Another error that the Clark people made was in starting and keeping up a prolonged demonstration in the middle of the night when Charles F. Murphy cast the ninety votes of New York for Clark, taking them from Harmon. If that roll call could have been speedily completed, the next following might have nominated Clark. But during the demonstration Bryan returned to the convention hall and laid his plans. When Nebraska was reached on the next roll call he secured the opportunity which he utilized to defeat Clark. He abandoned his instructions and asserted that, because New York had voted for Clark, he was branded, and as long as he had the support of men like Murphy, Ryan, and Belmont, he ought not to be nominated.

Meanwhile ballot succeeded ballot, on nine of which Clark had a clear majority of the convention. And all the time Bryan was waiting for the result he had anticipated. The delegates were besieged by telegrams from the old Bryan guard in every state. "Get behind Bryan," was the message they conveyed, and also warnings not to support the monopolists. Telegrams were stacked up on Bryan's table telling him what the people were doing.

"They're hearing from back home," was one of his smiling remarks. He knew that a large number of delegates were becoming uneasy.

Champ Clark went to Baltimore twice during the convention, but the battle had been lost when he arrived the second time. He might have been nominated if he had gone before the convention and demanded an apology from Bryan, or insisted that he present proof of the assertion that Clark was linked with the plutocratic interests. But it is almost certain that from the time Bryan turned and rent his personal and political friend of twenty years' standing, Champ Clark's ambition was doomed.

Politics is a game and very frequently a cutthroat game. Gratitude is often a by-word; honor an unknown quantity; loyalty and personal friendship disregarded. These things may be expected in politics. But in a long period of political observation I never have known a case of political treachery equal to or even approaching that of William J. Bryan towards Champ Clark at Baltimore in 1912.

When Clark reached Baltimore it was expected that he would address the convention. There were people who knew what kind of language Clark could use under great provocation, and they seemed to fear that if he spoke from that convention platform grave consequences might result. It was suggested to Clark that if he did make a speech he should use moderate language.

"See here!" and that fierceness in his nature blazed in a scorching flame, "I want you to understand that I am in no mood to make a goody-goody speech about Bill Bryan!"

While Clark was at Baltimore the second time his friends concluded that he could not be nominated. When they told him that such was their opinion, he said:

"We must not let Wilson's vote sag. He has been gaining on every ballot, but if he drops, that will be Bryan's chance and he will be nominated."

The other candidates whom Bryan had opposed seemed to be of the same mind. At least their friends saw to it that Wilson continued to gain until he received the necessary two-thirds of the convention.

This was the second time that the two-thirds rule was used to defeat a man with a majority of the delegates. It was first invoked seventy-five years before. The rule has been kept more as a tradition than because it was necessary, and also because a condition might arise where it could be used to defeat a man who had by underhanded means or corruption secured control of a majority of delegates. The silver men in 1896 would have abrogated the two-thirds rule if it had been necessary to name a candidate, and the Cleveland men in 1892 were ready to abrogate the rule if more than one-third of the delegates had held out against Cleveland's nomination.

Bryan's expressed hope, that it would not be necessary to nominate a third ticket in order to secure a progressive candidate, scared a great many Democrats who wanted party success rather than the success of any one man. On that account Bryan was given a great deal of authority in the convention. As a member of the resolutions committee he dictated the platform, and in it he wrote the celebrated one-term plank.

At any and all times Bryan found an opportunity to speak. As soon as he appeared on the platform or stood where the crowd could see him and seemed to want recognition, the crowds surrounding the delegates, and many delegates also, vociferously shouted for Bryan, and the convention could not proceed until he had his say. Bryan knew he possessed this power. It was in that way he secured an opportunity to deliver his fierce denunciation of the New York delegation, the Belmonts, and Thomas F. Ryan, who was at that time a delegate from Virginia.

Bryan's attack on Ryan and those Virginians who supported him called forth a fiery rejoinder from Congressman Henry D. Flood. Bryan has heard bitter things said about himself at other times, but it was

rather surprising to have a southern Congressman tell
him to his face that he was, and always had been, a
party wrecker.

There is one feature of the convention that never
received any comment. It was in the power of Oscar
Underwood and the delegates who were supporting him,
during the many ballots in which Champ Clark was
leading, to have nominated Clark. Underwood, was
no more of a possibility in that convention than were
Harmon, Marshall, Foss, Baldwin and others. Only
Champ Clark, Woodrow Wilson, or William J. Bryan
had a chance to be named. Underwood's delegates
could have nominated Clark, even after Bryan's
assault upon the Speaker.

After the convention was over Clark made a public
statement in which he spoke kindly of Governor
Wilson, and in which, after saying that in the Democratic primaries he had received 200,000 more votes
than Wilson, his nearest competitor, and that he led in
the convention on thirty ballots and had a clear majority of all the delegates on nine ballots, he added:

"I lost the nomination solely through the vile and
malicious slanders of Colonel William Jennings Bryan
of Nebraska."

A few years later I wrote an interview with Clark in
which he discussed the convention contest of 1912. He
referred to the candidacy of former Governor Folk in the
Missouri primaries, and said that, although Folk carried
only two counties in the state, he gave Clark's enemies
an opportunity to say that he (Clark) had opposition

in his own state, adding: "And even after the primaries had given me a solid delegation, Senator Gore continued to go up and down the country misrepresenting the situation and saying that Missouri was divided. Had it not been for this sort of thing I would have been nominated in spite of the treachery of Bryan at Baltimore."

Before it was published I showed a copy of the interview to Clark. It contained a remark he had made to me about Bryan.

"This must not go," he said.

"I suspected you would not care to be quoted on Bryan," I remarked.

"It's not that," he replied. "When I get ready to hang the hide of that skunk on the fence and shoot it full of holes, it won't be in a casual interview."

The mystery of the nomination of Tom Marshall for Vice President never has been fully cleared up. There was no necessity for the choice from a political standpoint, but it fitted in well with political conditions in Indiana to nominate Marshall. He might have interfered with political plans of the Democratic leaders if turned loose on the state when his term as Governor expired.

Marshall had been Indiana's favorite son in the early balloting for President. Tom Taggart wanted to do something for Marshall, and he had a conference with his long-time political pal, Roger Sullivan of Illinois. Not long after Sullivan swung the Illinois delegation, instructed for Clark, to Wilson and Indiana followed.

When it came to naming a Vice President the general rule was followed, which is that when an eastern man is named for first place, a western man is given the consolation prize, the Vice Presidential nomination. And at Baltimore the question was to whom this place should be given. The suggestion of Champ Clark brought such a storm of indignation from his loyal supporters as to cause its immediate abandonment. David R. Francis of Missouri wanted the nomination, but Bryan would not consent. He never forgot any man who voted against the regular ticket in 1896.

Then the balloting for Vice President began, and the delegates seemed inclined to honor the brilliant Governor of North Dakota, John Burke, who had been voted for during the balloting for President, and who had been elected Governor in a Republican state. Burke's vote was alarmingly large—alarming for those who did not want him named.

In one of the side rooms near the convention hall there was a hasty conference, in which nearly all the Wilson leaders participated. A dominating and commanding figure in that conference was A. Mitchell Palmer of Pennsylvania. One of the first conclusions reached was that Burke should not be named because he was a Catholic. It was feared that on account of religious prejudice such a nomination would be unwise. Discussion of various other candidates followed, but Palmer cut the conference short by asserting that an agreement to which he was a party was binding; that there was a fair understanding of just what was meant when Illinois and Indiana swung to Wilson, and so far as he was concerned there was nothing to do but vote for Marshall. And that settled the Vice Presidency. Thomas R. Marshall was nominated.

The Baltimore platform has received a great deal of attention ever since it was adopted. It was drafted almost entirely by William J. Bryan. At least nothing went into the platform which Bryan did not want and nothing was omitted that Bryan wanted inserted. Woodrow Wilson said of it: "Our platform is not to catch flies with." In fact, there was no need of making such a platform. The "flies," that is, voters, had already been caught. Success for the Democrats was assured by the split in the Republican party.

Always and always Bryan has made much of the platform at national conventions. He was first nominated because of the platform he helped to frame and upon which he made his great convention speech. At the time of his second nomination he insisted upon a declaration for free coinage of silver, and threatened to refuse the nomination if his demand was not conceded. In 1904 he fought all night to defeat a gold standard declaration. In 1908 he dictated the platform over the long distance telephone.

In 1912 he not only made the platform, but he introduced an innovation. He held it back until after the nomination, an unusual proceeding. And when it was read no one knew and few cared what was in it.

Platforms are a necessity of national conventions. Sometimes they are the only causes of strife at conven-

tions.   As a usual thing only a few sticklers care anything about a platform, the vast majority of delegates
agreeing with the hard-headed politician who remarked
that "platforms are to get in on, not to stand on."
Only once in a great while, as in 1896, do platform
pledges amount to anything, and only then on some
vital question.   A shrewd political observer has said
that the American people settle only one question at a
time.   If party platforms were confined to the vital
subjects, and were not long, rambling rigmaroles of
glittering generalities, they might be more effective in
political campaigns.

   If the declarations in the Baltimore platform received
any attention during the campaign of 1912, further
than Wilson's assertion that the pledges made were
to be kept, I do not recollect it.   There was enough to
talk about in 1912 without reference to party platforms.

CHAPTER XIV

THE EXPECTED HAPPENS

Republicans in a Crushing Defeat and Wilson Wins Easily—Almost a
Campaign of Tragedy Relieved by Bits of Humor—Many Prominent Republicans Defeated—Woman Suffragists Create a Sensation
with Their Parade—Mexico Gets a Place in the Sun—Charming
White House Régime of Mr. and Mrs. Taft.

THE Republicans in 1912 got just what they must
have expected. No Republican, unless blinded
by partisanship, expected anything but defeat. Of
course there are "possibilities," and there are "ifs,"
and there are any number of "alibis" connected with
the 1912 election, but the actual fact stands out clearly
that it was not a Republican year.

The members of the Republican national committee
who "went down the line" at Chicago did not expect
at that time that Taft could be reëlected. They were
close enough to the election of 1892 to know that
a man, nominated by southern delegates from states
that could not contribute a Republican vote in the
electoral college, and over the protest of the Republican
states in the North, could not be elected.

They remembered with bitterness that Roosevelt
had ruled them with an iron hand for seven and one-
half years, and then bequeathed Taft to them. The

opportunity was ripe to get rid of both Roosevelt and his bequest, although they had become reconciled to and satisfied with Taft. The Republican leaders saw defeat ahead, and, under the circumstances, they were resigned.

The campaign of 1912 was something of a nightmare and almost wholly a farce. The contest, as far as it could be considered such, was between an ex-President and a President, two men who had been fond and intimate personal and political friends and who had become bitter enemies, and were telling what they thought of each other.

It is only for the purpose of giving a few facts that any space is devoted to this campaign.

Roosevelt headed a third party because he overestimated the popular clamor for himself and underestimated the number of rock-ribbed standpat Republicans who never would have voted for him. It is doubtful if Roosevelt could have been elected even if nominated at Chicago. There were a lot of Republicans in the country who were very tired of him.

The campaign of 1912 was chiefly interesting on account of the brisk exchange of personal invective between the Republican and Progressive candidates and their campaign managers. The volume of language and criticisms of one against the other was vastly amusing to the Democrats who had nothing to do but await the counting of the votes.

"Taft wabbles," shouted Roosevelt.

"Roosevelt is like Louis XIV," said Taft.

The Expected Happens   199

Both were on the stump. Roosevelt's onslaughts were so fierce and fast that the President had to do more than reply through the papers, or at least he felt called upon to make speeches in the campaign and be the first President to go out on the stump and plead with the voters for reëlection.

President Taft also felt called upon to issue a statement denying that he had favored Catholics. His management of the friar land dispute in the Philippines, his negotiation with the Vatican, his appointment of a Catholic as Chief Justice of the Supreme Court, his frequent appearance in public with Cardinal Gibbons and other dignitaries of the Catholic Church, had been commented upon to an extent which finally produced an atagonism in other denominations throughout the country. The President denied that he had unduly favored Catholics during his Administration. So intense was the feeling on this subject that a White House statement was published before the national convention, and reiterations were made during the campaign.

While speaking of this religious issue in politics—and so many people seem to fear to give the facts or mention the subject—it may as well be told now as at any other time that even in the campaign of 1908 many persons had conscientious scruples about voting for Taft because he belonged to the Unitarian Church. It was pretty hard for many of the members of various sects to reconcile their ideas of orthodox religious faith with that of a man who belonged to a denomination as liberal as the Unitarian.

There were just a few things that stood out in the campaign of 1912 above the vociferous demonstrations of rival Republican and Progressive chairmen, and the extravagant claims and fulsome literature of the press agents.

One of these was a story told by Dr. Harvey W. Wiley. Wiley had been forced out of the Bureau of Chemistry and the administration of the pure food law by a cabal in the Agriculture Department. He went on the stump against both Taft and Roosevelt. In his speeches he told of the occasion when Roosevelt called the eminent food expert an idiot.

"It was in regard to saccharin," Dr. Wiley said. "I was opposing saccharin as a substitute for sugar, and was met by interests close to the President who were manufacturers of the substitute. I said that saccharin was not only contrary to the pure food law, but that it was unhealthy."

"'Any one who says that saccharin is unhealthy is an idiot,' asserted Roosevelt before all those present. 'Dr. Rixey gives it to me every day.'

"That," remarked Dr. Wiley, "was the reason for the establishment of the Remsen Board, which, with the organization in the Department of Agriculture, did so much to destroy the pure food law."

It was a tragic campaign, that of 1912. It was a tragedy from the beginning, when the two friends of more than twenty years became fierce rivals for the office both had held. The defeat of Champ Clark was another tragedy—a piece of political treachery which almost stamped the word politics with infamy.   It was tragic to see an ex-President and a President squabble for the nomination, and afterwards contend fiercely to be elected.

Then on October 14, about three weeks before the election, Roosevelt was shot by a fanatic in Milwaukee, Wisconsin.   The shot would have killed an ordinary man, but Roosevelt speedily recovered.

Vice President Sherman, who was renominated with Taft, died October 30th, less than a week before the election.

The expected occurred.   Woodrow Wilson was easily elected.   It would have made no difference if McCombs, the national chairman, had been allowed to run the campaign instead of Wm. G. McAdoo.   Managers were not important.   With the Republican party defeated, even before the split, it was an easy matter to elect Woodrow Wilson when the division was complete.

It matters not that he lacked 2,450,000 of having a majority of the popular vote and to that extent was a minority President.   He received 435 electoral votes to 88 for Roosevelt and 8 for Taft.   The farcical features of the campaign just saved the situation from being one of the most tragic in our political history.

Not only was Wilson easily elected, but a Democratic House was returned, and the doubtful Republican majority in the Senate was supplanted by a real Democratic majority, the first in eighteen years.

It is interesting to point out the effect of the split in the Republican party on the Senate.   In 1910 the

Democrats elected nine Senators to seats occupied by Republicans. In 1912 nine more Democratic Senators were elected to take the seats of Republicans. In 1914 the party split gave the Democrats six more Republican seats.

All of these were in northern states, with the exception of one border state. In all that time, six years and three campaigns, the Republicans were unable to gain a single senatorial seat.

President Taft contributed his share to the humorous aftermath of the campaign when he said that he would not leave the White House a future candidate for the Presidency. He made another remark which was generally enjoyed, when some one said that he would have to ride with Wilson to the Capitol. "It might have been worse," was his reply, and everybody knew that he meant that it might have been Roosevelt.

Mr. Taft also took occasion to relieve the tension by a humorous speech in which he spoke of the incubus which ex-Presidents became. He suggested that they be chloroformed or given a lotus leaf, anything that would put them away quietly where they would cease from troubling the people.

Many prominent members of both Houses went down to defeat in 1912, though several of them became members of the famous "Come Back Club," and were in the congressional harness again in a few years.

Senator Heyburn of Idaho died in the autumn. He was a distinct loss because of his absolute and outspoken independence. There was not the least trace of a demagogue in him, and his perseverance was remarkable. To him, more than any one man, is due the credit of passing the pure food law. His dogged persistence forced it through an unwilling Senate. His Republicanism was intense, and he allowed it to run back to Civil War times. It was due to the position he took on various occasions that there was a revival of the almost dead embers of that period.

Senator Bailey retired from the Senate during the short session. He had not sought reëlection, and after the Democrats of Texas chose Morris Sheppard, Bailey resigned. Whenever a reference was made to Sheppard as Bailey's successor he resented it.

"You must not speak of that man as my successor," he would reply, "I took care to interpose a good man between myself and the other."

Through Bailey's influence R. M. Johnston had been appointed by the Governor of Texas to serve the short term.

Joseph W. Bailey came to Washington a pronounced radical. Long before his services closed he was a pronounced conservative. As he saw it, his party had departed from Democratic principles, and he stood almost alone. An able man, a strong constitutional lawyer, and a vigorous personality, he lacked just something which prevented him from becoming one of the great men of his time. But he achieved leadership in both House and Senate; he could have long remained a leader of his party in the Senate if he had followed the progressive tendencies of that party, curbed his personal views, and been content to accept to some extent the views of others. Bailey never was in accord with Bryan, and that kept him out of harmony with a large wing of his party, and finally built up a strong opposition in his own state.

Woman suffragists created a sensation on March 3, the day before the inauguration of the new President. In the first place there had been a "suffrage hike" from New York to Washington, when a number of women dragged themselves over the slushy roads for 230 miles in order to impress the idea upon the country that they wanted the ballot.

On March 3, they staged a great demonstration, taking advantage of the big crowds which were in Washington for the inauguration. There was a very large parade, with the usual floats and other paraphernalia. Then there was something like an allegorical play presented on the broad steps of the Treasury Department the women posing on the cold stones with bare feet and in gauzy costumes.

During the parade the crowds broke away from control of the police and closed in upon the marchers, stopping the parade and jeering the women. It was an unruly crowd, more jovial than ugly, and the police were powerless. A detachment of cavalry was brought from Fort Myer to restore order.

Late that night there was a scene in the House over the affair. Advocates of woman suffrage took up the matter and denounced the men responsible for lack of police protection.

Tom Heflin of Alabama made a notable speech against suffrage and referred to the suffrage marchers as "hens and chickens." This caused a still greater uproar.

Hobson of Alabama took up the cudgels for suffrage. "A woman has just telephoned me," he said, "that a ruffian jumped upon a float in which her daughter was riding and seized her by the knee."

Minority Leader Mann, who had earlier in the evening been presented with a testimonial on account of his service, started a fierce storm by saying:

"She ought to have been at home."

"Don't let the fact that you received a testimonial to-night make a damned blackguard of you," shouted Cooper of Wisconsin, angrily.

Congressman Kent of California took a hand in the mêlée and denounced Mann, and the latter told Kent to "go to hell."

Altogether it was a wild scene, almost as great in disorder as ever seen in the House. Strange, is it not, that very little of what happened, is found in the *Congressional Record?* Many other similar scenes have been suppressed in that publication, which is supposed to record everything that is said.

Mexico had a place in the sun before the close of Taft's administration. Senator Fall of New Mexico and Senator Lodge of Massachusetts, both Republicans, severely criticized the Mexican policy and the failure to protect Americans. Senator Stone of Missouri, who had been a critic, but who, since the election, was a prospective manager of Foreign Relations, became more conservative and less rampant for the movement of troops across the border.

Tales of horror were brought to President Taft, and he issued a warning, which was called an ultimatum, directed to the various chiefs in that revolution-torn country. In Mexico City and other places there were riots in which American lives were lost and American property destroyed. Then came the deposition of Madero and the proclaiming of Huerta as President, followed a few days later by the assassination of Madero. Meanwhile American troops were in camp on the border.

President Taft did not recognize Huerta as President of Mexico. It has been said that he would have done so, but for the courtesy he desired to extend to his successor. In a matter of so much importance he thought that it might be taking an advantage to recognize a new President of a disturbed country whose accession had taken place within ten days of the close of his own term.

A short time before he left the White House President Taft, in the course of a semi-humorous farewell speech to the Press Club, told the assembled newspaper men that his "besetting sin was disinclination for hard work." Perhaps that accounts for many things which happened during his Administration. As a subordinate to others he was a very hard worker. I never knew of a man in the Cabinet of any President, with the exception of Elihu Root, who worked harder than

Taft when Secretary of War. Those who saw him in the Philippines knew him to be a very glutton for work when under pressure.

After he became President the whole situation was changed. No one could tell him to do thus and so; he was his own master for the first time in ten busy, hardworking years and he made the most of it.

President Taft liked pleasure. He enjoyed golf by day and social relaxation by night. He liked to travel, and it was no rare thing for him to start off, almost unexpectedly, on a long journey, leaving much business stacked up in the White House. With the best of intentions he would go away determined to work while traveling, but that he found almost impossible.

He made a number of trips to Panama. On these occasions, particularly if it were just before Congress was to convene, he would take quantities of data, papers, etc., and several clerks, determined to finish his message before returning home. In most cases various entertainments would occupy his time, and the message would be postponed to the last possible moment.

President Roosevelt would have his annual message prepared long enough in advance so that it could be mailed to every part of this country and even reach Europe before delivery. The different news organizations, in spite of the utmost urging, were never able to get President Taft's message until within a day or two of its delivery.

One of the heartiest and most pleasant men that ever

occupied the White House, President Taft had a way of creating wrong impressions.

There was a man in Chicago who had been born an Englishman, but had become a naturalized American citizen, very proud of his adopted country and its institutions. He was a Republican and had contributed $15,000 to the campaign fund of 1908, but he asked no political favors. This man was about to return to England on a visit and was taking his ten-year-old son with him. He wanted the boy to see and talk with the President of the United States, so that he could tell his grandfather in England about it, tell him that he, an American boy, could and did meet the ruler of this great country.

Through one of the most prominent Republicans in Chicago an appointment was arranged at the executive offices for the man and his son. Together they entered the building, and after waiting more than four hours went away disappointed. It takes bitter language to tell how that man felt, and how that Republican politician felt, after this occurrence.

In regard to offices requested by friends, and the "lifting of the civil service lid" for the accommodation of men who had been his strongest supporters, there are many stories of how peremptorily they were turned down by Mr. Taft. In fact, it was at the executive offices that the President made himself unpopular.

In the White House proper, in the home of the President, Mr. and Mrs. Taft dispensed such hospitality as endeared them to all who were their guests. The White

House receptions were most enjoyable; the early garden parties, the musicales, dinners, dances, and small gatherings were delightful affairs. As hosts President and Mrs. Taft were never excelled. They were in no sense homespun; neither were they exclusive; they were charming people who seemed glad to welcome and entertain their guests. Mrs. Taft replaced the policeman who, up to that time, had opened carriage doors, received the cards of callers, and performed other incongruous duties, with colored attendants in unobtrusive livery; and in many other ways imparted to the White House the atmosphere of a dignified and hospitable home.

CHAPTER XV

WILSON SELECTS HIS CABINET

Choice of Bryan for Secretary of State Arouses Unheeded Protests—
Texas Favored—Colonel House the Man of Mystery—Open Door
Policy Proclaimed.

WOODROW WILSON assumed the rôle of President soon after the election in 1912, though he continued to hold the office of Governor of New Jersey up to within a short time of his inauguration as President of the United States.   As soon as the result was known he began to lay plans for his administration of what we Americans are pleased to call the greatest office in the world.   There never was a time from the moment of his election when Woodrow Wilson did not feel amply competent to meet every contingency which could arise, and without confiding in anybody or seeking advice.

Of course Cabinet discussion began immediately after the election.   Governor Wilson listened to suggestions, but there was one office and one man he would not discuss.   He would not discuss suggestions for Secretary of State and he would not discuss the name of William J. Bryan in connection with a Cabinet position.   From the time he was elected until the names of members of the Cabinet were sent to the Senate there was no official intimation as to Bryan, yet a few days before the inauguration Bryan appeared in Washington, bland and smiling, and answered when addressed as "Mr. Secretary." If there was a pre-convention offer of the premiership, it was carried out in good faith.

There were many protests against the selection of Bryan for the Cabinet as soon as it became noised about that he was to be given the most prominent position in the gift of the President. They came from the conservative or "reactionary" wing of the Democratic party; from men who had always been opposed to Bryan. These protests angered the President-elect. As soon as it became known that they were being sent to Governor Wilson the same old Bryan game was played. Letters in favor of Bryan began to pour in and the counteraction was four-to-one. Bryan men all over the country rallied to the support of their idol, and, always being an active element, they completely swamped the protests with their endorsements.

Soon after the campaign was over Wilson sought the seclusion which Bermuda is supposed to afford. But the man who has been elected President of the United States is bound to be in the glare of publicity no matter how carefully he may plan to conceal his movements.

It was while in Bermuda that Wilson fed a number of newspaper correspondents "salt water dope." They reported among other things that he would not attempt to dictate to Congress. There was more to the same effect, which seems strange to recall in after days when we realize that Congress never had such a dictator; not even Roosevelt could compel such obedience as Woodrow Wilson.

One incident at Bermuda showed clearly that Wilson intended to be President and that he was not to be second in command. In one of the newspapers was a cartoon showing Bryan busily engaged in making a Cabinet, accepting boards bearing the names of well-known Democrats and rejecting others.

"How little they know," remarked Governor Wilson. "Mr. Bryan is not selecting the Cabinet."

Very soon after he was elected Wilson began to display that imperious nature which characterized his Administration. When there was talk of a possible panic on account of new party policies, he threatened those who, because of prospective legislation, started panics with as severe punishment as the Government could inflict.

He created consternation in Washington when he demanded a simple inauguration. Those who always make the installation of a President a gala occasion were almost driven frantic. He relented to the extent of permitting a parade and the other usual ceremonies, but refused the inaugural ball. Now, the inaugural ball had been not only a time-honored quadrennial institution, but it is an important factor in furnishing funds for the inaugural committee. Not only that, but the thousands of visitors attend the ball, and when they return to their homes they have something to tell their friends which is out of the ordinary, and can give the impression that they were specially honored by invitations to the President's inaugural ball. Hence the disappointment extended to the visitors as well as to the inaugural managers.

And so it fell out that when inauguration day came there was no change in the traditional ceremonies except the absence of the ball. Mr. Wilson and Mr. Taft rode to the Capitol and returned amidst cheering throngs, followed by the customary long procession of soldiers, regulars, and militia, cadets and midshipmen, sailors and marines, civic and other organizations. The government of the United States was transferred from William H. Taft to Woodrow Wilson.

Previous to coming to the Capital the President-elect had obtained his ideas of Washington from sources generally antagonistic to the rich men and social leaders of the city. This was shown first in his declination to become a member of the Chevy Chase Club, the most exclusive country club of Washington.

His attitude was further shown when one of the self-constituted civic regulators visited him and gave him a view of the local government which was summed up in the words:

"The system of government in the District of Columbia is controlled by men with connections in speculative real estate; a triangle of profit and power manned by a triumvirate."

Governor Wilson made this comment:

"He (the visitor) excited me because he put my nose on a fresh trail, and the kind of a trail that I always follow with zest."

And when he came to the matter of appointments in the District of Columbia, Wilson showed a distinct aversion, if not hostility, to that element, which by reason of wealth and social position had always been prominent in Washington affairs.

While he was getting ready for his new duties Wilson announced an "open door" policy for the White House. From Trenton came the report that his private office would be open; visitors would not be turned away; the people would have access to their President; there would be no more closed doors.

Everybody in Washington laughed and made sarcastic comments, just as they did in regard to Wilson's comments on publicity and assertions that everything of a public nature should be done in the open.

They knew the situation of old.

Of course Wilson did not realize the impossibility of conducting the Presidency as he did the Governorship of New Jersey. To maintain the open door would have afforded him no time for work or recreation. As to publicity, that was long ago stifled by the bureaucrats in Washington who have built up a system of secrecy in the National Government that cannot be broken down. Every new administration is impressed from the beginning that only by the greatest secrecy can governmental affairs be conducted; that the public has no business to know how its affairs are conducted, and should only be apprised of what has been going on when the results are announced.

Wilson's plan of the "open door" for the White

House and publicity, of which he had spoken and written, went glimmering together. No administration was quite so secretive as his, and no President less accessible, or more aloof from the people.

E. M. House, the "Man of Mystery," became an important figure at that time, and in the papers was credited with great power and influence with the new administration. He was mentioned for the most important Cabinet positions and the most important foreign embassies. He was credited with having more to say about the make-up of the Cabinet than any other man. During all the preliminaries and also during the whole administration, this silent, secretive Texas man was the close confidant of the President. Four years later, during the campaign of 1916, a man who had intimate knowledge of the relations which existed, thus expressed it: "Colonel House is the only man who has the full confidence of the President."

He was an idealist and found in Wilson a man of sympathetic thought. He had been an admirer of the New Jersey Governor before he had ever met him, and in 1911 became active in his efforts to make Wilson President of the United States. His work attracted the attention of at least one man. That man was Woodrow Wilson.

The first meeting of these two men took place in 1912 at the home of Colonel House, who was then living in East 37th Street, New York. Governor Wilson frequently visited New York and on such occasions stopped at the Coddington, a small hotel in West 35th

Street.   It was an easy walk from his modest hostelry
to the home of the Colonel.   Many times during that
eventful year of 1912, before the Baltimore convention,
the Governor went to New York, took up his quarters
at the Coddington, and then went over to the home of
his friend.   There they discussed the political situation
in the Democratic party; there were planned the political maneuvers which helped to make Woodrow Wilson
President of the United States.

The little that became known of Colonel House developed after the Presidential election, when there was
bound to be publicity concerning every moth, big or
little, that came within the blazing light which beats
upon a man from the moment he is elected to the
Presidency.

Governor Wilson had observed that Colonel House
rarely said anything for publication and was comparatively unknown.   He did not even have a favorite newspaper man to whom he would give a story about Wilson.
The air of mystery which the Colonel created accorded
with a characteristic which became a dominant feature
of the Wilson administration and perhaps accounts for
the intimacy.   President Wilson was willing that there
should be mystery concerning himself and his acts,
and he seemed to enjoy the bewilderment and talk
which they created.

The President had not been long in office before he
learned that the majority of those who went to see
him had some selfish motive in view.   Speaking at
the Press Club he said that whenever he found a man

without an axe to grind and who was without selfish
motives, that man he held in close friendship and trust.
There could be no other to whom he referred than
Colonel House.

It may not have been due to the influence of Colonel
House, but Texas was very much favored during the
Wilson administration in the matter of Cabinet selections. Albert S. Burleson was appointed Postmaster
General, David F. Houston was nominally a St. Louis
man, but had been in that city only four years when
made Secretary of Agriculture. Before that he had
been a resident of Texas. When James C. McReynolds
was promoted from the Department of Justice to the
Supreme bench, another Texas man, Thomas W.
Gregory, was made Attorney General.

The favoritism shown Texas was recalled when the city
of Dallas, Texas, wanted the national convention in
1916. The national committee as usual assembled in
Washington. R. M. Johnston, the Texas member
of the national committee, called on Roger C. Sullivan,
the member from Illinois, who was working for Chicago,
and sought support for Dallas.

"What more does Texas want?" asked Sullivan.
"You've got three Cabinet officers and the Power
behind the Throne, and yet you're not satisfied?
Years ago," continued Sullivan, "the Italians crowded
out the Irish in one of the wards of Chicago. The
Irish boss remained and controlled the Italians for a
time, but finally there were evidences of a revolt. At
one of the meetings an Italian complained that although

they (the Italians) furnished nearly all the party voters, the Irish held the offices and it was about time the Italians received recognition.

"'Wha'd'ye Eyetalians want, annyhow?' asked the Irish boss. 'Haven't ye got the Pope?'"

Of course no other appointment caused the amount of discussion as did that of Bryan. It was asserted by his warm admirers that he would "dominate the Administration." Close friends of Wilson said that Bryan had been selected because the President wanted Bryan where he could be watched; that he preferred to have him on the inside of the house shooting out rather than on the outside shooting in. Bryan himself seemed highly pleased with his office. His smile was very expansive, and he appeared to be the embodiment of loyalty to his chief.

It had been said that "Bryan put one over on Wilson" when he wrote the one-term plank in the Baltimore platform. Moreover, he had much to say about keeping platform pledges. Early in the year 1913 he made a speech at Harrisburg, Pa., in which he said: "A man who violates a party platform is a criminal worse than a man who embezzles money."

He did not know at the time that there was reposing in the pocket of A. Mitchell Palmer a letter written by Wilson before the inauguration practically repudiating the one-term plank.

CHAPTER XVI

WILSON IN THE WHITE HOUSE

The New President Surprises the Country by Personally Presenting
His Message—Drives Two Important Bills through Congress—
Underwood in Complete Control in the House—Senate Brought
into Line—Lind Sent as Confidential Agent to Mexico—Famous
Carabao Dinner—Bryan in the State Department is not Entirely
Happy.

AFTER eighteen years the Senate was again, on
March 4, 1913, in the control of the Democrats.
From the time it was known that the Democrats would
be in control scheming began for the places of
honor and power in the gift of the party. About the
first thing was the organization of a progressive wing
under the leadership of Hoke Smith of Georgia, who
had been in the Senate only a year, but who was touted
as the Wilson leader in that body. Smith made an
issue against the seniority tradition, also against the custom that one Senator should hold two important committee assignments while other Senators had only minor
places. The movement was successful—for the men
who engineered it. Only a few years later Hoke Smith
was a member of Finance and Judiciary, two of the best
committees in the Senate, Chairman of Education and
Labor, and in addition a member of Agriculture, Rules
and Military Affairs.

In disposing of the great honorary position the Democrats not only upset tradition, but created a surprise for everybody. It was naturally supposed that Senator Bacon of Georgia, the senior in length of service (of all save Tillman and Martin, who were of the same rank, but who waived their claims), would be chosen President pro tempore with substantial unanimity. But Clarke of Arkansas was selected by the caucus. Clarke had been called a "White House Democrat" in the Roosevelt days, and had never been regularly on the Democratic reservation, always exhibiting an independence that was at times disconcerting to his fellow Democrats.

The defeat was crushing to Bacon. It was the highest position he could possibly attain. It was the one ambition of his life, and he looked forward to Democratic control of the Senate to see it gratified. He did not live long enough to allow the next reorganization of the Senate to bestow upon him the honor he coveted.

Bacon was the first Senator to be elected by direct vote of the people under the constitutional amendment, when he was chosen for a fourth term.

The best thing about Thomas Riley Marshall was that he never took himself or his office seriously. An official position that makes a man the presiding officer of a body that does as it pleases, overturns parliamentary law and its own rules at pleasure, reverses itself and makes the man in the chair the "goat," is not one to be taken seriously. There is, of course, one serious duty of the Vice President, that is, waiting for the President to die or resign.

Vice President Marshall took a humorous view of his position, and for that he should be thanked. Early in his career he said he would like a room in the Senate office building where he could put his feet on the table. Throngs of sightseers went into his room in the Capitol, and were sometimes introduced and at other times simply gazed at the man who was sitting there with nothing to do.

"I don't see," said Marshall, "that this room differs much from a monkey cage, except that the visitors do not offer me any peanuts."

When President Wilson called the Sixty-third Congress in extra session neither he nor any one else foresaw that the session which began April 7, 1913, would, in conjunction with the regular session, make the longest continuous sitting ever known in the country. Congress was in session for 567 days without an adjournment.

Talking day after day, in which the Senate indulged itself, seemed to strike the new President as rather amusing. He called Congress to revise the tariff, but when he saw that the Senate was taking its time he decided to put through a currency measure. The Republicans served notice of a long debate if that program was carried out, but that only made the President more determined than ever. Hence he kept Congress with its nose to the grindstone and said that, if an adjournment was taken before the currency bill was

passed, he would call another session. So both the
tariff and the currency laws were enacted.

Thus before a year had passed Congress realized
that there was in the White House a dominating personality, a man who made Roosevelt's bossism look
mild in comparison.

One of the first surprises which the President gave
Congress and the country was his determination to read
his message to a joint meeting of the assembled houses,
reverting to a practice which had been abandoned 112
years before. This idea was not well received and there
were many caustic comments. Senator Borah of Idaho
so thoroughly disapproved the innovation that he never
listened to a message delivered in person. For the
most part, however, the reading of the message was
regarded merely as a manifestation of harmless vanity,
as were other peculiarities in which the President indulged. But he caused attention to be focused on
what he had to say.

The tariff act of 1913 is known as the Underwood or
Underwood-Simmons law. It ought to be called the
Wilson law also, because Woodrow Wilson left his
stamp upon it. The way he handled the Democratic
protectionists in Congress was surprising. Grover
Cleveland could not cope with them, and if Woodrow
Wilson had had to deal with such Senators as Gor-
man, Brice, Murphy, and Jim Smith, who were in the
Senate in 1894, he might have failed.

So far as the protection Democrats in the House were
concerned—and every Democrat who shouts for a

revenue duty on any article produced in his state is a protectionist—the President found easy sailing. Oscar W. Underwood represented a steel and iron district and was credited with favoring protection on these articles, but he did not show it in writing the tariff bill. He reduced the duty on the products of his district, and insisted that products of other sections of the country be sacrificed also. When the President said he wanted free wool and free sugar, Underwood put those articles on the free list, despite opposition of men who represented wool and sugar producing states.

Taking his bill into a Democratic caucus Underwood made it a party measure, allowing the sugar men in Louisiana, and others who had pledges to redeem, to vote their convictions. He had a working majority of one hundred and fifty, besides about twenty Progressives, who supported tariff reductions, so he had no difficulty whatever in passing his bill.

"Wait till that bill gets to the Senate," said the wise ones, who remembered the last Democratic tariff bill. It was known that many Democrats were not at all in sympathy with many of the provisions of the Underwood tariff bill. Chairman Simmons of North Carolina had several times voted for protection. The Florida Senators were known to be much disturbed over the reduction of the fruit duties. The Louisiana Senators were outspoken in their opposition to free sugar, and it was supposed that they would be joined by a number of western Senators from beet sugar states, and also that Senators from wool producing states would protest vigorously. Well, they did. They were about ready to "kick over the traces," and it was intimated that sugar and wool must be cared for or there might be a revolt. Then they were given a hint, and with the exception of the Louisiana Senators, there were no Democrats who refused to support the tariff bill.

When President Wilson was told that there must be a duty on sugar and wool or the bill could not pass the Senate, he remarked: "What a pity. We shall have to go to the country again on this tariff issue."

Then he went further, and one day when he received the newspaper correspondents he said that an "insidious lobby" was in Washington and haunting the Capitol in an effort to defeat the tariff bill. Just what he wanted printed was handed to the newspaper men by White House clerks when they left his room, and within twenty-four hours the country was ringing with the words "insidious lobby."

And the Senators took it up. Senator Cummins introduced a resolution for an investigation, and finally the celebrated "lobby committee" was sent on its long, long journey, for at this writing the end is not yet.

But the threat of going to the people, and the intimation that tariff reform was being prevented by an "insidious lobby," were sufficient to bring the doubtful Senators into line. They could not afford to be branded as succumbing to an "insidious lobby," and they well knew what would happen if they had to go before the people after defeating a tariff reduction bill.

Of course, no one found the "insidious lobby," or any

other kind of lobby that had very much influence. There were men in Washington representing various interests who were trying to secure higher rates of duty, but there were others working for lower rates. As to sugar, the chief bone of contention, the investigation developed the fact that the lobby for free sugar was more "insidious," or at least was spending more money, than the lobby for protection.

The committee never completed its investigation and never made a report on the particular subject for which it was created. It would be interesting to know whether it ever found even a semblance of the "insidious lobby" it was created to unearth. What is also unsettled is whether the President was misled as to the existence of such a lobby. At all events he made good use of it as a "bogey man." The whole affair seemed so much like the famous "five-million-dollar conspiracy," which Roosevelt worked so successfully for his own interests, that I am inclined to bracket that sensation with the "insidious lobby" and let them go together as two of a kind.

It has often been said that President Taft bequeathed to President Wilson the Mexican situation. At all events the new President found a serious condition in Mexico when he took charge.

No doubt the altruistic ideals of Bryan were the cause of Wilson's first move in Mexico, and led him to refuse recognition of the de facto government of Huerta and later encourage Carranza and Villa. The sympathy of Bryan was with the 15,000,000 poor, ignorant, and down-trodden Mexicans. Carranza and Villa represented this large mass; they said so. Huerta was said to be the legitimate successor of Diaz, who had ruled Mexico with an iron hand so many years. Huerta stood for the capitalistic class, the 2,000,000 who could read and write and had property; besides, he was a murderer.

Hence John Lind, Bryan's intimate friend in Minnesota, was sent to Mexico to tell Huerta to get out. President Wilson had Congress assemble in joint session so that he could tell them what he had done, Lind being already in Mexico.

Bryan had not been long in office, and had really performed no particular service, when his most vociferous friends proclaimed him "the greatest Secretary of State since Thomas Jefferson." As the intervening list of Secretaries included John Marshall, James Madison, James Monroe, John Quincy Adams, Henry Clay, Daniel Webster, John C. Calhoun, William L. Marcy, William H. Seward, James G. Blaine, Richard Olney, John Hay, Elihu Root and Philander C. Knox, it may be remarked that the Bryan admirers were inclined to be extravagant in their praise.

There was one feature of Bryan's office-holding wholly unexpected by his newspaper friends. He had been a newspaper man, reporter, correspondent, editor. He had been an advocate of publicity. It was expected that the State Department would cease to be a sealed mystery, where gum shoes and cloth slippers are used; where everybody says, or looks as if he were about to say, "hush! hush!" But Bryan proved to be the greatest stickler for the maintenance of secrecy ever at the head of the Department.

"I shall say nothing about any matter pending in this Department until a conclusion has been reached," he would remark when asked about a subject that might be under consideration in the Department, and he would shut his large mouth grimly, leaving across his face a long line, which was the embodiment of firmness.

As to discussing the phases or conditions of negotiations, or making suggestions, or talking confidentially with any of his most intimate newspaper friends, that was taboo. All this was so much unlike the pleasant manners and customs of John Hay, Elihu Root, and Philander C. Knox, that it proved a rude shock to the Washington correspondents. And yet to those who knew the real Bryan this secretiveness was no surprise. No man had Bryan's confidence; no man could speak for him or tell what he would do in a given case. As long as he was Secretary of State he maintained his uncommunicative, determined attitude.

Bryan's life in the State Department was not happy. He was not the kind of man to be shut within four walls. The grinding detail of office was not congenial to him. And he did not permit himself to be so confined. He went out on the lecture circuit and gave as a reason that the salary of $12,000 paid to a Cabinet officer was not sufficient to meet his living expenses. This statement was stunning to those humble followers, the plain people, who thought a thousand dollars a month was "a pile of money." His frequent absences would not have been noticed had he been away for health or pleasure, but when devoted to lectures for pay they caused a great deal of adverse criticism. Bryan resented the criticisms because he had carefully figured out the absences of his predecessors, Hay and Knox, and found that they had spent less time in the State Department than himself. He said he was simply taking the leave which was accorded all government employees, and it was his own business as to how he employed his time.

The fact that these thrusts irritated him showed another Bryan different from the one we had known for twenty years. Previously no one ever heard him acknowledge that the many shafts aimed at him had taken effect, and he always welcomed an attack because he was so absolutely sure of himself that he feared no one, and was never quite so happy as when in a wordy combat either through the papers or on the platform.

There was another amazing feature of his officeholding, due to his supposed power. A man who runs for President three times leaves a trail of many actual or implied "promises to pay." Many Democrats went to see Bryan and asked for places. Those who had been wandering in the wilderness with him for sixteen years wanted some of the honey. Bryan made every effort to care for "deserving Democrats," and what proved a real marvel was the fact that he was so successful. There was not a department in which several Bryan supporters were not placed. This activity of

Bryan and interference in other departments sometimes caused grumbling and complaint, but the other
Cabinet officers seemed somewhat in awe of the premier,
the man who for so long had been Democracy's boss
and, possibly, still retained that position.

Then there was injected into the diplomatic affairs
of a great government as a serious matter—grape juice.
Oh, the laughs that it caused! To those who took
our diplomatic relations seriously, who really cared
about the punctilious observance of all ceremonies in
dealing with the representatives of foreign governments, the grape juice reign was a tragedy. But to
the country at large it was a comedy. Instead of wine
Secretary Bryan served the diplomats with grape juice.
Then he made matters worse by issuing an explanation
to the effect that he was an abstainer from liquors.

Altogether, Bryan's life in public office was not pleasant. During all the years of his prominence he had
aroused antagonisms, created various impressions, and
left a trail of enmities for acts both wise and foolish.
They sought him out when he became the premier in
the Cabinet, and he was a target for criticism, much of
it unjust, but all of it embittering his official life.

Huerta resented the intrusion and interference with
the sovereignty of Mexico, particularly as other foreign governments had recognized his government.

Henry Lane Wilson, the Republican hold-over ambassador, had been handling the Mexican situation for
years. He recommended the recognition of Huerta and
was recalled and also discredited. There was one

amusing incident connected with the service of Ambassador Wilson under the new Administration. While he was still at his post he received a cable from Secretary Bryan warmly commending his course. The ambassador had it published. Bryan was about to deny its authenticity when he was confronted with his signature to the original dispatch. Then it was explained that the dispatch had been written by a clerk in the usual course of business, but knowing that it was important he attached a red tag to the paper. In State Department parlance a red tag means "danger," or "go slow," or "look out," and its actual interpretation is "read this." The tag was displaced in some way, and Bryan signed the paper in a perfunctory manner without reading, as every Cabinet officer does, a rubber stamp not yet having been provided for such signatures.

Lind was a Confidential Agent in Mexico, and in that way he was addressed by the representative of Huerta. In the exchange of notes it was observed that Huerta employed men who could command language far superior to that used by the United States diplomats. In the battle of notes the victory was with Huerta. Lind was not the only "confidential agent" in Mexico. There were several. One of them I interviewed after his return. He had learned nothing and had done nothing for the Administration. He was full of mystery and clammy with secrecy. Afterwards, he turned traitor to Wilson and became one of the most abusive opponents of the President.

The Mexican situation was still in an unsettled condition when Congress assembled in December. Again the President read his message to the joint session. It was in this document that he used the words "watchful waiting" in regard to his course in dealing with that country. Minority Leader Mann asserted that Wilson's course ultimately meant war with Mexico.

Incidentally it was in that message that President Wilson gave the Democrats, especially those from the South, another great shock by recommending a presidential primary law. The Democrats feared that it would do away with state lines. But although a dictator, and the most successful boss any Congress ever had, Wilson was shrewd. He knew when he was up against real opposition. That was the last we ever heard of national presidential primaries.

In December, 1913, the Military Order of the Carabao afforded the National Capital amusement by giving a dinner during which fun was poked at some of the policies of the Administration. President Wilson took the affair seriously and made an official matter of it.

The Carabao is a society of Army and Navy officers, limited to those who had service in the Philippine Islands previous to the end of the insurrection against the United States. For years it had been the custom of the members of this organization to get together with invited friends at an annual dinner, revive old times, sing the songs they had sung in days when they first fought the Spaniard and then the Filipino, and, in a spirit of fun and relaxation, have a genuine good time.

But the fun at this particular dinner reached the sensibilities of those in authority. One of the stunts was a moving picture of the arrival of a Filipino in a flying machine. This Filipino told of the difficulties he had in his quest of "Hon. Wm. Jenny Bryan." "Search me," said an assistant in the State Department, "but go to the Chautauqua and you may find him." The Filipino said he followed one date after another, but could not catch the Secretary as he jumped from town to town.

Bryan had asserted that if he had his way he would cease to build battleships and cruisers, and in their stead would construct two great peace ships and call them "Friendship" and "Fellowship." At one stage of the dinner there was a procession of floats, three alleged battleships, pasty looking objects of paper and cloth. One was labeled "Friendship," the next "Fellowship," and the last "Piffle." That was what really hurt, because a New York paper, opposing the Administration, had run a cartoon almost daily in which the battleship "Piffle" was a prominent feature.

By direction of the President the officers who were responsible for the dinner program were called to account. One charge was that they had sung offensive songs, which ridiculed the policy of the Administration in trying to give independence to the Philippine Islands. The offending song in particular was carried by the air of "Tramp, Tramp, Tramp, the Boys are Marching," and had this chorus:

Damn, damn, damn the Insurrectos,
Cross-eyed Kakiack ladrones;
Underneath the starry flag,
Civilize 'em with a Krag,
And return us to our own beloved homes!

Years before in the Philippines the word "Filipinos"
was used instead of "insurrectos," but in deference to
the wishes of Governor Taft the substitution was made.
The "Krag" was the regulation army rifle.

Both President Roosevelt and President Taft had
attended Carabao dinners and listened to this and other
songs, but never had raised any question about them.

While the songs were made the main source of the
complaints against the Army and Navy officers, the real
cause was the belittling of the peace plans of the Administration and the severe "roasts" of Bryan. President Wilson ordered an investigation, and when the
report was made, wrote a severe reprimand of the officers
connected with the dinner. It was a stinging letter in
which he derided the so-called "fun" which "ridiculed
their superior officers and the policies of the Government." He spoke of "childish wit" and "silly effer-
vescences."

It was the last Carabao dinner for several years.

Secretary Bryan was very active in his advocacy of
peace, and as long as he remained in the Cabinet he
had the President with him. It was early in the Administration that the first war scare occurred. California was about to pass a land law designed to prevent
Japanese from acquiring lands in that state. Japan

protested and Secretary Bryan made strong representations to Governor Hiram W. Johnson, but without avail. Then he was sent to California to expostulate in person and had no better success.

This attempted interference of the Federal administration in the affairs of a sovereign state was a shock to many southern men in Congress, who positively announced their intention of standing by California. Even those who had voted against battleships and an increase of the Army were for the time ready to tell Japan that our states had a right to manage their own affairs in their own way, and to back up their opinions with force.

Secretary Bryan frequently gave utterance to his peace ideas. He declared there was no need of wars, and was constantly advocating disarmament, and urged that the United States take the lead in disbanding the navies of the world.

Occasionally he had another view. For instance, in dealing with situations in the Caribbean he found that force was the only thing which the people of that region understood. One day he rushed into the office of the Assistant Secretary of the Navy, Franklin D. Roosevelt, who was acting in the absence of Secretary Daniels.

"Roosevelt, I want a battleship sent at once to Santo Domingo," said he. "I have a dispatch which shows a serious condition there, and I must have a battleship within twenty-four hours."

"It's a physical impossibility, Mr. Secretary," explained Roosevelt, "there isn't a battleship within five days' sail of Santo Domingo."

"But I must have one at once," insisted the Secretary of State.

"There are no battleships in those waters," argued Roosevelt. "It will take twenty-four hours to coal a battleship for such a voyage. I could get a cruiser there from Guantanamo, and that is the best I can do at the present."

"I know nothing about the difference in ships," said Bryan. "When I said battleship I meant a ship with officers and guns and sailors. That is what I want."

He found as Secretary of State that "something with guns" was necessary, but he went right along negotiating treaties which were to do away with guns and secure universal peace.

President Wilson decided to get along with the newspaper correspondents in Washington and afforded them an opportunity to see and question him twice a week. President Taft had tried something of the same kind. The hour of four o'clock one day in the week was fixed to meet the President, but Taft would often cause them to wait until 6 o'clock or 6:30, and the meetings were not popular.

President Wilson fixed 10 o'clock in the morning, and promptly at that hour he stepped into the oval office and faced from seventy-five to one hundred newspaper men and answered their questions. Occasionally the most important subjects were barred, especially when

relating to foreign affairs. As to others Mr. Wilson
handled them so adroitly that he accomplished a double
purpose. He secured publicity for such matters as he
desired, with his view prominently presented, and he
minimized and practically suppressed those things
which might have been made sensational. In fact, these
interviews often acted as an extinguisher. Men with an
inkling of a big story would have it discredited by a few
words from the President. Referring to these interviews in a speech he made at the Press Club the President said: "Often when I meet you at our morning
talks I know what is in the back of your heads. I
could tell you sometimes more than I do tell you."

Of course he could. It was this very fact that made
the interviews of little value. Then these open interviews also destroyed that old-time, always reliable
friend of the Washington correspondent, the "highest
authority."

"I can state on the highest authority," the special
commissioner would write, while the more modest
correspondent would say, "It can be stated on the
highest authority." The writers wanted to create the
impression that the President had given them their
information. That was the implication. But the bi-
weekly conferences, which every newspaper man was
privileged to attend, made the President the actual
"highest authority," instead of the fictitious character
created by the staff correspondents and the commissioners, and thus limited the scope of imagination.

There was one contingent which received a rude

awakening during the first year of Wilson's occupancy of the White House. They were the "fair-haired boys" of the Democratic party; those self-constituted advisers and mentors who had found Wilson so accessible and sympathetic when Governor of New Jersey, and during the campaign. They were in Democracy what an amalgamation of the "tennis cabinet" and "fair-haired boys" of the Roosevelt days would have been. Being an amalgamation they called themselves "the Common Council." But there was one great difference. Wilson did not see them, listen to their advice, tell them what to do, or give them any opportunity to become mouthpieces of the Administration. He gave most of them jobs in the Federal service, but so far as seeking their opinions,—well, he never had much use for anyone's opinion but his own.

Late in the year occurred the first of three weddings in the Wilson family. Miss Jessie Wilson became the wife of Francis B. Sayre. Like all White House weddings it was a very great social event, attended by the high officials in civic and military life and the Diplomatic Corps.

President Wilson had a way of doing what he called the "obvious thing," a term reminiscent of his college professor days, and then expressing surprise because it called forth remark. For instance he seemed to steal about the city, making unexpected calls at the departments and still more unexpected visits to the Capitol. On several of these occasions he would say or do something that made a newspaper story, such as getting lost in the Capitol building or in the corridors of the departments and inquiring his way.

And he wondered why his doing the "obvious thing" should seem so strange to Washington people.

"I tremble to think of the variety and falseness of the impressions I make," he told the Press Club. He did not realize that it was because his actions were so at variance from those of his predecessors that there were comments and wonder as to what he would do next.

CHAPTER XVII

PANAMA CANAL MYSTERY

President Wilson Forces Congress to Reverse Itself and Repeal Free Tolls for American Coastwise Ships Going Through the Panama Canal—Great Britain a Potent Influence in Securing the Change of Front—Situation in Mexico Grows Worse—Fleet Goes to Mexican Waters and Vera Cruz Is Taken—The European War Brings About a Marked Change in America.

THE year 1914 was one of important events. Even without the overwhelming and all-absorbing conflict in Europe, the effect of which was so quickly felt on this side of the Atlantic, the year was an eventful, nay, even a history-making one for the United States.

In the National Capital the year opened without a time-honored ceremony, the reception at the White House. That function has always been a resplendent and gala affair. The diplomats are there in their glittering uniforms and decorations. All the army and navy officers are present in full dress uniforms, and gold lace, yellow, red and blue stripes, denoting the different branches of the service, make a brilliant showing. The women are handsomely gowned. All in all the New Year's reception at the White House is one of the most distinctive and spectacular functions of the season. President Wilson was at Pass Christian, Miss. The White House was closed, but the Cabinet officers kept open houses, and so the day was not entirely devoid of all that it has come to mean in Washington.

It was early in February, 1914, that President Wilson announced that he would seek a repeal of the clause in the Panama canal act exempting American coastwise ships from the payment of tolls in passing through the canal. The announcement came as a great surprise. Before the Baltimore convention a Democratic House had adopted a free tolls provision. While the bill was still pending in the Senate the convention met and included this plank in its platform:

"We favor the exemption from tolls of American ships engaged in the coastwise trade passing through the canal."

The Senate soon after, aided largely by Democratic votes, passed the bill containing the exemption clause. Senator Walsh of Montana, who was on the sub-committee which drafted the platform, said the free tolls plank went in with Bryan's consent, though as Secretary of State Bryan favored the repeal.

From the time the free tolls provision had been enacted into law there had been vigorous protest on the part of Great Britain. She claimed it was a violation of the Hay-Pauncefote treaty, which provides that all nations should have equal treatment in the use of the canal. When the Hay-Pauncefote treaty was pending Senator Bard of California offered an amendment specifically exempting coastwise ships, but it was voted down. Senator Spooner of Wisconsin explained at the time that coastwise trade was so exclusively an American institution that we would not make it the subject of a treaty with any foreign country. But Great Britain had again outwitted us in diplomacy. The man who could stand up and say that "all nations" in a treaty did not include the United States had a mighty weak argument. The real facts were that, having been bested in a diplomatic deal, the United States had taken occasion to correct the mistake by legislation. It wrote into law what the legislators said was intended when the treaty was ratified. And it has always been held that legislation supersedes a treaty.

President Wilson went to Congress with a special message asking for the repeal of the free tolls clause. After explaining what he wanted, he said:

"I ask this of you in support of the foreign policy of the Administration. I shall not know how to deal with other matters of even greater delicacy and nearer consequence if you do not grant it to me in an ungrudging manner."

These cryptic words never have been officially explained. No one has told how the foreign policy of the United States was to be affected if the repeal was not granted. No official explanation ever has been given of what was meant by "matters of even greater delicacy and nearer consequence." The meaning could only be conjectured. The best guess was that the foreign policy was one of peace at almost any price. Great Britain was threatening, and it was supposed had the backing of other nations. It also was surmised that the Japanese situation was involved. Japan and Great Britain had a treaty of alliance. Japan was supposed to be aiding the Huerta Government in Mexico. By bowing to the demand of Great Britain it is said that the United States secured the influence of England to force her ally, Japan, to cease any activities antagonistic to the United States in Mexico. Many years later a writer in one of the well-known reviews stated that English statesmen interested in the Tehuantepec Railroad, which crosses Mexico at its narrowest point, were much concerned over the effect of free tolls for American ships, and shrewdly playing upon President Wilson's dislike for Huerta, had, it was said, promised to prevent support of Huerta by the Japanese if the President would secure the repeal of the free tolls provision.

One of the explanations as to why the Administration insisted upon the repeal of the law allowing free tolls for American ships going through the Panama canal also relates to Japan, but gives a different motive. When California decided to exercise her rights as a sovereign state, and determine for herself as to what should be done in the matter of public schools and what races should or should not be permitted to attend such schools, and also to decide what kind of people should have the right to acquire title to land in that state, Japan became very much offended. Secretary Bryan made a flying trip across the continent to tell the Californians what they ought to do, but notwithstanding his views California went on and did as she pleased. Meanwhile Japan sent what might be considered an

ultimatum; that is, Japan informed the United States
that the proposed legislation in California would be
considered a national affront by Japan.   That was one
of the non-justiciable questions between nations.   A
national affront can only be settled by resort to arms.
It meant war.   At this point, according to the story,
Great Britain took a decided stand and said to Japan:
"Treaty or no treaty, war with the United States means
war with Great Britain," and the British Lion, whenever he shakes his mane, expects to get something for it.
In this instance the *quid pro quo* was the repeal of the
law giving free tolls to American ships going through
the Panama canal.

While it seems inconceivable that there could have
been any fear on the part of the Administration regarding Mexico, the threatened Japanese assistance in that
country may have had some weight.   However, it ap-
pears that the mysterious reason advanced by the
President was to some extent as surmised.   It later
developed, according to unofficial reports, that Japan
was threatening to take over and occupy one of the
islands in the Pacific Ocean.   The island did not
amount to very much, but there would have been resentment if it had been taken by Japan; the United
States had made no move about it, and the attitude of
the Administration at that time was to preserve peace.
Great Britain came forward with a proposition to hold
off Japan from taking United States property, if the
United States would repeal the free tolls provision for
American ships passing through the Panama canal.

These were probably the "other matters of even greater delicacy and nearer consequence" referred to in the Presidential message.

Before the President went to Congress with his canal tolls message, he had taken the matter up with the Foreign Relations Committee of the Senate. He had a secret meeting of the committee called, and they arranged themselves in a semicircle about the President in much the same manner as a post-graduate class might have surrounded a college professor.

"I have a letter from our Ambassador to Great Britain," he began. Walter H. Page was then our representative at the Court of St. James's. The President drew a letter from his pocket as if to refresh his memory, and referred to the ambassador as "Walter." It seems that Walter had been the guest of Rudyard Kipling, the author and poet, who had spent some time in the United States. The distinguished English author spoke very highly of this country in general and expressed a liking for our people, but added: "You have one grievous fault; you do not keep your treaty promises."

Ambassador Page inquired for particulars, and the creator of Private Mulvaney explained that for more than half a century England had been equally interested with the United States in a canal connecting the Atlantic and Pacific Oceans; that England had always been ready to co-operate with the United States in regard to the canal; and that finally a treaty had been made, the Hay-Pauncefote Treaty, in which both nations had agreed that all nations should receive equal treatment as to vessels passing through the canal, and yet the United States had repudiated that part of the treaty by allowing the coastwise shipping of the United States to go through free of tolls. "Walter has been very much impressed by the conversation," the President told the committee; he had written the President very earnestly concerning the subject. The President then urged that the free tolls be repealed, and insisted that the whole foreign situation would be improved, and that this country would no longer stand before the world as a treaty breaker. When he hinted that international complications with other nations might be avoided by repealing the tolls provision, he was asked if he referred to Japan, and replied that in a measure Japan was involved, but there was no pressing danger in that direction.

The President then asked individual members directly what they would do, beginning with William J. Stone of Missouri, chairman of the committee. Stone explained that only about a year before he had voted for free tolls and believed in free tolls for the coastwise ships, but if the President, who had charge of our foreign relations, said that a repeal was necessary he would subordinate his own convictions and vote for repeal. Other Senators, with a few exceptions, promised the President support, among them four Republicans.

Senator O'Gorman of New York was one of the last to be reached in this individual catechism. O'Gorman had been one of the early Wilson men, and supported him in spite of the fact that in 1912 the New York delegation was opposed to Wilson at Baltimore. O'Gorman was Chairman of the Committee on Interoceanic Canals, and, as the repeal of the tolls was a legislative proposition, it would naturally have been considered by his committee instead of the Foreign Relations Committee, but the President had almost pointedly shown that he was skeptical as to O'Gorman, for he had said, earlier in the discussion, that he did not want racial prejudice to influence anyone in the performance of an act of national honesty. O'Gorman was aware that the "racial prejudice" suggestion was aimed at him, and it also became clear in his mind why the President had taken the matter to the Foreign Relations Committee instead of the Committee on Interoceanic Canals. O'Gorman talked very plainly, saying that his Irish ancestry did not affect his judgment in regard to the relations of the United States with foreign governments. He said that the free tolls act had been passed by a Democratic House of Representatives, had received a large Democratic vote in the Senate, and was endorsed by the convention which nominated Mr. Wilson for President. He further said that he was open to argument, but in his opinion the President had not yet presented sufficient reasons to convince him that there should be a repeal of the free tolls act.

That was the first important difference between the President and the New York Senator. It is true that

Senator O'Gorman was one of three Democrats on the Banking and Currency Committee who had refused to accept the currency bill as it was handed to them and, with the Republican members, had remodeled and reformed the measure, but the canal tolls opposition of O'Gorman was something different. It was opposition in the face of a personal demand by the President. From that time until the end of his term the New York Senator had no influence and almost no relations with the White House.

All the leaders in the House were against the repeal of the free tolls provision—Speaker Clark, Leader Underwood, Chairman Fitzgerald, and Claude Kitchin, later successor of Underwood as leader. Leader Mann of the Republicans and Victor Murdock of the Progressives were both vigorously opposed to the repeal. All these leaders fought the so-called gag rule, under which the repeal bill was hurried through. All, save Murdock, had supported gag rules when such rules were for measures they wanted, but they protested vigorously when the gag was used against themselves.

There was much talk about violations of platform pledges, talk that in later debates only caused derisive laughter. Some of the remarks made in the debate will live in history. Here are a few:

Champ Clark, Speaker of the House:

"The amazing request of the President for the repeal, like the peace of God, passeth all understanding."

"We want war with no nation, but rather than surrender our right to complete our sovereignty over every square foot of our globe-encircling domain we will cheerfully face a world in arms."

Leader Underwood:

"Our whole difficulty arises from the un-American spirit of surrender. Can any one tell us plainly why we surrender and what is to be accomplished by it?"

Pat Harrison, Democrat, of Mississippi:

"Are we now to bow in humility to Great Britain, and surrender national honor to an unjust and unreasonable demand for the sordid consideration of assisting in settling another question?"

Frank E. Doremus, Democrat, of Michigan:

"I will not revert to the fact that the assault upon our national honor came from within and not from without."

But the demand of the President was not to be withstood. Many Republicans joined the Democratic majority in passing the bill. Some of these were actuated by a belief that the Canadians would close the Welland Canal to American ships. James J. Hill of St. Paul exerted a tremendous influence; a number of votes for repeal could be traced directly to him.

In the Senate the bill was vigorously opposed, but the changes of many Democratic Senators from their attitude of two years before insured its passage. The support given the bill by Root of New York, Lodge of Massachusetts, Burton of Ohio, and McCumber of

North Dakota prevented the Republicans from making a party issue of it in political campaigns.

Eleven Democrats voted against the repeal. Among them were Senators O'Gorman, Chamberlain, Walsh, Ashurst, and Vardaman. Nearly all these men, as well as others, used strong language in stating their views.

In connection with the repeal and the insistence of Great Britain that "all nations" included the coastwise ships of the United States, there came the interesting development that both Secretary Root and Secretary Bryan had negotiated treaties with Colombia, in which the ships of that nation were granted use of the canal free of tolls, and that England had consented to the arrangement.

The conditions in Mexico grew worse instead of better. The mission of John Lind, his mysterious conference with the President at Pass Christian, his return to this country for a "vacation," and his second trip availed nothing. Although it was known that he wanted to get Huerta out diplomatically, he had authority to and did tell the Mexican ruler that the United States would use force to remove him. Even that had no effect upon the old Indian, who was often inflamed with strong drink, and stubborn.

Meanwhile the embargo on arms was raised and the Carranza and Villa forces procured all the arms and munitions they could pay for. Then came a series of Tampico incidents. American citizens were rescued by foreign war ships. American war ships were ordered

away from Tampico while Americans were pleading
for protection. A detachment from the *Dolphin*, a
paymaster and several sailors, were arrested by a
Mexican force. Rear Admiral Mayo demanded an
apology and a salute. Huerta apologized, and the
officer who made the arrest was punished, but Huerta
would not salute.

There followed a surprising naval demonstration.
The whole Atlantic fleet, battleships, cruisers, and
smaller craft, all went ploughing down the Atlantic
coast and through the Gulf of Mexico. The Mexican
Government had two little gunboats to oppose this
great mass of floating steel. There was already in
Mexican waters at that time a large squadron of United
States battleships and cruisers. "I do not know what
we shall have to do, but we are ready," was the parting
remark of Admiral Badger, in command of the fleet.
Perhaps this was a paraphrase of the slang expression,
"We don't know where we're going, but we're on our
way."

All that happened in Mexico belongs to history, but
the historians will have difficulty in explaining, in the
light of what was accomplished, why after Vera Cruz
was taken and held for months, the forces withdrew.
Perhaps it was part of the scheme to make Huerta retire from Mexico. In that case Carranza, who was
aided by such a move, did not treat us appreciatively,
for he ordered us to get out of Vera Cruz. He said that
by taking Vera Cruz the United States had committed
an act of war against Mexico. That the Americans

while occupying Vera Cruz gave that city a better government than it ever had had in its history made no impression on Mexican leaders.

Finally, Huerta resigned as President of Mexico and left the country. This was a triumph for the Wilson administration, but it did not bring peace to Mexico, nor did it settle the disturbed conditions in that distracted country. First Chief Carranza and his aid, the bandit Villa, continued their careers of murder, robbery, and rapine, and finally occupied Mexico City.

The American people had begun to be very much dissatisfied with the Mexican situation, and it may have been that public opinion would have forced some definite and important action, if the great European war had not dwarfed everything in its terrible whirlwind of destruction. It brought about a marked change in this country, particularly in business, politics, and financial conditions. The business situation had been rapidly approaching panicky conditions. Factories were shutting down and men were out of employment. President Wilson realized the depression. After a talk with a delegation of business men, the White House gave out a summary of what occurred, in which it was stated:

"The President said that, while he was aware of the present depression of business, there was abundant evidence that it was merely psychological; that there is no material condition or substantial reason why business should not be in the most prosperous and expanding condition."

The words "merely psychological" rang from one

end of the country to the other, and the levity and
sarcasm they engendered must have irritated the President. There was an evidence of this on the golf links
not long afterwards. Players ahead of the President
courteously waited for him to pass them. Sitting on
a bench at the tee, they waited for the President to
make his stroke.

"I always take an iron here," the President explained,
it being a place where a wooden club ordinarily was
used in making the drive; "some way I never am able
to do anything with the driver."

"A mental hazard," remarked one of the men on the
bench.

The Presidential frame stiffened.

"Not at all, not at all," he replied coldly, and proceeded on his way.

Like his predecessor Mr. Wilson was a devotee of
golf, though his appearance on the links did not receive
as much attention as did Mr. Taft's. Mr. Taft played
at the fashionable country club. Mr. Wilson played
at various clubs of less pretension with Dr. Cary
Grayson, the White House physician, his constant
companion.

Very soon after the war in Europe began the President issued a proclamation of neutrality on the part of
the United States, and urged the people to take no action that could cause offense to either side. "We must
be impartial in thought as well as in action," he said.

Then began the long effort to secure recognition and
observance of the neutral rights of the United States.

There were repeated warnings, many notes, continuous protests, and insistent messages. They continued as the war progressed, but the interference became more pronounced, the restrictions more aggravating, and it finally seemed to be recognized that international law and the rule of the high seas were to be changed and regulated to suit the nations engaged in the great conflict.

Many were the incidents that caught the public mind as the war progressed. It had been raging for six weeks when Secretary Bryan said in a speech, "The era of war has ended in the United States and is drawing to a close in Europe."

Bryan also signed peace treaties with four foreign nations, two of which were then engaged in the war. These treaties provided for a year of investigation of any disputed point before war was declared. In celebration of the signing of the treaties he gave a luncheon to the envoys, the menu starting off with "neutrality soup."

There arose soon after the war began a clamor by the men in Congress from the cotton and copper producing states. In view of the great demand which the war later created for these products the fears of the Congressmen were not justified. Copper was properly contraband and the men from the copper states, while protesting against the zeal which Great Britain exercised in preventing shipments to the Central Powers, saw that they could do nothing.

Cotton was not then contraband, but Great Britian

established a blockade, and cotton could not go to Germany, Austria, or Belgium. The utmost effort was made to compel England to permit cotton exports to go through Holland and other neutral countries, but the British Government was firm. Then it was proposed that our government should issue $250,000,000 in bonds and buy and store cotton. Other schemes like the Populist sub-treasury plan of 1890 were suggested. Senator Sheppard of Texas organized the "Buy-a-Bale-of-Cotton Club," and many individual purchases were made to help out the southern cotton planters. Hoke Smith of Georgia was a very vociferous cotton Senator, and at one time it seemed that he might break with the Administration, but such a break on the part of the southerner was avoided by the increased price of cotton which soon followed.

One of the first results of the war was the bill to increase the revenue, called a war tax. Such a measure, it was realized, was bound to come sooner or later. Probably it would have been postponed until after the election had there been no war, but it was urged by the President in a message, in which he pointed out that the falling off in imports due to the war necessitated additional revenue.

The President was urged by Democratic Senators and Representatives not to force an additional tax levy at that time.

"It is unpopular," they told him.

"Yes, what of it?" he asked.

"It will injure the party," they argued.

"I can't help that," he replied.

"It will defeat fifty Democrats who are seeking re-election," they told him.

"That is their misfortune," was his response.

"But why not wait until after election?" they asked.

"Because it is right," the President said. "We will show the people that we are not afraid to act when action is necessary, and that we are not afraid to trust them."

And the war revenue bill was passed, but not without a great deal of opposition by the Republicans, and many misgivings on the part of the Democrats.

The war created an era of high prices in the United States never before known. The high prices of the Civil War were based upon a depreciated paper currency, and so they were really not as high as they became during the European war. The first effect of the declaration of war was to cause something of a panic in finances, a great depreciation of railroad and industrial stocks, the assumption being that all securities held abroad would be dumped on the American market and that this country would be drained of gold. The stock exchanges were closed in order to prevent a tremendous slump in all stocks.

How differently it all turned out. The demand for American products, arms and munitions, foodstuffs, horses, mules, and other supplies, everything that was produced in this country, turned a golden stream into the United States, and caused a prosperity the like of which was never before known. Money filled the banks and coffers of the fortunate, men grew rich as the destruction and disaster increased. Every battle with its rain of shell and explosives and awful toll of human life meant an addition to the prosperity of a portion of the people of the United States, a prosperity which became a battle cry in a great political campaign.

An event of the autumn was the return of Colonel Henry Watterson and Colonel George Harvey to the Wilson reservation. Harvey had been *the* original Wilson man. While he was working hard for the New Jersey Governor for President, and had secured the assistance of the brilliant Kentucky editor, Wilson discovered that Harvey's close relations to men of great wealth might injure him, and Harvey was kicked into the discard and Watterson went with him. The affair caused a great commotion at the time, questions of veracity were raised, and Colonel Watterson asked that a "court of honor" be created to settle the controversy. Governor Wilson chose to ignore the whole matter.

For more than two years Harvey and Watterson kept aloof, but upon invitation both visited the White House, and this act of reconciliation was featured for several days as a notable event.

CHAPTER XVIII

WAR AND POLITICS

Drift Towards Depression Checked—Republicans Seek Methods for Restoring Party Harmony—Congressional and Other Elections of 1914—Bitter Clash Between Mann and Heflin—Another White House Marriage.

THE war in Europe was of great service to the Democratic party. It was evident that the party in power was going on the rocks when the outbreak in Europe changed the whole course of events. The demand for war supplies checked the rapid drift towards business depression. A market was created for American products. More than that, the party was relieved from the odium of enacting a special revenue law increasing taxation in time of peace. The bill to meet the deficit in the revenues was called a war revenue measure. The Mexican question was nearly forgotten, as was the canal tolls repeal, and other subjects which had caused division in the Democratic party seemed to be swallowed in the war.

The Republicans discovered as soon as they were out of power that they were unhappy. They liked to run the Government, and set about scheming how they could regain control. Late in 1913 the national committee was called to meet in Washington to decide upon a plan of getting together, of bringing back the Progressives. At first it was decided peremptorily that there could be no change in the method of representation in national conventions. But men of progressive tendencies, who had remained with the party, said that there would have to be such a change if there was to be harmony; that the control by southern states as in 1912 would not be tolerated by the progressive element. A committee was appointed to see what could be done, and a way was found to change the basis of representation.

Chairman Hilles gave a dinner to the committee at the Metropolitan Club, so that the discussion could be absolutely private with no danger of a leak. After the waiters and everybody save members of the committee had been excluded, the heart-to-heart talk began. When the question of southern delegates and the seating of contestants in 1912 was mentioned, one of the Old Guard remarked that there was no call for a bolt that year on account of the action at Chicago, which had been just and fair.

"We had better not go into that," retorted Senator Borah of Idaho; "if we do, we shall soon find ourselves hopelessly divided. I participated in that proceeding and know that at least fifty legally elected delegates were deprived of their seats."

After this warning the discussion took a turn for harmony.

In both Senate and House efforts towards conciliation were evident. Minority Leader Mann, though sometimes exasperated by Victor Murdock, leader of the Progressives, worked hard for harmony, and tried in every way to be personally agreeable to the third party members.

Theodore Roosevelt was still a political problem for the Republicans. He had kept himself continually in the public eye. In 1913 he had brought a libel suit against a Michigan editor, who had accused him of drunkenness, and won his case. In 1914 he made such vicious assaults upon William Barnes as to cause that politician to bring a libel suit, an action which injured Barnes, did Roosevelt no harm, and reflected credit upon Charles Evans Hughes by reason of the facts brought out.

Roosevelt, with his restless spirit, had dashed off to South America, and as a faunal naturalist had sought adventures in the depths of the unhealthy forests of Brazil, contracting a fever from which he suffered as long as he lived. He discovered a river, the River of Doubt, and started a controversy, a thing he dearly loved.

Coming back to the United States after a hurried trip to Europe, he dipped into politics and seemed almost on the point of telling the Republicans of New York whom they should nominate for Governor, but, taking another tack, announced that the Progressive party had come to stay and selected his own candidate for Governor.

Roosevelt took particular interest in Pennsylvania, where Gifford Pinchot was the Progressive candidate for Senator against Penrose. The Colonel said about everything a man could say about Penrose, but the Pennsylvania boss had been used to that kind of treatment and it did not harm him. In Illinois Roosevelt championed the candidacy of Raymond Robins for the Senate, and was very severe on Senator Sherman, who was the nominee of the Republicans. In both Pennsylvania and Illinois the Republican candidates secured a plurality of the votes, beating both Progressive and Democratic nominees. Roosevelt supported Beveridge, the Progressive candidate in Indiana, who received enough votes to insure the election of a Democrat.

As in every campaign, New York became the center of interest. When the election was over Charles S. Whitman, the Republican candidate for Governor, who carried the state by 140,000, became a Presidential possibility. James W. Wadsworth, Jr., defeated Ambassador Gerard for the Senate, thus succeeding Elihu Root.

It was generally believed that Root declined to run because he feared defeat. That might have been the case, but he positively disliked the scramble for the primary nomination, and also the fight before the people, which meant two campaigns, a vastly different proposition from that of going to a legislature and being elected without fuss or trouble.

Roosevelt's Progressive candidate received such a small vote that it seemed quite likely that the Progressive party was disintegrating. Still it was potent enough to save the Democratic party from defeat in the congressional elections. Democrats were elected in at least thirty congressional districts where Progressives were candidates for whom enough votes were cast to have elected Republicans. In the House the Democrats had twenty-five majority over the Republicans. Five Republican candidates for the Senate went down to defeat because Progressive candidates in their states gave Democrats a plurality of the votes.

Although the Democrats gained seats in the Senate and held a majority in the House, the Republicans considered that they had won in the mid-term election a victory which pointed to success in the Presidential election in 1916. Computations were made showing that, on the basis of the votes cast in 1914, the Republicans would have 303 votes of the 531 in the electoral college. At all events a number of "favorite sons" came forward, and there was promise of a lively contest for the nomination.

One of the features of the campaign that year was the slogan that appeared on bill boards, and in black faced type in Democratic newspapers, and on the Democratic campaign text books. It read:

"War in the East; peace in the West; thank God for Woodrow Wilson."

It was effective in some parts of the country, and particularly in the western states, where opposition to the war made itself manifest on several occasions. The people became deeply impressed with the idea that Woodrow Wilson was a peace President.

James R. Mann, minority leader of the House, had

realized for a year and a half that he had made a mistake
in speaking as he did about the woman suffrage parade
the day before the inauguration. He had been roundly
abused by the suffragists and had been blacklisted by
them; that is, he was included among the Senators and
Representatives marked for defeat in the elections of
1914. His opportunity to square himself came during
the consideration of a Philippine government bill, when
he offered an amendment for woman suffrage in the
islands.

William A. Jones, of Virginia, who had charge of the
bill, said that Mann had changed his position. During
one debate on suffrage, he reminded Mann, that Heflin
of Alabama had yielded time to the minority leader to
speak against suffrage.

"I am ashamed that I ever spoke on the same side
with him," said Mann.

"You are not more ashamed than I am," retorted
Heflin.

Jones read from the *Congressional Record* to prove
that Mann on March 3, 1913, when informed that a
young woman had been insulted during the parade, had
said: "She ought to have been at home."

"I thought it was better for her to be at home," retorted Mann, "for fear the gentleman from Alabama
should have seen her. He would have been sure to
have insulted her."

The remark aroused the Democratic side. James
Hay of Virginia demanded the words be "taken down,"
which is the preliminary method for censuring a mem-

ber or expunging the language from the *Record*. Discussing the motion to expunge the words, Mann said he used them because he recollected that, in a speech Heflin had made in regard to granting permission for the parade, he had "used language which made everybody blush with shame, most of which had been left out of the *Record*."

"I protest against this cowardly man using such language about me," shouted Heflin.

"What I have stated is true," went on Mann. "That speech was an insult to womanhood."

"I pronounce the gentleman from Illinois a liar," Heflin roared, his whole frame shaking with anger. "I ask him not to indulge in any more of that kind of talk," added Heflin, and everybody who saw him thought that he meant fight.

But Jim Mann never was a coward or without nerve. He went on in the same line. "If I had made such a speech against womanhood, I should never want it referred to again."

In the end Mann's critical words were stricken from the *Record*, but he had gained his point and retrieved himself for the unfortunate remark of March 3, 1913. "Expunging from the *Record*" is not very severe punishment. In all legislative bodies the words "taken down" and "expunged" from the records are those that get the greatest publicity and remain in history.

Vice President Marshall created a mild sensation a short time before the adjournment of Congress by allowing a moving picture operator to film the Senate.

It was on a day when the Senate stood in recess and the Vice President and Chaplain held a sort of mock session of their own, going through the forms of calling the body to order, having a prayer, and the reading of the Journal. Senator Luke Lea of Tennessee stood up and introduced a bill. Senator Kern, the majority leader, sat at his desk busily engaged in writing. A little later the movie man caught Senator Hoke Smith of Georgia setting his watch by the grandfather clock in the corridor.

Next day when the Senate met the storm broke. Senator Overman, Chairman of the Committee on Rules, told the Vice President very plainly that he had exceeded his authority; that the Senate wing of the Capitol was wholly under the control of the Committee on Rules, and that the dignity of the Senate had been rudely shocked by any such performance as being made the subject of a moving picture show.

Finally, it was shown that Senators as well as the Vice President had been to blame for the infraction of the rules; mutual apologies were made, and the whole matter eliminated from the *Record*, so that no trace of any untoward controversy should be embalmed in that journal of congressional debates.

There were a number of interesting incidents connected with the Administration during the year 1914. One of these was in regard to Memorial Day exercises at Arlington. The Grand Army of the Republic asked President Wilson to deliver an address, and he declined. Then they sought Champ Clark, and he accepted.

Subsequently the President withdrew his declination, and addresses were delivered by both the President and the Speaker of the House.

Early in the year Secretary Daniels issued the famous order prohibiting alcoholic liquors on naval ships and at naval stations. It excited widespread comment. Naval officers felt that it was a reflection upon their habits and a restriction of their personal rights, but when prohibition was established in the military services of a number of the European countries at war, and it became apparent that the Secretary's order was proving beneficial to the Navy, these criticisms ceased.

John Bassett Moore remained as Counselor of the State Department for one year under the new Administration and then resigned. This valuable diplomat did not find the conditions congenial. Upon his retirement Robert Lansing was chosen for the place.

The second White House marriage took place May 7, when the youngest daughter of the President, Miss Eleanor Wilson, was married to Mr. William G. McAdoo, the Secretary of the Treasury. This was more of an event than the previous marriage, on account of the high position of the bridegroom. He was a member of the President's official family, one of his trusted advisers in political as well as in administration affairs. He now became one of the President's personal family. Again all officialdom assembled in the East Room of the White House and witnessed the interesting ceremony. Although Secretary McAdoo had a family of grown children he did not look his years, and had an attractive personality which might well captivate so young a woman.

In August, 1914, death visited the White House, taking the wife of the President and the mother of his three daughters. The whole nation mourned with the President and extended its sympathy. This was expressed by resolutions in Congress and by letters and telegrams from all over the world. In a democracy like the United States the President stands in close relation to the people, and much sympathy was expressed for the lone man in the White House, whose public burdens, great as they could possibly be, were augmented by the death of his beloved life partner, who for so many years had shared his joys and sorrows as he went onward and upward to the highest pinnacle of fame.

CHAPTER XIX

GETTING CLOSE TO THE WAR

World Conflict Involves the United States in Many Controversies—
Interesting Contest Over the Shipping Bill—Prominent Men Re-
tire from Public Life—Bryan Disagrees with the President on
Account of Notes Sent to Germany and Resigns—Great Britain
Disregards American Neutral Rights—Ford Peace Ship Fiasco.

THE short session of the Sixty-third Congress which
ended March 4, 1915, was enlivened by a successful filibuster against the ship purchase bill in the Senate. The bill was strongly urged by the President and
passed the House. It provided for the purchase of
ships by the United States Government, and it was
believed that under its terms the German ships interned
in American harbors could be acquired. At least that
feature of the bill was made the chief point of attack
by its opponents. As the discussion proceeded, a
situation developed which made it certain that the bill
would be defeated. It was found that there was not an
active majority in the Senate for the bill, and that
a number of Democrats, who felt called upon to vote
for it if a vote was reached, wanted the bill defeated.
In fact, many Democrats were indifferent and supported
the bill simply because it was an Administration
measure. The opponents prevented a vote on the bill

by talking day after day. A threat came from the White House that there would be an extra session of the Sixty-fourth Congress in order to pass the bill if it was defeated, but that did not deter the Republicans from carrying on the filibuster.

Finally, came an unexpected attack. Senator Clarke of Arkansas, always independent in his actions, moved to recommit the bill to the Committee on Commerce. Taken by surprise, the supporters of the measure secured a vote on a motion to lay the motion of Clarke on the table, when it was found that, in addition to Clarke, Bankhead of Alabama, Hardwick of Georgia, Hitchcock of Nebraska, O'Gorman of New York, Camden of Kentucky, and Vardaman of Mississippi, all Democrats, were against the shipping bill, and had joined the Republicans in the movement to secure its recommittal, which meant its defeat. These seven more than offset the votes of La Follette of Wisconsin, Kenyon of Iowa, and Norris of Nebraska, three Republicans who supported the bill.

Then followed a filibuster by the supporters of the bill with a view of preventing a vote on Clarke's motion, during which Senator Stone of Missouri assumed the duty of whip wielder for the Administration, and bitterly assailed the seven Democrats for deserting their party and conspiring with the Republicans.

Senator O'Gorman replied, and in the course of his speech said that, if the policy of those in control of the party was to be pursued, "the likelihood of New York remaining in the Democratic column is doubtful."

Amendments were then proposed to the bill which
secured a doubtful majority for it, and the filibuster
against it was renewed. There were several very long
speeches. The rules as interpreted by former Vice
President Sherman and others, with the object of limit-
ing debate, were rigidly enforced. No adjournments
were permitted and no Senator was allowed to yield for
an interruption without losing his right to the floor. It
was during this term of severity that Senator Smoot
broke the long distance record of continuous speaking
without interruption, holding the floor for eleven hours
and thirty-five minutes.

The most interesting plan to pass the shipping bill
was never put in operation. It was known as the
"strong-arm" method. A motion was to be made to
close debate, and was to be put through by the presiding
officer regardless of rules. Everything was arranged
for the exciting event, but Vice President Marshall refused to be a party to it. He was willing to call a Senator to the chair, and Senator James of Kentucky and
Senator Swanson of Virginia were willing to take the
responsibility, but another difficulty arose. The vote
of the Vice President, it was found upon careful canvass, was necessary to adopt the motion and Marshall
would not vote. Bryan, who in the last term of his
service in Congress had filibustered long and earnestly against "gag" methods to pass the silver repeal
bill, and who had disturbed the serenity of the Parker
convention of 1904 by a fight against what he called
"gavel rule," went to the Capitol and urged Marshall

to assume the responsibility and save the Administration's shipping bill.

An interested body of spectators had gathered for the final performance. Many high officers of the Government and their wives were in the galleries and Cabinet officers were on the floor of the Senate. It was believed that Bryan could persuade Marshall to reverse his decision, but after a long effort to win him over the Vice President still refused, as presiding officer, to take any step which was not in accordance with the rules of the Senate.

Incidentally the refusal of Marshall to take a revolutionary stand at that time started a movement for another candidate for Vice President in the next election. Close friends of the President began to give out intimations that this or that man would be a good candidate for Vice President in 1916.

With the failure of the "strong-arm" plan the death knell of the shipping bill was sounded. The President consented to have it laid aside and the appropriation bills were rushed through. All thought of an extra session was abandoned.

The President did not want Congress in session. There were two great overshadowing problems to face, the European war and Mexico, and he did not want Congress interfering with his policies in regard to either. Not even his desire to pass the ship purchase bill, and it could have passed the new Senate, would induce him to call Congress in extra session. He wanted the intervening nine months without "Con-

gress on his hands," to debate, and possibly pass, resolutions of inquiry regarding the administration of
foreign affairs.

With the end of the Sixty-third Congress the senatorial careers of Elihu Root of New York, George C.
Perkins of California, Theodore E. Burton of Ohio, and
Joseph L. Bristow of Kansas came to a close. Two of
these, Root and Burton, were candidates for the Republican nomination in 1916, although both of them
disavowed any such ambition several times during the
short session of Congress. Several times when they
were opposing the shipping bill their Democratic colleagues charged them with being Republican Presidential possibilities, but both of them treated the
allusions as jests.

Root's retirement was a distinct loss to the
country. He was one of the best equipped men in
public life to render good service. As a Senator
he continued to do the big things that characterized
his service in the War and State Departments. He
was never small, he had no petty meanness, and his
sense of humor was never wanting. With few words
he often relieved a tense state of feeling, and again he
would scorch an opponent with his delicate sarcasm.
On one occasion Senator Newlands of Nevada made a
rather bombastic speech of criticism and flourishes,
parts of which were directed against Senator Root.

"If the Senator from Nevada," responded the New
Yorker, with the utmost affability, "would lend us the
charm of his genial personality more frequently he

would not have expended his eloquence and energy for nothing. The matter which has been the subject of the Senator's protracted and illuminating remarks was disposed of several days ago during the lengthy and lamented absence of the Senator."

There were a few Senators who liked to get into a controversy with Senator Root. There was a certain pride in having been in a tilt with Elihu Root, even if it were a one-sided contest. On one occasion when Senator Root was making a speech Senator Martine of New Jersey, who would break into anybody's speech, interrupted Root and roared out one of his impassioned and vociferous utterances.

"The Senator from New Jersey," remarked Senator Root, in that halting manner so effective in his humor, "the Senator from New Jersey should not make my poor feeble speech the setting for his brilliant gems of oratory."

When Root decided to retire I wrote a short article about him for a periodical. In it I told a story about the Senator and Colonel Roosevelt, a story that never can be published, as shown by the following letter, written after I had submitted my manuscript to Senator Root:

"UNITED STATES SENATE,
"WASHINGTON, Aug. 12, 1914.
"MY DEAR DUNN:
"The little article you sent me is very nice and I am very much obliged to you. I see nothing in it to object to except a single paragraph about Mr. Roosevelt. I

don't want that published. I have felt that the relations between Roosevelt and myself have been such
that any controversy between us would necessarily de-
generate into the kind of recrimination and exposure of
confidences which accompany a divorce suit, with a
loss of personal dignity to both. Accordingly I have
carefully refrained from saying anything at all about
him personally. I don't want to do so now. I return
the paper which you sent with the paragraph to which
I refer, on page four, crossed out in blue pencil.

"With kind regards, I am

"Faithfully yours,

"ELIHU ROOT."

Senator Perkins of California was one of those remarkable products of our country, a self-made man who
is a credit to his maker. A state of Maine lad, living
on a farm until thirteen years old, he then became a
sailor. In 1855 he sailed before the mast around Cape
Horn and located in California. He became a successful business man, and after holding a number of offices
he was elected Governor. In 1893 he succeeded Leland
Stanford in the Senate, and when he retired in March,
1914, was third Senator in length of service.

During his career Perkins devoted himself to California and the Pacific coast. He took special interest
in the extension of American interests in the Pacific,
particularly in Hawaii and the Philippines. He was a
staunch friend of the American Navy.

"I would rather be an officer in the Navy, wearing
the uniform of my country, and in command of one of
our magnificent ships, than hold my present position in

the Senate," he once told me, and I knew that the lure of seafaring life still called him.

Senator Burton and Senator Bristow were both men of strong personal characteristics, men whose integrity was never questioned. Both had been independent in the first part of their senatorial careers; Bristow inclining toward insurgency and Burton toward mugwumpery. Both became better party men near the close of their terms than at any time during their six years of service. They were not alike, yet both were serious-minded men, hard-working and studious, and forceful enough to make for themselves a place in the Senate.

The first break in President Wilson's Cabinet was the resignation of his Secretary of State. William J. Bryan resigned as Secretary of State because he feared the Administration he had created was growing too warlike. Bryan would not sign a note which Wilson had prepared to be dispatched to Germany in regard to the *Lusitania*.

Of all the tragedies of the war that which aroused this country, which seemed to be the one real reason for going into the war, was the sinking of the English liner with the loss of 125 Americans who were peaceful passengers on a merchant ship. It was all the more shocking because Count von Bernstorff, the German Ambassador, had published advertisements in the newspapers warning Americans not to take passage on the *Lusitania*.

"If I had been President," said Colonel Roosevelt, in discussing the *Lusitania*, "I would have called Count Bernstorff to the White House and told him to disavow the advertisements or receive his passports. I would also have told him to tell his Government that American lives must not be destroyed; that if submarines sank peaceful ships and Americans were lost, it would mean war. I know the Germans. The advertisements would have been withdrawn and the *Lusitania* would not have been torpedoed."

Soon after the sinking of the *Lusitania* President Wilson delivered an address in Philadelphia, in which he declared that the example of America should be for peace and used the expresssion "too proud to fight," which sent a chill down the spines of people who were ready to go to war with Germany, not only because the sympathy of the country was with the allies, but on account of the *Lusitania* and numerous other outrages the Germans had perpetrated.

The firm and almost warlike note which later was sent to Germany in regard to the *Lusitania* caused a strong reaction. This note was signed by Bryan. The German reply was inadequate, almost offensive in terms, and a second note was prepared. It was this note which Bryan refused to sign and he tendered his resignation, which was accepted. For a few days there was grave apprehension, and a belief that the second note must be strong, indeed.

"God bless you, Mr. President," said Bryan in his good-bye at the White House, and as he passed out the pacifists thought that the one tie which would keep this country out of war had been broken. Robert Lansing became Secretary of State.

And then the second note was published, and it was found to be not only less warlike than the one which Bryan had signed, but much milder than the "strict accountability" note which had been dispatched upon the first threat of Germany to sink merchant ships. Bryan said that the note had been changed; that the note he had refused to sign was modified after he had tendered his resignation, but evidently not to such an extent as to cause him to withdraw his resignation.

The retirement of Bryan was for several weeks a matter of much speculation and discussion. Those who could not find as much war in the note that he refused to sign as in the two previous notes he had signed sought for other motives. The general opinion was that Bryan had become convinced that Wilson would not abide by the one-term plank in the Baltimore platform, and that he wanted to be in a position to run for the Presidency if there was a favorable opening.

The facts are that Bryan was not happy in the State Department. Four walls, unless they confined a multitude of people whom he was addressing, were too small for Bryan. Besides, he was no longer Democracy's boss, and he was not wholly dominant in his own Department. Although the position of Secretary of State carries with it the title of Premier of the Cabinet, it does not follow that the Secretary can even control his own Department. It had become known that President Wilson was writing the notes which were signed by Bryan.

Bryan suffered in leaving the Cabinet when he did

and for the reasons he gave. He was charged with disloyalty at the moment when partisanship had been laid aside and every American citizen was called upon to stand by the President. A great many people feared that Bryan's popularity might bring about a division in the country at a time when an unbroken front was most essential. No one knew what Bryan's large following would do, particularly if he should use his wonderful oratorical power in opposition to the President. Had war followed the bold utterances in the first *Lusitania* note, a division such as Bryan might have created would have been serious.

But the temperament of the American people is such that they soon recover from what seems to be a calamity or irreparable loss. They soon learn that no one man is absolutely necessary in this great nation; that any man, no matter what his position or ability, may die or resign and the Government will still live.

Finally, there was a partial settlement of the *Lusitania* controversy. A promise was obtained from Count Bernstorff that merchantmen would not be sunk without warning. Later Germany came along with a declaration of the same sort and a demand that merchantmen should not carry guns to be used against the submarines. Of course, the United States could not prescribe what the merchant ships of other nations should carry in the way of defense.

About the middle of June our people learned that Great Britain was rifling our mails and that our commerce had been detained. We had been restricted from dealing with neutral countries in non-contraband articles. By orders in Council Great Britain was making or unmaking international law as best suited her designs. Goods which United States merchants were not permitted to deliver in Holland, Sweden, and Denmark were sent from Great Britain, and British merchants were making large profits.

Besides rifling our mails, Great Britain had been making use of our flag, hoisting it over merchant ships in order to deceive enemy ships and thus escape capture or destruction. The seizure of American ships and their detention while mails, not only to Germany, but neutral nations as well, were opened and their contents disclosed, became a regular practice. American merchants began to complain that their trade secrets were thus obtained and that their customers were being taken away and turned over to British merchants. By July 18, 1915, it was shown that more than 2,000 American ships had been seized and taken into British ports.

Notes of protest were sent on several occasions, but in every case, whether concerning the seizure of ships, or concerning the mails, Great Britain rejected the demands of the United States, and maintained that all her acts were a war necessity.

"Dollar chasers" was what Americans were called in the British and Canadian press, because objection was made to the interference with the neutral rights of American citizens engaged in legitimate commerce. Every act which was against Germany was loudly applauded, and every demand upon England was denounced.

By the middle of September American cargoes valued at $15,000,000 had been confiscated. Meanwhile Great Britain was successfully floating a loan in this country and raising $500,000,000 to pay for the war supplies furnished by citizens of the United States.

One position taken by the United States, particularly pleasing to England, was the refusal to create a new international law to the effect that belligerents could not purchase arms and munitions in this country. A great many of our people would have been glad to have an embargo laid upon death-dealing supplies, but it would take an act of Congress to lay such an embargo, and the State Department in a note to Austria and in representations to German officials showed that it would be contrary to all usage to deny any government the right to purchase arms in a neutral country.

Possibly the determination of the Government on this subject led to the formation of plots to destroy munition plants, and otherwise to make this country the base of operations and intrigue which we regarded as contrary to international law. The arrest of an American on board a ship touching at a British port with letters and papers from the Austrian Ambassador, and letters from attachés of the German Embassy, still further complicated the situation.   In one of the letters written by Baron Dumba he said: "Having regard for the self-willed temperament of the President," etc.   He also referred to the President as "intransigeant." The publication of this letter caused a demand on the Austrian Government for the recall of the Ambassador. Captains von Papen and Boy-ed, military and naval attachés of the German Embassy, were also involved by the capture of the letters, and the Government had them removed from the country. Captain von Papen had referred to our people as "idiotic Yankees."

There had been a long delay in sending one note to Great Britain concerning the interference with American shipping. Our government did not feel justified in calling Great Britain to account for the violation of our neutrality rights while Germany ruthlessly continued to sink non-combatant ships with the loss of lives of Americans who were passengers. Germany intimated that in view of the dangers to such ships Americans should not take passage on them, particularly when they carried munitions of war for use against the German and Austrian soldiers.

The note of Secretary Lansing to Great Britain was published November 8, 1915, and it was found that he had taken very strong grounds against the methods of the British Government. The United States as the greatest of neutral nations became the champion of neutral rights. The note questioned the effectiveness of the blockade, and as applied to the ports of neutral nations, asserted that it was "ineffective, illegal, and indefensible." The "relations between the United States and Great Britain must not be governed by expediency, but international law." The determination was announced to "contest the seizure of vessels at sea upon conjectural suspicions," and also to unhesitatingly protest against the lawless conduct of belligerents.

The tragedy which covered Europe was given a touch of humor towards the end of the year by the entry of Henry Ford as the peacemaker and the sending of a "peace ship" to Europe, with Mr. Ford's avowed intention of "getting the boys out of the trenches by Christmas." His intentions were good and no doubt he hoped that such an appeal as he was making would in some way end the war or bring about negotiations for peace. But at that time, as for a long time afterwards, neither side was willing to enter upon negotiations for peace which would restore conditions and territory as they had been before the war, and the allies would not accept the suggestion of peace with Belgium, Serbia, and parts of France and Russia in the possession of the central powers.

There were many who gave Mr. Ford credit for sincerity of motives and, could his original plan have been carried out, it might have been a dignified attempt to bring peace. He invited many very distinguished people to go on the peace ship, but the onrush of cranks, grafters, junketers, and all sorts and conditions of men and women caused the others to withdraw their acceptance, and the expedition degenerated into a sorry comedy.

At first the peace ship movement threatened international complications. Foreign governments were somewhat doubtful about its character and mission.

But England rose to the occasion. While the British Government had to take official cognizance of the ship and examine it and the tourists, the people of England treated the movement as an American joke.

The bickerings and quarrels among those on board the peace ship, the selfishness displayed by many of the passengers, the intent of others to make what they could out of it, the schemes of the grafters, and the idea which prevailed among a large number that it was simply a junket out of which they were to get all the pleasure they could, converted a serious movement into a farce, and heaped lasting ridicule upon a man whose intention gave every evidence of sincerity.

CHAPTER XX

YEAR BEFORE THE BATTLE

Republicans Look Over the Field—Roosevelt Would Support None but Hughes—No Opposition to Wilson among Democrats—Mexico Becomes Important and the President Recognizes Carranza—Pan-American Conferences—President Wilson Weds Mrs. Galt—Harding in the Senate.

THE political game for the great stakes in 1916 was played without intermission during the year 1915. For a long time after the election of 1914 the Republicans believed that all they had to do was to name a candidate and he would be elected. When the European war brought so much prosperity to the country, they began to see that it was not going to be so easy, yet they still believed that they could win.

At that time—before it became evident that the support of Theodore Roosevelt was necessary to Republican success—the Republican leaders desired to get the consent of Elihu Root to be a candidate. Very particularly did that element in the party known as the Old Guard and residing in New York, want Root for the candidate, so that they would have a man to rally around and prevent the selection of a Whitman delegation to the national convention. They did not want Whitman.

Root as a candidate was discussed by a group of men in Washington, and one of them who was to see the ex-Senator in New York was instructed to tell him that the hard work of the administration would be taken off his hands, and that he could give his whole attention to the big questions of government.

"You are all bent on killing me," was Root's rather plaintive remark when the matter was put up to him. "You know that a man seventy-two years old, as I shall be when the next President is inaugurated, cannot bear the burdens imposed by the Presidency."

"But why is it necessary for you to take up all the cares? Why cannot you leave all the troubles about appointments, save the very important places, to Cabinet officers, and refuse to be bothered by the applicants?"

"There will be a thousand men seeking office," he replied, "who will not be satisfied unless they see the President and present their cases to him. I know a thousand men, some of them deserving party workers but unfit for office, who would not be satisfied with a 'no' from a Cabinet officer, but would insist upon seeing me personally.

"There is a great work for a President to do, and if I could take up the problems of administration and the foreign complications which arise, and confine myself to these alone, I should be glad to do so. But there is now too much laborious duty in the Presidency for a man of my years."

A little later I saw Colonel Roosevelt and discussed

the political situation with him. It was my opinion that he could return to the Republican party and make the race for President and win. But he would not align himself with the Republicans—not at that time, although he made no objection to his followers returning to their old allegiance. The question as to whether he would support any of the men then mentioned for President if nominated by the Republicans was brought up. One after another he wiped the different names off the slate. Root had presided over the convention which robbed him of the nomination in 1912. Fairbanks was a delegate to that convention and voted for every robbery that was committed. Burton had been a party to the manipulation of the Ohio state convention which deprived him of a number of delegates. Whitman he pooh-poohed at, and Weeks he did not consider at all available.

"How about Hughes?"

"I'll support Hughes," was the quick reply. "I'll support Hughes, but not unless he declares himself. We must know where he stands on national honor, national defense, and all other great questions before we accept him."

It was my inference that the Colonel wanted Hughes to make his declaration before the nomination, something that was impossible as long as Hughes continued in the attitude of not being a candidate. The Colonel was intent upon "smoking out Hughes," either with a declaration as to his attitude on public questions or, preferably, with a declaration that he would under no

circumstances be a candidate or allow the use of his
name in the convention. But Hughes would not be
"smoked out."

On the Democratic side there was only one candidate,
Woodrow Wilson. Efforts to bring out Champ Clark
failed, the Speaker himself putting an end to all talk
of that kind.

Both national committees met in Washington in
December, 1915, and called the national conventions
for 1916. The Democrats fixed on June 14, and the
Republican committee, having met later, selected June
7, bringing both conventions very close together. The
Republicans were still in doubt as to their candidate.
They did not want Hughes, but feared they would have
to take him. Roosevelt was still the uncertain quantity in their computations. They knew that the Progressives must be brought back if the Republicans were
to win.

The Democrats were in high feather, although not
showing the confidence expressed by President Wilson
at a dinner which he gave to the members of the national
committee. Although this dinner was in no way public, the President, in the course of a general talk and in
conversation with members, was quoted as giving
voice to the following expressions:

"I shall enter the next campaign with confidence."

"The Republican party is running up a blind alley."

"Our foes are talking through their hats."

"The Mexicans will continue to raise all kinds of
trouble until they are through."

A political event of national interest was a dinner given in New York by President Gary of the Steel Corporation, attended by a score of magnates, at which Theodore Roosevelt was the guest of honor. Various interpretations were given to the affair, the one most exploited being that Roosevelt was to be the candidate of the great financial interests.

Just as Bryan's statement, that he could not live on $12,000 a year, had chilled to the marrow a large number of his followers, so the Gary dinner struck a chill to the hearts of many of Roosevelt's supporters throughout the country. However, it was not the Gary dinner which prevented the nomination of Theodore Roosevelt by the Republican party.

The troubles in Mexico continued.

Early in January President Wilson delivered his Indianapolis speech on the occasion of a Jackson Day dinner. He was in an unusually good frame of mind and the speech was full of pleasantries. He reviewed the Mexican situation and seemed perfectly satisfied with the policy of the Administration. It was in that speech that he said:

"When some great dailies not very far from where I am temporarily residing thundered with rising scorn at watchful waiting, Woodrow sat back in his chair and chuckled, knowing that he laughs best who laughs last."

It was in that same speech that he said that the Mexicans had a right to spill blood if they wanted to and it was none of our business.

The President, however, continued his efforts to bring about a settlement of the affairs in Mexico. He tried to have the chiefs who were leading warring factions get together and settle their differences, but without avail. Plans made by Pan-American governments to bring about peace were thwarted by First Chief Carranza, who took the position that he could not confer with outside governments regarding the internal affairs of Mexico. Finally, the United States recognized Carranza as head of the *de facto* government of Mexico.

A Pan-American conference was held in Washington in 1915, called by Secretary McAdoo of the Treasury Department. It was called a "financial" conference, because it was under the auspices of the Treasury Department and the subject of finances as they related to the southern republics was made the important feature, although commerce, trade, shipping, and other subjects were considered.

An interesting by-play was observed in connection with this particular Pan-American conference. The conference was engineered and handled by Secretary McAdoo. John Barrett, who had long been at the head of the Pan-American Union, was a secondary figure, though the meetings were held in the building over which he presided. Even the President in his speech went so far as to allude to the meeting as the first of its kind and expressed surprise that it should never have been thought of before. This rather nettled Barrett, and he took occasion when he addressed the conference to point out what had been done, referring to the Pan-American conference called by Blaine in 1889, and subsequent gatherings in Mexico, Rio de Janeiro, and Buenos Aires. Barrett made it very plain that the efforts to unite the nations of the American continent in closer relations, both diplomatic and commercial, had not been allowed to slumber until the year 1915.

As to the outcome of the conference it may be told in a few words. The men in these southern nations wanted money. They wanted large loans, but particularly they wanted large investments in their undeveloped resources. The United States as a nation was not authorized at that time to make loans or investments. The men with money in this country do not look with great favor upon loans or investments in other countries on this continent. There are too many opportunities in the United States. Not only that, but they preferred to make large loans to the war torn nations of Europe, and to invest in large enterprises in China, rather than to undertake the development of those still wild regions of South America. As to the financial affairs, such as exchange, etc., they will follow when trade warrants the establishment of banking facilities. Trade and commerce will increase when the southern countries produce in large quantities those articles which are not produced in the United States. In the meantime the great commerce of the world will go on as it has from the beginning on lines of latitude rather than lines of longitude.

A grand sight, though somewhat pathetic, was the

march of the veterans of the Grand Army of the
Republic in the fall of 1915, at the time of the annual
encampment of the organization in Washington. Fifty
years before, some of them, then forming part of the
wonderful armies of Grant and Sherman, one just from
the victorious fields of Richmond and Appomattox, and
the other from the famous march to the sea and the
sweep through the Carolinas, had marched in Grand Review at the close of the great Civil War. A half century
had made a wonderful change. In 1865 it took two days
for these soldiers to pass in review, in 1915 they passed
by in less than two hours. The young men and boys in
1865, joyous and hearty with life before them, happy
with their safe return to their homes, were old men with
tottering steps, their ranks decimated, a mere skeleton
of the victorious army of 1865. But the sentiment was
there; the years had softened all animosities; the
country was again united. At the close of the
encampment the "boys in blue" mingled with their
old enemies, the "boys in gray," and "Yank" and
"Johnny Reb" shared each other's tents and hospitali-
ties on the field of Gettysburg. Both the semi-cen-
tennial of the Grand Review, and the joint encampment
of the survivors of Gettysburg were historic events,
each contributing a chapter to mark the milestones of a
nation.

The suffragists were very active during the entire
year. Congress was not in session, and they devoted
themselves to work about the White House, trying to
secure a declaration from the President. The President

had once positively stated that suffrage was a state issue, but the women seemed determined to get him to reverse his views. Once when the members of a persistent delegation announced that they would remain until the President saw them, he slipped away to the golf links, returning late in the evening.

Early in October President Wilson announced that he would vote for woman suffrage at the New Jersey election in October. A number of Cabinet officers and other men connected with the Administration followed his lead. A few weeks later woman suffrage was overwhelmingly defeated in New Jersey. In the November elections three other states, New York, Massachusetts, and Pennsylvania, gave strong majorities against suffrage.

On October 9, 1915, the engagement of the President and Mrs. Norman Galt, of Washington, was announced. Rumors there had been, for the frequency with which the White House limousine stopped at the modest little home in 20th street had not escaped the neighborhood eyes, and there was gossip of long evening drives about the beautiful avenues and of other incidents that betokened an interest more than friendly, but nevertheless the announcement was a great surprise, even to Washington. The public generally had believed the President wholly engrossed in the serious affairs of government.

On December 18 the marriage took [place. The ceremony was performed at the residence of Mrs. Galt, with only the relatives of the principals present. It was known that the honeymoon was to be spent at Hot Springs, Virginia, and the President's car was to leave the Union Station on the evening train after the ceremony. There were great throngs at the station to see the bride and groom. They waited a long time, until long after the train had departed, and then went away disappointed. The President and his bride had circumvented the curiosity seekers. The White House limousine, instead of going to the Union Station, sped away southward, across the long bridge and down to Alexandria, where the bride and groom boarded the private car and were on their way to the Virginia resort.

They remained away during the holidays, and again the annual New Year's reception at the White House was omitted. Soon after the New Year, however, the White House resumed social activities. The first function normally would have been the reception to the Diplomatic Corps, but the war in Europe had made it impossible to invite all the diplomats to any affair at which they would be obliged to be present. So in lieu of the diplomatic reception, one was given in honor of the Pan-American representatives. This answered every purpose, and diplomats who had been on friendly terms before the war were not compelled to meet as enemies. This reception was Mrs. Wilson's first appearance in the rôle of First Lady of the Land, and she proved a very charming hostess to the thousands who thronged the White House.

Warren G. Harding was sworn in as a Senator from Ohio when Congress met in December, 1915, to begin the first session of the Sixty-fourth Congress. He was then known as the publisher of a thriving country newspaper, a man who had been active in politics in his state and who had been a state senator and lieutenant governor.

Joseph G. Cannon again returned to the House after what he called "an enforced absence of two years."

CHAPTER XXI

NATIONAL PREPAREDNESS

President Wilson Executes a Quick Change in Regard to Preparation
for Defense—Derides Agitation in 1914 and Becomes Chief Agitator
in 1915—Prophet Ezekiel Quoted—Secretary Garrison Resigns.

AMONG the strange—almost unaccountable—shifts
in the policy of the Administration was that in regard to national defense which occurred between December, 1914, and August, 1915. When Congress met
in December, 1914, the demands for Army and Navy
increases were ringing loud and earnestly. Many Republicans were making a party issue of it. Colonel
Theodore Roosevelt added his voice to the general
demand. The Colonel's relative, Franklin D. Roosevelt, a Democrat, who was Assistant Secretary of the
Navy, contributed his share by saying the Navy was
short 18,000 men.

Long before the war in Europe there had been an
active propaganda to create a sentiment in this country
for an increase in the Army and Navy, and the addition
of larger ships, greater guns, and larger munition supplies. With the war came renewed activity by those
who were most interested. Many people were fearful
that the country was in real danger. Opponents of
military preparation said it was absurd to think that

any one of the powerful nations at war desired to take on the United States as an additional antagonist, but in spite of their arguments there was a general feeling that serious danger threatened the United States.

President Wilson was more amused than disturbed by the clamor. He blew it away like a puff of smoke in his address to Congress on December 8, 1914. He was outspoken against compulsory military service, and declared that there was no reason for fear from any quarter. "We never shall have a large standing army," he said. "We shall not turn America into a military camp. We will not ask the young men of the country to spend the best years of their lives making soldiers of themselves." "Nervous and excited," he characterized those who were agitating for a greater military establishment.

In April, Secretary Daniels wrote a letter on the state of the Navy and asserted that the Navy was fit, with plenty of war munitions and fully recruited. A month later, indicating a change of mind in the Administration, the Secretary said that the Navy was strong, but not strong enough. Early in July Secretary Daniels announced his intention of organizing a naval advisory board of scientists, inventors, and business men to determine what was needed and to make recommendations for improvements in the Navy. Like several other moves of the Secretary, this was not pleasing to naval officers. They had put in four years of highly specialized study at the Academy, and throughout all their service they had been studying naval construction and naval needs in machinery and ordnance, and thought they were more competent than a civilian board of inventors and scientists to plan and prepare the best naval equipment. Towards the end of July Secretary Daniels declared for a larger Navy, and it was known that Secretary Garrison was preparing for a larger Army.

On August 4 it was announced that President Wilson in his next annual message to Congress would urge that immediate action be taken towards preparation for national defense. He had become a convert to preparedness. Nothing was said as to what had occurred to change his mind since December, 1914, but in August it became known and was the talk in Administration circles that President Wilson was the man around whom to rally for national defense. Early in October the President made his first public declaration on the subject of preparedness and in favor of such national defense as "to command the respect of other nations for our rights." The popularity of the President's position was evident, and a little later he said that he wanted the United States second in sea power. In November the President made a speech at the Manhattan Club in New York which was practically the forecast of his message to Congress a month later. He said that there was no need of being panic stricken, but that it was evident that a larger Army and Navy were needed. He approved the Garrison plan of an increase of the regular forces and a reserve of 400,000 men.

William J. Bryan, who several months before had re-

tired from the Cabinet, became active about this time as
an opponent of militarism. He rated President Wilson
as a "jingo" on preparedness. He said he read the President's Manhattan Club speech "with sorrow and concern." "He has announced a policy which has never
been adopted by any party or any authoritative organization in the Government." Bryan went to Washington about the time Congress was to assemble, and
it was understood that he intended to make a fight; to
rally all his following, and if possible defeat the President's plans. But the opposition of Bryan never
materialized. He was too busy on the lecture platform
to give his whole time to the subject. While he made
a number of speeches in various parts of the country
against militarism, they did not seem to have much
influence upon Congress.

The amusing side of the President's position for national defense was developed when he quoted the
prophet Ezekiel as in favor of preparedness. The next
day Roosevelt came forth with the statement that
three months before he (the Colonel) had quoted
the same words from the same prophet in an address
at San Francisco. This was followed by a statement
from the White House denying that the President had his
knowledge of Ezekiel by reading the works of Theodore
Roosevelt. Bryan, who would not be left out of any
public matter coupled with the Bible or advertising,
also took up Ezekiel and quoted from the prophet to
prove his theories. As a final touch Ezekiel was the
topic assigned to Senator Penrose at a dinner of the

Gridiron Club. In the most solemn way, and with an erudition and research that few believed possible, the Pennsylvania Senator discussed Ezekiel, while the diners were convulsed with laughter. Not all of them, perhaps, for to this day there is doubt among those present as to whether President Wilson enjoyed this part of the entertainment.

It became evident that Congress, or at least the House of Representatives, would not accept the Garrison plan for an army reserve. James Hay, Chairman of the Committee on Military Affairs, was very much opposed to the plan; in fact, he was opposed to any general increase for the regular army. He was supported by Claude Kitchin, the House floor leader, who was opposed to the entire military and naval program of the Administration. Champ Clark, the Speaker, supported the President's program, but gave it a back-handed slap, saying that we could maintain peace if we deserved peace and that "we have forced every war we have ever fought."

During the last part of January and the first part of February, 1916, President Wilson went before the country and made his campaign for military preparation. The first speech was made in New York, and was so different from the placid utterances of his message to Congress as to create some alarm. He gave a warning of grave perils and the necessity for war preparation:

"I cannot tell you," he said in his speech, "what the international relations of this country will be to-morrow and I use the word literally. And I would not dare keep silent and let the country suppose that tomorrow was certain to be as bright as to-day."

. . . .

"What America has to fear, if she has anything to fear, are indirect, roundabout, flank movements upon her regnant position in the Western Hemisphere."

The day this speech was delivered another note of protest to Great Britain was made public. It had been understood for some time that the differences with England were not being adjusted, and this may have led James R. Mann, the Republican leader, to say in the House that England was the menace to the peace of America, that war with her was more likely than with any other country.

As if to give color to the attitude of Mann, Senator Walsh of Montana, an ardent admirer and supporter of President Wilson, made a speech in the Senate vigorously assailing Great Britain, and denouncing the attitude that country had taken respecting the neutral rights of the United States.

About this time Bryan, exercising his knowledge of the data in the State Department, challenged President Wilson to produce facts and reasons for his change of front in regard to military preparation. Of course, the President paid no heed to the challenge.

Continuing his campaign for preparedness, the President made a tour of the West. Speaking at Cleveland, Ohio, he said:

"Gentlemen, let me tell you very solemnly you cannot afford to postpone this thing. I do not know what a single day may bring forth."

"I know that we are treading daily amidst the most intricate dangers."

"The world is on fire. Sparks are likely to drop anywhere."

"If all could see the dispatches I read every hour, they would know how difficult it has been to maintain peace."

At Pittsburgh the President was less alarming. He repeated that the "world is on fire," but added that it had not reached the United States, and, "I do not believe that the fire is going to begin, but I would feel surer if we were ready."

At Milwaukee and Chicago the President was still milder, though continuing to urge his policy of preparation. At Des Moines he took a shot at Roosevelt. "Some men are actually preaching war," he said, replying to a remark of the Colonel that "America should not be an ostrich." Roosevelt, apparently taking the war talk seriously, said that he and four sons were ready to volunteer.

The newspapers strongly favoring preparedness, basing their opinions upon the Milwaukee, Chicago, and Des Moines speeches, criticized Wilson's efforts. His speeches were called weak and not impressive. This seemed to result in a change, for at Topeka, Kansas, the President became more vigorous. He asserted the right of Americans to travel where they desired, declared that the right to send food, cotton, and manufactured products to peaceful populations in open neutral markets should be maintained, and uttered a sentence indicating that England might be the enemy against whom strong military preparation was necessary.

"It may be necessary," he said, "to use the force of the United States to vindicate the rights of American citizens to enjoy the protection of international law."

At Kansas City, Mo., the President said:

"I say to you in all solemnity that there is not a day to be lost, not because of any new critical matter, but because I cannot tell what may happen in twenty-four hours."

"I haven't enough men to guard the Mexican border. I haven't enough even to keep bandits from raiding into United States territory."

Possibly the most important statement was made at St. Louis. The President was speaking of the Navy:

"It ought," he said, "in my judgment, to be incomparably the greatest Navy in the world."

That caused a shudder among the Democrats in Congress, particularly the so-called "little Navy men" and many others who had persuaded themselves to vote for only part of the preparedness program of the Administration. They gathered some comfort out of a statement by Admiral Strauss to the Naval Committee, made public the same day that President Wilson made his St. Louis speech, to the effect that Secretary Daniels had lopped off estimates of $12,000,000 recommended by Strauss for guns and munitions for the Navy.

The St. Louis speech ended the campaign of the President for preparedness. To this day there has not been a statement showing what nation was threatening this country at that time. We never have known whence came the dispatches that so unnerved the Chief Magistrate of the Nation. Considerable wonder was expressed as to why, in view of threatening conditions, the entire situation was not placed before Congress in order that immediate action might be taken, and also why an effort was not made to secure the enormous output of war munitions which were being daily shipped from our ports to the warring countries in Europe.

Less than three weeks before the end of President Wilson's second administration one of his closest friends, speaking of this excursion of the President in behalf of preparedness, gave me information which is simply astounding. My informant quoted Mr. Wilson directly and in such detail that he impressed me with belief in his statements. The President, according to this close friend, went on that memorable trip in 1915 and 1916, making vigorous speeches in behalf of a large Army and Navy, not so much for the immediate effect that it might have upon Congress, but for the effect in the future upon the people of the country when the President would have to resort to conscription to raise an army. He knew that the people would not stand for conscription unless they were convinced that a great emergency existed, and without conscription Germany

would win the war. It seems incredible that such a
motive could have animated Mr. Wilson at that time.
It was in 1915 and 1916, nearly a year before he was
re-elected on the sole ground that he kept us out
of war; and in the campaign he promised that we should
not go to war. It was a year before the "peace without
victory" speech; two years before he told this country
in an address that the warring nations seemed to be
fighting for the same object; it was more than a year
before he went to Congress and asked for a war declaration against Germany. For fifteen months then, according to this close personal friend, he had been laying
his plans to keep Germany from winning the war.
Long before declaring war he saw the necessity for conscription to raise an army to fight that war. Fifteen
months before asking for conscription, he took steps to
set in motion the forces which would educate the people
to a point at which they would support conscription in
order to send a great army to the battlefields of Europe.
He knew at that time (1915–1916), this friend told me,
that his supporters and best friends in Congress would
not vote for conscription, unless the impression had been
created in the minds of the people of the country that
conscription was necessary. Again, I say it seems incredible, in view of what happened in the intervening
months, between the preparedness swing around the
circle and the declaration of war, that in 1915 and 1916
Woodrow Wilson was planning to prevent Germany
from winning the war. Were it not for the high standing and character of the man who gave me this informa-

tion, I would not here record the statement. It is another chapter of mystery in the public life of the mysterious man who for eight years was President of the United States.

The country soon had another subject to interest it. Secretary Garrison resigned, also the Assistant Secretary, Henry Breckinridge. Garrison had reached a point at which he could not remain in the Cabinet. He had been supported all the way by the President for his continental army plan of 400,000, and an increase of the regular army. But Chairman Hay would not accept the Garrison plan. There were several conferences, and finally the President yielded to Hay; this left Garrison in the air, and he promptly resigned. In doing so he gave as the principal reason the determination of the President to reject the army plan of the War Department, "the policy recommended to you and adopted by you," said Garrison, in a letter to the President. He had another reason, the President's acquiescence in the Clarke amendment to the Philippine bill. This amendment provided absolute independence for the Filipinos in four years, and was adopted in the Senate by the deciding vote of Vice-President Marshall, who could vote only when there was an equal division. The President told Garrison that, while he thought the Clarke amendment "unwise at this time, it would clearly be most inadvisable for me to dissent if both houses agree."

So on two grounds Lindley M. Garrison resigned, and President Wilson lost a very strong member of his

Cabinet. Of course, it was impossible, under the circumstances of Garrison's retirement and the short time before the expiration of the Presidential term, to find a man of conspicuous ability and standing to accept the position of Secretary of War. Newton D. Baker of Ohio was named for the place.

With the retirement of Garrison all hope of accomplishing very much for the Army ceased. Congress rallied to the President, for only a comparatively few members desired a large regular army. The militia men had made themselves felt, with the result that the army legislation was for their benefit rather than that of the regulars. There were increases, but entirely insufficient to meet anything like the alarming conditions which had been pictured by the advocates of military preparedness.

CHAPTER XXII

YEAR OF ACUTE SITUATIONS

President Wins in a Skirmish with Congress and has McLemore and
Gore Resolutions Tabled—U-boat Crisis and Threatened Break of
Diplomatic Relations—*Deutschland* Makes Two Visits—U-53
Arouses Indignation—Mexican Situation Sends 100,000 Troops to
the Border—Nation-wide Railroad Strike Averted by the Adam-
son Eight-Hour Law—Child Labor Law—Hazing Harding.

THE year 1916 was not one of ease for the President
or the country. A political campaign was in full
blast, and there was the ever-recurring crisis over the
submarine boats and the interference with our rights on
the seas by Great Britain.

An acute situation arose in the last part of February
when the McLemore and Gore resolutions were introduced in the House and Senate. The Texas Representative and the Oklahoma Senator introduced resolutions to the same purport, calling upon the Federal
Government to warn American citizens off ships of
belligerent nations. At one time it seemed that both
houses might pass the resolutions, but the pro-ally feeling, supplemented by the determination of the President, soon procured a majority against them. It was a
very trying time for pacifists who were also Democratic
leaders. Senator Stone in the Senate and Congress-

man Kitchin in the House were in a very uncomfortable position.

President Wilson insisted upon a vote on the two resolutions and in the end he emerged triumphantly, for both houses, each by a large majority, laid the resolutions on the table. Kitchin went so far as to declare that Congress would not follow the President into war, indicating that the policy of the Administration was in the direction of war.

In April President Wilson threatened to break off diplomatic relations with Germany on account of unsatisfactory negotiations over the submarines. Germany then sent a note to the United States saying that submarine warfare would be modified to the extent of giving persons on unarmed ships an opportunity to escape.

The President seemed intensely in earnest in his determination to keep the country out of war. In a speech delivered at the New York Press Club he said that he would sacrifice his political career in order to preserve peace. It was apparent that his remarks applied not only to the European situation but also to Mexico.

During the summer the people were brought in closer touch with the submarines through their activities along our shores. The undersea German freighter, *Deutschland*, made two trips from Germany to the United States, appearing first in the Baltimore harbor and the second time at New London, Conn. In October a German submarine was at Newport, R. I., and a few days afterwards sank six British ships not far from Nantucket Island. The people of the country became more intensely antagonistic to Germany than ever before by reason of these submarine exploits.

So great was the interest of the people in the European war that the Mexican situation became of secondary consideration, but it was still a matter that received attention. President Wilson caused a flutter among those persons who had talked to him about the Mexican situation by saying:

"I found out what was going on in Mexico in a very singular way—by hearing a sufficiently large number of liars talk about it."

People throughout the country were shocked and those of the Catholic faith deeply incensed over the reports from Mexico of outrages perpetrated by Carranza troops upon the churches, clergy, and religious orders, including the nuns in their convents. Carranza made no effort to curb his soldiers, while his attitude towards the Catholic Church was extremely hostile. As President Wilson had recognized Carranza as the head of a **de facto** government in Mexico, the Catholics in the United States held him responsible to some extent, and voiced their opinions at times in severe criticisms.

Two outrages by the Mexicans aroused a feeling which almost caused the Senate to pass a resolution of intervention. A dozen or more Americans were massacred at Santa Ysabel, Mexico. Then Villa made a raid across the border at Columbus, New Mexico. The massacre and raid caused our Government to act. It was decided to pursue Villa and his nondescript army, but first the consent of Carranza had to be obtained in order to permit our troops to enter Mexican territory. This negotiation took up much time. Carranza would not permit the use of the Mexican railroad to transport troops and supplies. That made the pursuit of Villa more difficult. A detachment under General Pershing followed the trail of Villa, but so much time had been lost that the wily bandit was able to retire into the rough mountain country where he was safe.

Pershing had not been long in Mexico before Carranza insisted that the American troops be withdrawn. Whether or not it was at the instigation of Carranza it is impossible to say, but American soldiers belonging to the Pershing expedition were ambushed at Carrizal by Carranza troops and many were killed and twenty-three taken prisoners. It then seemed as if war with Mexico was inevitable, especially as there was a delay in securing the release of the captured troops.

We were making ready for war. Under the army bill it was found that the militia could be drafted into the service of the United States, and the state troops were called out for service on the Mexican border. The process of making United States troops out of the National Guard was simply that of calling them into service and having them take the oath under the new law. There was some dissatisfaction. Many National Guard soldiers did not understand that the Hay bill, which had been regarded as giving the National Guard so much and doing so little for the regular army, also

contained provisions which could take the militiamen
away from their homes on short notice for service on
the border or elsewhere.

To many of these citizen-soldiers the duty was a
great hardship. It took them from their regular employment and gave them the small pay of regular soldiers. Many families were left without means of
support. Congress remedied this to some extent by
appropriating money for the relief of families left
destitute. But there was still another element of dissatisfaction. Many men of the National Guard were
engaged in prosperous occupations and could serve
only at a great loss. While they expressed themselves
willing to serve in any emergency and danger to the
country, they did not like the idea of going down to the
Rio Grande simply for patrol duty, for it was well
understood that their only duty would be to patrol the
border and prevent bandits from entering the United
States. It was true that they could have declined the
oath and were afforded the opportunity of so doing, but
men do not like to back out under such circumstances.
They did not want to be put in the attitude of earning
a white feather, even if the service was to be more of
a frolic than a fight.

"I know my business will be ruined," explained one
guardsman. "I know that my wife and children are
going to suffer; but we have talked it all over and
agreed that I have got to go because I cannot spend
the remainder of my life explaining why I did not
go."

And so 100,000 National Guardsmen were sent to the Mexican border.

One night the extra editions of the newspapers announced that the soldiers held as prisoners after the Carrizal ambush had been released. I happened to be a guest that evening at a social function which was attended by a large number of Democrats, everyone of whom, so far as I can remember, was an officeholder. There were Cabinet members, Senators, Representatives, and officeholders of lesser degree in the assemblage. Not one among them expressed any joy over the release of those troopers. On the contrary, I heard numerous regrets that the Mexicans had acceded to the demands of the Administration. The current opinion was that the failure of Mexico to comply with the demand of the United States for the release of the soldiers would have meant an invasion of Mexico by the large army assembled on the border.

"A war in Mexico," said one man very frankly, "would re-elect the Administration and insure Democratic control in the Senate and House. Frankly, I am sorry that Carranza has acceded to the demands of our Government. Sooner or later we must intervene with armed forces, and I would prefer that it should be done during this Presidential campaign."

Following the release of the Federal troopers at Carrizal—and they were a ragged, half-starved, and sorry looking lot of men when they reached the American lines—Carranza resumed his demands that the United States troops should withdraw from Mexico.

As if to add a touch of comedy to the Mexican situation, Villa also made demands for the withdrawal of the troops, not seconding Carranza exactly, but basing his demands upon the same grounds, that the presence of the United States troops was an invasion of the sovereignty of Mexico.

Second only to the wars—European and Mexican— was the railroad situation which developed during the summer and became acute in a business and political way in the early autumn before the adjournment of Congress. It was a contest between capital and labor, though this time labor was represented by the highest class of workingmen in the country.

The difference between the railroads and their train employees reached an impasse when the brotherhoods demanded an eight-hour day, with the ten hours' pay they were receiving. The railroads insisted that the matter should be arbitrated. A deadlock ensued and President Wilson intervened. He first attempted to secure mediation through the labor conciliation board created by the Government. Then he asked both sides to submit the whole matter to him. This was done. The employees refused to recede and the railroads would not grant the eight-hour day; they insisted on arbitration and the employees rejected arbitration. The President decided—so far as he could—in favor of the contention for the eight-hour day, but the railroads refused to comply.

President Wilson went to Congress with the entire proposition, and the Adamson law was hastily framed, granting the main contention of the employees, the eight-hour day, which was in reality a wage increase.

This bill was speedily rushed through the House. In the Senate there was a little delay, while the committee listened several hours to the railroad operators and the brotherhood representatives. In the end the Adamson bill was presented to the Senate without amendment.

There was a great emergency. Orders for a strike of the conductors, brakemen, engineers, and firemen on all railroads of the country had been issued. Only a few days remained before the strike order would go into effect. Meanwhile there had been an embargo on freight, and starvation and suffering stared the whole country in the face. It was a hold-up.

The bill was passed by the Senate late on Saturday, September 2. The strike was called off. President Wilson was in New York when the bill passed, and he signed the bill while passing through Washington Sunday morning on his way west. Then, to make sure that there was no illegality because of his signing it on Sunday, he signed it again when he returned to Washington.

And so the great railroad strike was averted—for a time.

I have referred to the Adamson law as a hold-up— and it was the most stupendous legislative hold-up ever known in the history of the country. Four hundred thousand railroad employees actually forced through Congress legislation of doubtful legality and compelled the executive department to assist them. Of course, there was much at stake. There was a question of moving troops in case such movement should become necessary. There was the possibility of the starving of hundreds of thousands of people in cities, of babies without milk, of hospitals without supplies, of a congestion of traffic nation-wide in extent. Such was the threat when the President and Congress acted, and the legislation known as the Adamson eight-hour law was passed. The Government and the people of the United States were at the mercy of these men. Our civilization had advanced to a point at which every industry and food supply depended upon the keeping of all machinery in motion—particularly the transportation machinery of the country. To stop this traffic meant chaos, and 400,000 trainmen were willing to precipitate that chaos in order to secure ten hours' pay for eight hours' work.

It was a hold-up which grated upon the nerves of the public and irritated everybody who was forced into compliance with the terms of the four brotherhoods. It was a hold-up which came near to being an overshadowing issue in a Presidential campaign. It would have been an important issue but for the prosperity caused by the European war, and fear that this country might be drawn into that war. The Adamson law and the method of its enactment became secondary in importance to money and peace.

A considerable flurry was caused by the nomination of Louis D. Brandeis as Associate Justice of the Supreme

Court. The nomination was sent in early in the year and there was a long fight over it; there was an investigation of the career of Brandeis as an attorney, and his whole life as a lawyer was brought to light.

As a matter of fact, a majority of the Senate was against the confirmation of Brandeis. All of the Republicans, save a few Progressives, were bitterly opposed to his elevation to the Supreme Bench. There were at least a dozen Democrats who felt the same way, and for a time it looked as if this nomination might be defeated. But in the end the President won.

Confirmation of Brandeis was made a party question, and this was of great advantage to the nominee. Then the race question was raised and allegations were made that Brandeis was being opposed because he was a Jew. This was also a powerful factor in his support.

Finally, he was confirmed and the politics of the situation was all in favor of President Wilson and the Democratic party. Republican opponents of Brandeis were placed in the attitude of having opposed him because of his Progressive tendencies or because he was a Jew, both of which implications were detrimental to the party.

Probably one of the most remarkable instances of the manner in which President Wilson had his way with Congress was in regard to the child labor bill. This measure had passed the House and was before the Senate. It had a few friends on the Democratic side; there were a good many who were indifferent, and a large number who were bitterly opposed to the legislation. The strongest opposition came from southern Senators, who had served notice that if the bill was presented it would be debated at great length. This, of course, meant a filibuster. The Senate leaders decided to abandon the measure, but that determination lasted only for a few days. It was not long before Senator Kern, the majority leader, after a visit to the White House, went to the Senate and said that the child labor bill must be passed before Congress adjourned.

Then began a fierce struggle. There was very bitter feeling—under cover for the most part—among the Democratic senators who were against the legislation, but there was no way to defeat the measure. Criticisms, as usual, were more severe in the cloak room than in the Senate chamber. It was attacked as unconstitutional and unnecessary. The bill prohibited the shipment by interstate commerce of goods any part of which was made by children under fourteen years old. At one time opponents proposed to attach the immigration bill, with its literacy test, as a rider to the child labor bill. Then came an intimation from the White House that there would be a veto and that Congress would be expected to remain in session until the child labor bill was passed. And the President had his way. The bill became a law, and it was a distinct political asset for the President in the northern states during the Presidential campaign, although it was afterwards declared to be unconstitutional by the Supreme Court.

One of the interesting incidents of the session happened early in the year. Senator Harding of Ohio was then a new member of the Senate, but he had been lieutenant governor of Ohio, and was used to presiding and familiar with parliamentary law. One day Senator Newlands of Nevada, one of the prominent Democrats of the Senate, took the floor to deliver a set speech. Vice President Marshall sent for Senator Harding, and when the Ohio Senator went to the desk, he was thus admonished:

"It is the custom of the Senate," said Marshall, "to haze new senators. This form of punishment usually consists in calling one of them to preside over the Senate when Newlands makes a speech. It is your duty to remain in the chair until he concludes."

The Vice President departed and Newlands went on with his speech. It was out of the ordinary. He reviewed the shortcomings of the Democratic party, pointed out its omissions and failures, predicted defeat and disaster if it did not mend its ways.

Some time after Newlands had concluded the Vice President returned.

"You have served your sentence," he remarked to Harding. "Hereafter you will be considered a full-fledged Senator."

"You may think that you have hazed me," replied Harding, "but I have been enjoying myself, having a better time than I've had in years. I have listened to the worst lambasting of the Democratic party that it was ever my good fortune to hear."

"Do you know," remarked the Vice President, pensively, "I have come to the conclusion that Newlands is the original fat boy who spilled the beans."

CHAPTER XXIII

NATIONAL CONVENTIONS OF 1916

The Inevitable Happens at Chicago—Hughes Named by the Republicans—A Convention Without Enthusiasm—Democrats at St. Louis Carry Out the Program and Nominate the Old Ticket—A Platform Flurry, But the President Has His Way—Democracy Transferred from Bryan to Wilson.

IT was not a happy political family which gathered at Chicago in 1916. With the nomination of Charles E. Hughes inevitable, the Republicans assembled in a disgruntled mood to go through the form of naming a candidate they did not want, but whom they expected to elect. In fact, the prospects in June for Republican success were very bright. It appeared to be very simple. Nominate a man whom Roosevelt would support; bring back the Progressives; count on a large German vote; and they had enough to spare. And, as a matter of good measure, there were the Catholics, who were intensely dissatisfied on account of the recognition of Carranza in Mexico. So there was ample assurance of success.

The Progressives had called their convention at the same time and in the same city as the Republicans, the avowed object being to agree upon one candidate who would run against Wilson and unite the Republican

party. The real object of the Progressives was to force
the Republicans to nominate Roosevelt. The thousand Progressive delegates who assembled there had no
thought of compromising upon any man except Roosevelt. They were opposed to Hughes, just as they were
opposed to any of the other men who were candidates
before the Republican convention. They could see no
man other than Roosevelt.

What made the nomination of Hughes inevitable
was the fact that he was the one man of prominence in
the country to whom Roosevelt could make no valid
objection. Hughes had neither participated nor taken
sides in the proceedings which prevented Roosevelt's
nomination in 1912. There were other men, Senator
William E. Borah of Idaho was one, and Senator
Albert B. Cummins of Iowa another, who might have
been satisfactory to Roosevelt, but were not satisfactory to the men who were in control of the convention; besides they were not the second choice of a
sufficient number of the delegates.

Although there was uncertainty about the candidacy
of Justice Hughes, many delegates were elected for him.
Oregon in a primary instructed its delegates for him.
In New York, with former Senator Root the candidate
of the Old Guard and Hughes supported by Governor
Whitman, the delegation split even between these favorite sons. Other states elected Hughes delegates, and
before the convention met Hughes had more delegates
than any other candidate.

Notwithstanding that Roosevelt was opposed to

them, and had so expressed himself, efforts in behalf of various favorite sons continued. John W. Weeks was a New England candidate. Former Vice President Fairbanks was Indiana's candidate and gathered scattering delegates in other states. Former Senator Burton was Ohio's favorite son and he, too, had outside support. Senator Cummins had Iowa and Minnesota. Senator La Follette had a majority of the Wisconsin delegation and the support of North Dakota. Henry Ford had Michigan, with the exception of two delegates. Senator Sherman had the Illinois delegation. Colonel Roosevelt had delegates from several states scattered over a wide area.

In the selection of delegates the candidacy of favorite sons afforded an opportunity for the old line Republicans to choose men of their own kind, who were sure to make the nomination of Roosevelt an absolute impossibility. As the Colonel was not in the Republican party, but an avowed Progressive, he was not before the primaries in the different states. Particular care was taken in the selection of delegates to see that none but anti-Roosevelt men were elected. Delegates might be for Root, Weeks, Fairbanks, Burton, Cummins, Sherman, La Follette, or Ford, but when it came to a second choice it was found that they were not for Roosevelt.

Just before the convention a tremendous sentiment for Roosevelt was aroused. Big business in New York endorsed him, and a certain American spirit developed favorable to his nomination. The Colonel made a trip through the West and his every appearance was marked by wild demonstrations. Had the Roosevelt movement started before the delegates were elected, it might have turned the tide and brought about his nomination, but it came too late.

With the arrival of the delegates at Chicago and during the preliminary skirmishes, one fact soon became apparent. Roosevelt could not be nominated. A careful canvass was made, and the men in charge of the anti-Roosevelt forces counted 700 of the thousand delegates who never would vote for his nomination. They allowed 100 for accidents and mistakes, but that left 600 of the "hand picked" kind that could not be shaken. George W. Perkins, the Progressive leader and Roosevelt manager, was shown these figures and given such straight information as to convince him that Roosevelt could not be nominated by the Republican convention.

Then began a series of negotiations to prevent a third party ticket. This was a very difficult task. The Progressives went to Chicago for the sole purpose of nominating Roosevelt and compelling the Republicans to accept him. If the Republicans would not do so then let them take the consequences, was their attitude.

Meanwhile the Republican managers worked night and day in an effort to bring about a combination which would name a candidate to their satisfaction. They did not want Hughes. They were all against Hughes with the exception of W. Murray Crane of Massachusetts and Senator Reed Smoot of Utah. These two men were working earnestly for Hughes, although willing to confer with others who were trying to unite on some other man.

The leaders did not want Hughes because they believed he would be unsatisfactory from a party and personal standpoint after he was elected. This view grew as New Yorkers told incidents of his career when Governor of that state. One of the stories that circulated in the rooms of the leaders related to a conversation between Hughes when Governor-elect and Job Hedges, a spellbinder and very popular member of the New York machine. In the campaign Hedges had made fifty speeches for Hughes. They met in a train, and Hedges opened the conversation by saying:

"Governor, if any one comes to you in my behalf and urges my appointment for any office, I want you to know it is without my authority or by my request. I am not a candidate for any position whatever. However, if you should consider that I may be of service to you, I want to say there is one position that would be agreeable, because I have given attention to the work and duties of the office, and I think I could accomplish a great deal for your administration."

Hedges named the position and then noticed a great change in the Governor-elect. He stiffened, and Hedges could feel the temperature drop several degrees.

"Mr. Hedges," said Mr. Hughes, with cold formality, "the fact that you have been so actively campaigning in my behalf precludes the possibility of my appointing you to any office. I cannot have it said that I have distributed offices as a reward for support."

Other stories of like character were retailed during the days before the convention, and it was often said that the "best way to secure recognition and offices from Hughes in case he was elected was to be one of those who had done nothing for him."

At all events, the New Yorkers belonging to the Old Guard, the men who had for so many years been the managers of the Republican party in New York, were firmly opposed to Hughes and took no pains to conceal their opposition; on the contrary, they took frequent occasion to warn those who were supporting him that they could not expect recognition when Hughes was elected.

As showing the effect of foreign interests on the convention, the German-American Alliance was represented at Chicago and promised the Republicans the united support of the German voters if any man other than Roosevelt were named. The delegates from the West brought reports of a strong peace feeling in that region, which made the leaders believe that Roosevelt could not carry that section of the country, where he had been so popular. In the discussion of the availability of Roosevelt, and he was discussed, especially in conferences held with Perkins and other Progressives, the opposition which Roosevelt would arouse among the Germans and the peace people was brought forward as showing that Roosevelt could not be elected if nominated. This view was shared by a number of ardent Roosevelt men among the Republicans.

The Chicago convention was scheduled to be one of the most exciting ever held. With this expectation thousands of people went to that city. But it turned out to be a very tame and uninteresting convention. The real interest centered in the movements and negotiations of the leaders before the convention met and while it was in session up to the very last day. The "underground" work and the efforts of the leaders to bring about the nomination of a man more to their liking than Hughes were the only features that relieved the convention from extreme dullness. And these negotiations would have been more exciting if they had promised results. But every plan was blocked. The secret conclaves where plans were discussed became a farce, because no set of men could agree on anything, nor could any man promise to deliver delegates from his state or section.

There was nothing in the early sessions of the convention to give color or interest to the proceedings, save, perhaps, the speech of the temporary chairman, Senator Harding of Ohio. He had been frequently mentioned as a "dark horse," in the days preceding the convention. Senator Harding never gave the slightest indication that he considered the discussion of his name anything more than newspaper compliments. As a presiding officer he was a success, keeping good order and good feeling among the crowds, and occasionally injecting a little humor into the proceedings.

The Progressives upset the routine for a time, when they sent a communication to the Republican convention asking for a joint committee of consultation. This was agreed to, and for two nights the joint committee discussed and contended, but nothing came of it. The Progressives would have no one but Roosevelt, while the Republicans suggested the names of all the candidates, including Hughes, only to have them rejected. In connection with the report of the committee to the Republican convention, Roosevelt's letter, in which he suggested Senator Lodge, was read, but this fell as flat as anything in the convention.

The expected happened when the nominations were made. Each candidate was accorded a "demonstration," largely manufactured and kept going far beyond the natural enthusiasm which the name provoked.

The name of Theodore Roosevelt produced more genuine enthusiasm than any other, but it was in the galleries and among the spectators. During the demonstration the delegates remained silent, although according the Roosevelt supporters full sway. In fact nothing was said or done during the convention which would in any way offend the Colonel or his supporters. As the handful of delegates marched about the hall shouting "We want Teddy!" echoed by cheering galleries, it was observed that most of the delegates stood or sat patiently without manifesting emotion of any sort. One coatless enthusiast trudged up one aisle and down the other shouting:

"We want Teddy! We want Teddy! Everybody's for Teddy!"

Then, as he looked at the undemonstrative delegates, he again shouted:

"Everybody's for Teddy!   Everybody's for Teddy— but the delegates!"

That fellow had a sense of humor.

After a long day of oratory and without adjournment or recess, the convention went to the first ballot with the expected result. Each favorite son received the vote of his state and scattering support from other states. The second ballot followed, and a mild sensation was created when a poll of Massachusetts was demanded and disclosed that there was a bad break from Weeks, the New England candidate, Crane and McCall voting for Hughes and Lodge for Roosevelt. All the other delegations remained with their candidates. The shifts showed a gain for Hughes.

The Hughes leaders on the floor of the convention, Governor Whitman of New York and former Senator Fulton of Oregon, decided to push their advantage and nominate their candidate before adjournment. But it was late at night, the convention had been in continuous session nearly twelve hours without rest or meals, and on a roll call a very large majority voted to adjourn.

On account of this vote the opponents of Hughes took a new lease of life. They had defeated the Hughes men on a direct vote, and assumed that it might not be too late to prevent his nomination. Immediately negotiations were resumed and managers of the other candidates were called into conference. The anti-Hughes men said that if they could only prevent a nomination for a few ballots, the Hughes strength would disintegrate and could be concentrated upon a man who would be more satisfactory to them.

But the same difficulties confronted them that had blocked their efforts theretofore. They could not agree on any man, nor could they have promised the delivery of the delegates even had they come to an agreement. In the early morning hours of Saturday they were as hopeless and helpless as they had been from the first.

The convention assembled for its last session, but before the delegates had entered the hall it was known that Senator Sherman had released the Illinois delegation, and that nearly all of them had determined to vote for Hughes. The Iowa men held a caucus on the floor and decided to withdraw Cummins.

The stampede—which once had been expected to go for Roosevelt—had begun, and as the roll call proceeded it was seen that Hughes would be nominated. Indiana withdrew Fairbanks and voted for Hughes. Ohio withdrew Burton, and Senator Wadsworth withdrew Root. Senator Weeks withdrew himself in a graceful speech which made him many friends, while Senator Lodge, who had received a few votes on the strength of Roosevelt's letter, withdrew his name.

It was all over, except finishing the roll call and making the nomination unanimous. Hughes was the Republican standard bearer of the campaign of 1916.

It did not take long to nominate Fairbanks for Vice President and adjourn the convention before he could decline, and what had promised to be an exciting convention came to a tame end.

The Progressive convention, which had been held in leash for four days by Perkins, broke away early on Saturday morning and nominated Roosevelt before Hughes had been nominated by the Republicans. Parker of Louisiana was named for Vice President. This gathering was much disgruntled. The majority wanted to nominate Roosevelt at the beginning and let the Republicans do the worrying. But they had been held back, and the convention killed time with speeches, marching, singing, and noise. At the close they had nothing but what they had in the beginning, a ticket named, but with the possibility that their candidate would not run. They believed they could have forced an acceptance from Roosevelt if they had nominated him at first, and thus held the whip hand over the Republicans.

Perkins and other leaders had argued with them to the effect that their convention had been called at the same time and place with that of the Republican convention for the express purpose of getting together, and it was due to the Republicans to afford every opportunity for a compromise and to take steps for harmony. Because action was postponed the Progressives lost and the Republicans gained. The Progressive delegates were far from satisfied. In fact, most of them left in a very ugly frame of mind, particularly as a telegram from Roosevelt foreshadowed his purpose of declining the nomination.

It was not a vociferous nor an enthusiastic crowd of Republicans that gathered in the hotels after the convention. The streets were not crowded and about the only activity to be observed was the rush to the railroad stations.

In one hotel a group of Hughes men were exchanging felicitations over their success. Arthur I. Vorys of Ohio joined them.

"When you fellows want something during Hughes's administration," said Vorys, "come to me. I'll be in a position to do something for you. You've been for him and you'll get nothing. I've been against him and for that reason I'll stand in with him."

The high light of the convention, and of the campaign, for that matter, came after the convention adjourned. It was the telegram of acceptance which Hughes sent to Chairman Harding. That patriotic and stirring utterance put more life into the Republicans than anything that happened before or afterwards. It paved the way for Roosevelt's support and sounded a keynote which cheered the Republicans as they went back to their homes.

There was nothing of any moment in the Democratic convention at St. Louis. That convention met for the purpose of renominating Woodrow Wilson for President and Thomas R. Marshall for Vice President. All efforts to sidetrack Marshall had failed. He was like the "Old Man of the Sea" and remained astride the Democratic Sinbad. When efforts were made to unload him, Kern and Taggart of Indiana, with all their friends, showed their teeth.   Various men were mentioned, but very few men of prominence desired to become aspirants for the Vice Presidency.   So it was known long before the convention assembled that it was to be the old ticket and a platform which President Wilson desired.

The essential features of the platform were taken to St. Louis by a member of the President's cabinet. There were two matters of importance, one the declaration for woman suffrage and the other the plank in regard to Americanism, the latter in its terms very offensive to the Germans.   Senator Stone of Missouri was chairman of the committee on resolutions, and while the sub-committee was putting the platform into shape he spent a number of unhappy hours, particularly after the President's instructions had been received.   Senator Stone, residing in a state where there was a large German vote, did not want the anti-Teutonic declaration.   Nor did he like the suffrage plank.

Senator Stone's colleague, James A. Reed, was a candidate for re-election in 1916.   He was much disturbed over the anti-hyphenate declaration which the President insisted should go into the platform.   It might mean the loss of Missouri.   Reed sought Stone at the hotel where the sub-committee was at work, and both Senators argued for some time and tried to secure a more moderate declaration, but without avail.   The President was firm, and of course had his way.

After many hours of weary waiting the platform was brought into the convention.

"We've got everything except the kitchen stove and

a few farming utensils in it," remarked Jim Nugent,
the Democratic boss of New Jersey, who was a member
of the committee, and very much opposed to the platform as agreed upon.

In the convention the fight was over the suffrage
declaration. It went hard with the old line Democrats
to swallow that plank. They did not believe in it, but,
as Senator Walsh of Montana explained to the convention, it was necessary to secure the support of a number
of Western states. Who at that time believed that
Walsh was such a prophet and that the woman suffrage
states would determine the election? But the control
of the Administration was supreme. The platform
which Wilson wanted was adopted.

Like all conventions of the Democratic party, it was
oratorical. From the beginning to the end most of the
time was occupied in speechmaking. Governor Glynn
of New York had been selected for temporary chairman
and made the opening speech. It had been prepared
in advance and approved by President Wilson. It was
saturated with peace sentiment. All past difficulties
with foreign nations which had been settled without
war were reviewed and commended. It was evident
that the Democrats believed, when this keynote speech
was prepared, that Roosevelt, a war advocate, would be
nominated by the Republicans. Senator Ollie James
of Kentucky, the permanent chairman, also talked
peace and asserted that "President Wilson had brought
the most militant and warlike nation of the world to
its knees without resort to war."

Of course, a Democratic national convention would not be complete without a speech from Bryan. Mr. Bryan had failed to secure a seat in the convention as a delegate from Nebraska, but he was conspicuous in the press section. He also timed his entry at each session so as to attract attention and cause the leather-lunged Bryanites in the galleries to set up their old war cry, which had been heard for a score of years.

"Bryan! Bryan! Bryan!"

From every part of the convention hall came the familiar chant; repeated whenever he entered the hall, when he left, and at intervals when there was a lull in the proceedings.

"Bryan! Bryan! Bryan!"

Democracy—or a part of it—was calling for its own.

Finally, one night, when the convention was waiting for the committee on resolutions, the demand for Bryan became so vociferous that nothing could be done until he was heard. He knew, and everybody familiar with the Democratic party knew, that the convention would never finish its business without a speech from Bryan.

Amidst the uproar a delegate moved that Bryan be heard, such a motion being necessary because Bryan was not a delegate. It was carried, and the man who had been defeated in three campaigns; the man who had defeated Champ Clark at Baltimore and nominated Woodrow Wilson; the man who had been in Wilson's cabinet and resigned at a most critical time; the man who had opposed Wilson's policies, notably that of preparedness, stood before a convention which was to renominate Wilson for President.

No wonder there was uneasiness among Wilson's friends. Securely bound and obligated as the delegates had been by instructions, there might be danger in Bryan's speech; he might oppose Wilson there as he had elsewhere; he might create a schism in the party which would spell defeat. Why, there were Wilson men who actually feared that Bryan might stampede to himself that "hog-tied" convention.

As Bryan stood facing a vast multitude of people, the sweetest sound to him, that which pleased him most, was ringing in his ears. It was the roar of Democracy booming forth the same wild acclaim which for twenty years had been his own and which had ever been on tap at his command.

He spoke. The same deep, penetrating voice; the same rounded periods; the same oratorical effects, so entrancing to his adherents and so effective in casting a spell over a multitude were employed. For an hour he spoke. He praised President Wilson to the skies, which was a relief to the Wilson men. So earnestly did he orate in favor of Wilson that only the most cynical were able to keep in mind the one-term plank which Bryan had inserted in the Baltimore platform.

He stopped; and even as he was leaving the platform men began asking, as they always have asked as soon as the spell of his magnetic voice is broken, "What was it all about?" and "Just what did he say?" In a few minutes the convention settled itself, and like Alice in

Wonderland seemed to think: "Well, we've got that
off our minds."

The one outstanding feature of the St. Louis convention of 1916, the big fact, which was plainly apparent,
was that the control of the Democratic party had
passed from William J. Bryan to Woodrow Wilson.

CHAPTER XXIV

WILSON DEFEATS HUGHES

Peace and Prosperity a Successful Slogan—Race and Religion Injected into the Campaign—Woman Suffrage States Turn the Scale—New York Loses its Place as the Pivotal State—South and West Unite in a Democratic Victory—Incidents of an Interesting and Close Election.

WOODROW WILSON was elected a second time by more contingencies, more sets of different circumstances, than any man who has become President. Almost any one of a dozen happenings might have elected Charles E. Hughes. In the final outcome Wilson's election did not hinge on as few votes as elected Cleveland in 1884, but in that year the Presidency depended wholly upon the vote in New York which was very close. In 1916 the result depended upon the votes in a number of states which were very close. And, what made it so much more interesting, these different states were affected by several divergent interests. It so happened that these interests favored Wilson, and this fact accounted for his re-election.

The factors which were favorable to Wilson for a second term were: The slogan: "he kept us out of war"; peace and prosperity; high wages for laborers and high prices for farm products; woman suffrage; the return of the Mormons to the Democratic party; popular legislation put through Congress for which many Republicans voted; the mobilization of troops on the Mexican border where they did patrol duty, but did not fight; and the Adamson wage law. When to these were added the blunders of the Republicans, it became possible for Wilson to be elected by a very narrow margin.

The Democrats had no difficulty in choosing a chairman of the national committee. President Wilson had selected Vance McCormick of Pennsylvania before the national committee was named.

The Republicans had real trouble in choosing a chairman. They had to reconcile the differences between the regulars and the progressives, which was not an easy task. Hughes had ideas of his own and his wishes had to be consulted as he was the arbiter. The choice finally fell upon William R. Willcox of New York, who was scarcely known outside of New York City.

On the face of the figures at the beginning of the campaign it was easy to see that Hughes would be elected. By adding the Republican and Progressive vote of 1912, even with a fair allowance for the Progressives that would go over to the Democrats, it was easy to elect Hughes. Based upon the Republican vote of 1914 the Republicans were sure to win. In addition, as before stated, there was the German vote, believed to be antagonistic to Wilson because the Germans assumed that the Administration was favorable to the Allies; the Catholic vote which was antagonistic to

Wilson on account of the recognition of Carranza; and also the opposition which an administration creates in four years. There was enough to give the Republicans that overconfidence which created the betting odds of two-to-one on Hughes at the beginning of the campaign, and lulled the Republican headquarters into that peaceful serenity from which there was no awakening—until after the election.

President Wilson had an advantageous position in the campaign. He was stronger than his party from the very beginning. There was a certain element in his party which disliked him, but like the elements which opposed Cleveland in his day, they strengthened Wilson with the people. Wilson had forced through Congress a program of legislation which had proved very popular, and for which many Republicans had voted.

The alluring phrase, "peace and prosperity," seemed founded on fact. The country was rich and growing richer; there was employment at high wages for every person who wanted work; manufacturers and producers were getting the highest prices ever known for their goods; and, more important than all else, the farmers were getting better prices than ever before known. But the one dominating influence was voiced in the popular slogan, "He kept us out of war."

Nine woman suffrage states voted for Wilson. Back in the days when Roosevelt was a power and the silver issue was no longer a party question, all of these states had gone Republican. With two or three exceptions they are normally Republican states. The women voted strongly for Wilson on the ground that the country was not engaged in war and Wilson was a peace President. Every battle in Europe with its awful tales of slaughter sent a shudder through the people of the United States, and caused every woman to thank God that her son was not sacrificed in a struggle of war lords for personal grandeur and pelf.

Woodrow Wilson proved himself a politician, a better politician than Roosevelt, because Roosevelt's virile and aggressive temperament blunted his usual keen discernment as to the sentiments of the country about war. Wilson knew that the people did not want war, and he gave them the best kind of an object lesson when he ordered the National Guard to the border. He made soldiers of the militiamen, and this gratified many of them; and he showed the parents, relatives, and friends of these soldiers how much better it was peaceably to police the Mexican border than to be at war. Very few people cared in the least about Mexico or what had happened there during the past four years; but they were grateful that their boys were not being killed in fights with Mexicans, nor dying in the chapparal or in the mountains of Mexico. As an object lesson it was a decided success, and Democratic orators found that when everything else failed an allusion to the safety of the brave soldiers on the border would always get a Wilson cheer.

But even with all the advantages of the "peace and prosperity" and "he kept us out of war" slogans, and

the aid of the Adamson eight-hour law, Wilson would
not have won without the Mormons. It would have
been impossible for him to carry the Republican states
of Utah, Idaho, Wyoming, and New Mexico without
Mormon support. Utah was the only state in the West
that voted for Taft in 1912. The same year Wilson
had only a plurality of 1,111 in Idaho over Taft, while
in New Mexico the Wilson plurality was only 2,704,
and in Wyoming but 750. It was the Mormon vote,
then cast for the Republicans, which held down the
Wilson pluralities in all the states where the Mormons
are numerous. There is quite a large Mormon vote
in both Colorado and Montana, but not enough to
have carried those states for Hughes in 1916. In Arizona, Nevada, and California there are enough Mormons to have changed the result, assuming that the
same influence was at work among the Mormons living
in those states as in Utah and Idaho, where they are so
numerous and hold the balance of power.

Various reasons have been given as to the change of
Mormon sentiment in four years. They are a peace
people, but there were deeper reasons, for the Church
authorities were not men to believe that President Wilson was responsible for the peace and prosperity the
country was enjoying. Possibly the Church became
antagonistic to Republican methods and managers.
At all events, no effort was made to save the Smoot
machine in Utah or similar organizations in other states.
For the first time since Mark Hanna made his deal with
the Mormons in 1900, the Mormons returned to their

former political affiliations and voted with the Democrats.

The injection of race and religion into politics is generally a dangerous operation, and it so proved in the campaign of 1916. While it is true that Hughes made gains in some sections on account of German support, the loss to Wilson was made up in other sections by a determined American vote which was cast for the President. There was no offset for the Irish Catholic vote influenced by antipathy to England. This was shown in the Hughes pluralities in both New York and New Jersey.

Although the Republicans counted on a very solid German vote, it turned out that they did not get all they expected. Before the election there came a change of sentiment in Germany. Wilson was preferred to Hughes. Through a useful servitor and mouthpiece of the German Government the preference was made known, and the public was informed by a metropolitan newspaper which was earnestly supporting Wilson. It was stated that "Wilson was bent on maintaining peace with Germany." Also there was a "fear that Hughes might be sterner." Long after the election it was learned that the Democrats, through Senator Stone of Missouri and others, had been able to reach the leaders of German influence in this country.

In summing up how the Republicans lost the election mention must be made of the evident failure of the first Hughes western trip, when he did not come up to the hopes of the people. How Hughes could go into a

state like California and ignore its Governor is another
mystery of his management. No doubt the manner
in which Hiram W. Johnson was treated at that time
cost the Republicans the state of California and the
election. Johnson had been candidate for Vice President on the ticket with Roosevelt in 1912. He was in
1916 Governor of California and the Republican candidate for United States Senator. Hughes and Johnson were in the same hotel at Los Angeles, but did not
meet. Hughes lost the state by a plurality of 3,773
and Johnson was elected Senator by 297,215. It was
such commissions and omissions that helped to defeat
the Republicans in that much mismanaged campaign.

John W. Dwight said that Hughes could have been
elected for a dollar. Dwight was a former New York
Congressman schooled under Tom Platt and Ben Odell,
and he had been also under the skillful tutelage of Alex.
Mackenzie when he was for a time a resident of North
Dakota.

"It is just this way," said Dwight, explaining his
remark. "A man of sense with a dollar would have invited Hughes and Johnson to his room when they were
both in the same hotel in California. He would have
ordered three Scotch whiskies, which would have been
seventy-five cents, and that would have left a tip of
twenty-five cents for the waiter. That's all that would
have been necessary. That little Scotch would have
brought those men together; there would have been
mutual understanding and respect, and Hughes would
have carried California and been elected."

The women's special political train was another campaign mistake, and while it is doubtful whether it did all the harm which many people allege, it certainly did no good. The women of the West did not like the idea. They felt that they did not need instructions from the women of the East as to how they should vote. It is probable, however, that the women's special lost more votes of men than of women.

One of the mysteries of the campaign is why Ohio, a normally Republican state, should have given such a very large Democratic majority when states on three sides, Pennsylvania, West Virginia, Michigan, and Indiana, voted Republican. Prosperous condition of the people, peace, and the eight-hour law have been assigned as reasons. They all helped, but why didn't the same sentiment affect adjoining states? The election in every other state can be reasonably explained, but there is no satisfactory solution of the difference between the people of Ohio and those of adjacent states. Local differences and factional fights, lack of organization, neglect by the national committee until it was too late, were all factors, but all this cannot account for 90,000 Democratic plurality when adjoining states were Republican by almost normal pluralities.

The election of 1916 was not entirely lacking in interest and picturesque incidents. The heckling of Hughes in southern states helped to carry Maine in the September election by a majority that pleased the Republicans. The attack of Hughes upon the Adamson eight-hour law was a bold thing. He called it a "force

law," and "labor's gold brick." It strengthened him
with the business element, but hurt him in Ohio where
half a dozen Republican Congressmen were defending
their votes for the law.

President Wilson did not actually take the stump for
his own re-election, but made one or two trips making
non-partisan speeches that did him no harm. At
Shadow Lawn, New Jersey, where he was spending the
summer, to large delegations of visitors he also made
political speeches which had more effect upon readers in
the West than hearers in the East.

On September 30 the President in an address at Long
Branch said:

"The certain prospect of the success of the Republican party is that we shall be drawn, in one form or another, into embroilments of the European war, and to
the south of us the forces of the United States will be
used to produce the kind of law and order which some
American investors in Mexico consider most to their
advantage."

Credence was given to this utterance because on
the same day Colonel Roosevelt made the speech at
Battle Creek, Mich., known as a "war speech," in
which he called President Wilson's European policy
"humiliating and ignoble," and his Mexican policy
"infamous." He said that, if he had been President,
he would have taken possession of every German ship in
our harbors after the *Lusitania* incident. This was the
speech which the Democrats printed and circulated in

peace-loving communities like North Dakota and other western states, and in sections where there was a large German vote.

On October 21 President Wilson delivered another speech in which he played the peace notes with strong effect, and in the course of which he said:

"I know that the way in which we have preserved peace is objected to, and that certain gentlemen [Roosevelt and those who believed with him] say they would have taken some other way that inevitably would have resulted in war, but I am not expecting this country to get into war, partly because I am not expecting those gentlemen to have a chance to make a mess of it."

The mystery which surrounds the second *Lusitania* note was injected into the campaign. We do not know exactly what occurred in regard to that note. It is known that Bryan resigned as Secretary of State rather than sign it. He stated that it had been modified after his resignation had been tendered, but to what extent no one can tell.

In the campaign some one talked too much. It was said that a memorandum of some sort was attached to the note which greatly softened it. So strong was the belief of Senator Lodge in regard to this statement that he used it during the campaign; used it with such effect that a denial came from the President.

But the incident did not end there. The President's indignation against Lodge was carried further. Long after the election there was a celebration of the one-hundredth anniversary of the establishment of St. John's Church in Washington. President Wilson accepted an invitation to speak. Senator Lodge also accepted an invitation to deliver the principal address. President Wilson withdrew his acceptance and did not attend. Senator Lodge was not for a long time included in invitations to the White House, or designated on committees to go to the White House, or to escort the President to the halls of Congress when he delivered his addresses.

Roosevelt was always interesting whenever he appeared in the campaign, but he sent a shiver down the backs of Republicans in German or peace communities whenever he was most vigorous. Roosevelt was an asset in bringing over the Progressives, but his well-known inclination for a fight, and the bitter feeling of the Germans against him, made his part in the campaign a liability in several sections.

Roosevelt had made Hughes Governor of New York, but they had never been closely associated. Roosevelt had a high appreciation of Hughes's character and ability, although there had been times when the Governor's indifference and independence exasperated the impetuous President. During the campaign of 1916 Roosevelt and Hughes were thrown together more frequently than ever before. A short time before the election several friends of Roosevelt were badgering him about his growing intimacy with Hughes.

"I am not nor ever have I been intimate with Hughes," he vigorously responded.

"Well, you know him quite well," remarked one of the group. "What kind of a man is he?"

"Well," replied the Colonel, as his teeth snapped, "Hughes is the kind of a man who would in this campaign vote for Woodrow Wilson!"

It was not until fifty hours after the polls closed that the result of the election of November 7 was known by the returns from California. On November 22, Mr. Hughes congratulated Mr. Wilson on his election as President of the United States.

CHAPTER XXV

WHITE DOVE HOVERS

Peace Prevails for Five Months—The President and the Germans Submit Proposals—"Peace without Victory"—Bryan Willing to Help —Women Picket the White House—Pershing Withdrawn from Mexico.

THAT the re-election of Woodrow Wilson meant peace was indicated during the first three months after that event. There was peace talk everywhere except in those countries where it could become effective. Germany and her allies talked peace. People in the United States talked peace. But England, France, and Italy, who had been standing firmly against the fierce onslaughts of Germany and her allies, did not discuss peace.

Congress convened in December, 1916, for the short session, and William J. Bryan, who might be called the leading pacifist of the United States, went to Washington and was received on the floor of the House by his Democratic friends with a demonstration that showed he was still ardently admired. He went with a dove of peace perched on each shoulder, so to speak. In addition to the many conferences which he held, he particularly preached peace at a dinner given in his honor. He at that time submitted a number of planks for the next Democratic national platform. One of these was to provide a referendum to the people before any declaration of war should be made unless the country was actually invaded. President Wilson did not attend this banquet, but he wrote a letter highly commending Mr. Bryan. A few days later Bryan issued a statement in which he urged the councils of the churches of America to send delegations to Europe to urge peace. About the same time the Woman's Peace Party went to the White House and urged the President to lead in a great peace movement.

Peace talk was somewhat jarred or interrupted when in the midst of it came the news that a German submarine had sunk two American ships without warning, causing the loss of a number of lives. But Germany did not allow such matters as that to interfere with her program, and requested that negotiations looking to peace be submitted to the other powers through the United States Government. While it created the impression in this country that the end of the war might be in sight, the rejection of the German suggestions by the entente nations, on the ground that the offer was not sincere, showed that those nations thoroughly understood Germany.

It was about that time that the President sprang the greatest surprise of the year in his note to all belligerents, asking them to state their terms of peace. One particular statement in the note caused a great deal of discussion among diplomats representing the allied nations. The President said that "the concrete ob-

jects for which it [the war] is being waged have never
been definitely stated. The leaders of the several
belligerents have stated those objects in general terms.
But, stated in general terms, they seem the same on
both sides." The diplomats, as well as the statesmen
of the countries which had been fighting Germany and
understood the German purposes as well as the barba-
rous war customs of the Germans, were rather shocked
at the idea that the Germans were fighting for the same
great principles as themselves.

The several explanations in regard to this peace note
would have been amusing, if the subject had not been
so serious. Interpreting it Secretary Lansing in the
first instance gave out a statement, in which he said
that one reason for the note was that "the United
States was drawing nearer the verge of war," and that
the sending of the note "will indicate the possibility of
our being forced into the war." Later in the day
Secretary Lansing was called to the White House, and a
second statement was made, in which he said, "I did
not mean to intimate that the Government was considering any change in its policy of neutrality."

It was almost two weeks later when one of those
semi-official statements appeared saying that the President was "very greatly embarrassed by the extraordi-
nary manner in which the note has been misinterpreted
both in Europe and in the United States. The note
was not conceived as a peace move, it was conceived as
a warning that the United States was in danger of being
drawn into the war." While this last statement was

not official, it was convincing evidence that the first statement of Secretary Lansing was correct.

One of the early effects of both the German move for peace and the President's peace note was a panic in the stock markets, particularly with the stocks of those concerns which dealt largely in war munitions. Out of this stock market gambling proposition came an investigation of what was called the "leak," on the allegation that the knowledge of what the President was going to do was in the hands of certain stock manipulators long before it was published, and that they were enabled to take advantage of the information, and, selling the market short, reaped a rich harvest. The investigation which followed did little save to prove that the information did get into the hands of these stock gamblers, but further than that, like hundreds of other investigations of the same class, in net results it amounted to nothing.

Although it was near the middle of December, 1916, when the President made his peace suggestions to the allies, their reply was not made until January 11, 1917, when all jointly said that it was no time to talk of peace.

On January 22, 1917, President Wilson again surprised the country and the world by a speech delivered in the Senate, which had been cabled to all European capitals. This was the somewhat famous "peace without victory" speech, so-called because the President used that expression in urging that something be done to end the war. "Victory would mean peace forced upon the loser," he said, "a victor's terms imposed upon the vanquished."

At that time, it would appear, that the relations between the United States and Germany, notwithstanding the *Lusitania* disaster and the loss of many hundreds of American lives as well as the loss of property by submarine sinkings, were without serious danger of interruption. On January 7, 1917, Ambassador Gerard in a speech at Berlin had said: "Never since the beginning of the war have the relations between Germany and the United States been so cordial as now."

And while the Government of the United States was making its greatest efforts to bring about peace in Europe, the belligerents on both sides were interfering with American rights. The manner in which Great Britain outraged our commercial rights was notorious. She stopped our ships and confiscated their cargoes; she blacklisted our business men and arrogantly supervised our trade with the world, particularly in South America. Altogether it seemed that our grievances against Great Britain were almost as great as those against Germany, but while the English captured and confiscated American property the Germans destroyed not only American property, but also American lives.

One of those incomprehensible manifestations, which cause one to marvel at the curious twists of human intelligence, developed when Congress convened for the short session. It was a systematic heckling of the President of the United States by one branch of the suffragists. The heckling began the day the President addressed Congress. While he was speaking the suffragettes suspended from the rail of the gallery a large banner inscribed, "What are you going to do for suffrage, Mr. President?" This was followed up by "picketing the White House." The "picketing" was done by squads of women, who stood day in and day out in front of the White House with banners and placards addressed to the President; often they were disrespectful, many of them offensive. Occasionally a feeble attempt was made to remove these women, but when arrested or imprisoned they were released, and this disgraceful proceeding was allowed to continue. The President in 1916 had a plank inserted in the Democratic national platform declaring for woman suffrage to be granted by the states. The picketing women were not satisfied and insisted that the President should urge a constitutional amendment by Congress. They even went so far as to intimate that they could compel him to yield to their demands and also that no power dared to stop the picketing. The President passed among them daily as he drove in and out of the White House grounds, but gave no signal of displeasure, and so this unseemly demonstration was permitted to go on in front of the White House for nearly two years.

Again there was no New Year's reception at the White House, and Washington came to the conclusion that this social event, which was once an institution, was to be permanently abandoned, at least during the Wilson régime.

General Pershing was withdrawn from Mexico. He

had been sent there to capture Villa, but had not succeeded. Twice had our forces gone upon Mexican soil
with hostile intent and without any formal declaration
of war. Twice had they been withdrawn before accomplishing the results for which they had been sent. But
the people for the most part were satisfied, for they did
not want war with Mexico, nor with any other country.

When the Sixty-fourth Congress closed its session
President Wilson was inaugurated for his second term.
It had been customary for the retiring President to ride
to the Capitol with the incoming President, but there
was no retiring President at this time, and so Mrs. Wilson occupied this distinguished post of honor in the
trip from the White House to the Capitol and the
return. As Wilson had made this journey four years
previously, Mrs. Wilson attracted far more attention
than the President.

CHAPTER XXVI

UNITED STATES IN THE WAR

President Wilson Forces an Unwilling Congress to Declare a State of War—Waste and Extravagance Run Riot—Congress Most Subservient to the Executive—Both Parties Support the President—The Disloyal Element—Uncertain Outcome—Politics and War—Republican Success in the Congressional Election of 1918.

BY the end of January, 1917, it was known that Germany intended to continue her ruthless undersea warfare. On the first of February Germany's note to that effect was made public. Two days later the United States severed diplomatic relations with Germany. In announcing this fact to Congress and telling of Germany's determination to renew the submarine warfare, the President said: "I refuse to believe that it is the intention of the German authorities to do in fact what they have warned us they will feel at liberty to do." The President had more confidence in the Germans than other people had. Nearly everybody knew that war was inevitable and some preparations were made for it. In fact, it had gone so far that William J. Bryan urged a vote of the whole people on the war proposition before war should be declared.

On the 26th of February events had reached such a stage that the President went before Congress advising armed neutrality and asked permission to arm the merchant ships. At that time he said, "It is devoutly hoped that it will not be necessary to put an armed force anywhere into action." About that time the State Department made public the Zimmerman note in which it was shown that the Germans months before had been making an effort to unite Japan and Mexico in war upon the United States, and had offered as a prize to Mexico the states of Texas, Arizona, and New Mexico.

The House of Representatives promptly complied with President Wilson's request and passed the armed neutrality bill and also a bill granting the President permission to arm merchant ships, but the bill failed in the Senate mainly on account of the filibuster conducted by a dozen ardent peace men, who were afterwards severely scored by President Wilson as the "willful few" who prevented the legislation. There was still hope that war would be avoided. President Wilson called the Sixty-fifth Congress to meet in the middle of April to pass appropriation bills which had failed, but not with any view of having war measures adopted.

On March 18 three unarmed American ships with American officers and crews were sunk by German submarines. This created a great wave of indignation throughout the country, and the question was frequently asked whether that was not an act of war. A week later a more warlike tone by the Government was evident. The militia of the several states were called

out for guard duty. The Navy and the Marine Corps
were enlisted to full strength. Flags appeared on almost every building, and a general wave of patriotism
swept over the country.

President Wilson changed the date for the meeting of
Congress from April 16 to April 2. Late at night of
the day Congress convened, after the House had spent
an all-day session in organizing, the President went to
Congress and delivered his war message. It was a
very dramatic close of a long day's session. The President was loudly cheered until he reached that part of
his message wherein he advocated conscription to
raise an army. That sent a cold chill down the spines
of most members of the House.

Congress did not delay long in carrying out the President's wishes for a declaration of war. Late at night
on April 4 the Senate by a vote of 86 to 6 passed the
war resolution. At 3.10 on the following morning the
House voted 373 to 50 for the war.

Thus the country was embarked upon the great
war. It is an interesting fact in connection with the
vote that Congress actually felt that it had been
dragooned into declaring war. No one can tell what
would have happened had the vote been secret, but
those who were very familiar with conditions that
existed in the House at that time are convinced that
on a secret vote a majority of the House would have
voted against war. For some time afterwards it was
asserted that the press of the country aided the Administration in forcing the country into war when there

was a very strong sentiment against war. However that may have been, the fact remains that when the President asked for war Congress voted war.

President Wilson seemingly was imbued with the idea that war could be made on individuals and governments and not upon the people of a country. On both occasions when armed forces of the United States invaded Mexico he made it plain that war was not made upon the Mexican people, but against individuals. The first time the movement was against Huerta and the second time against Villa. In the war message of April 2, he said: "We have no quarrel with the German people. We have no feeling toward them but one of sympathy and friendship." A few months later he said in another speech: "We know now as clearly as we knew before we were ourselves engaged that we are not the enemies of the German people and they are not our enemies." Such impressions did not prevail among those who came in contact with persons of German birth and blood in this country, most of whom were German to the core. They were from the beginning the earnest supporters of the German Government, and even after this country went to war many of them were pro-German in thought and deed, and enemies of the United States. Even those who were in the government employ, and they were numerous, were German sympathizers and many were suspected of being German spies. It may be supposed that Germans in Germany did not differ much from Germans in America. In fact, it developed later, and was so promulgated by the peace conference in a statement by the Allies. that:

"Throughout the war, as before the war, the German people and their representatives supported the war, voted the credits, subscribed to the war loans, obeyed every order, however savage, of their government, for at any moment, had they willed it, they could have reversed it."

We are too close to the war at this time to write dispassionately and impartially concerning it; that must be left to future historians who may be able to tell all the facts without incurring the criticisms and arousing controversies that such an attempt would evoke at the present time.

The people of the United States could not believe that we would actually send our troops to the trenches in Europe. Even while reluctantly voting conscription many men in Congress expressed the hope and belief that Americans would not be called upon to sacrifice their lives on European battlefields. The debates in Congress showed that it was the hope that we would go into the war lending our moral support to the Allies, just as Japan did throughout, but without sacrificing lives and treasure. That was the talk. And meanwhile we went forward with preparations on a gigantic scale. It was a stupendous undertaking, the engagement of the United States in the European war.

Right here it seems proper to state a fact which the war demonstrated. It was only at a tremendous cost, and with the assistance of the fleets of England and

France aided by our own, that the United States was able to land an effective army on a friendly shore. No army was landed on any hostile shore of any nation during the war, save at Gallipoli; and that was a disastrous venture. It seems quite evident, therefore, that it would be utterly impossible for a hostile nation to land and maintain an effective force on the shores of the United States.

War incurs waste and extravagance, much of it inevitable, some of it criminal. Every war develops an army of pirates and profiteers who use patriotism as a cloak to legally despoil the taxpayers. For years after the Civil War there was much discussion about the "camp followers," as the profiteers of those days were called. Even the Spanish War lasting but three months had its grafters and money sharks. But never in the history of our country was there such infamous waste and extravagance as during the twenty-two months the United States was engaged in the world war. Four long years of desperate struggle to save the Union cost less than one fourth as much as twenty-two months of war with Germany.

These multiplied extravagances were everywhere apparent. Waste ran wild. Money seemed to be of no object save to spend extravagantly. It is impossible to enumerate the various methods of the waste. But the multiplication of government employees was one of the most apparent in Washington. Commissions and boards without number were created. There were enlargements of every branch of the public service.

Washington was flooded with army officers who seemingly knew not what to do. At one time, it was asserted, there were 9,000 of these officers in the national capital. Every man with a pull could get a commission. New branches of the military service were created. Thousands of useless clerks were employed. All the old forgotten junk-piles in Washington, passing under the name of buildings, were rented at extravagant rates by the government and equipped with expensive mahogany office furniture. In addition, hundreds of new structures were erected on vacant ground, while city parks were destroyed in order to find shelter for the boards, commissions, army officers, and clerks who were brought to Washington and placed upon the government payroll. In erecting the structures in Washington and elsewhere government officials bid against each other for materials and labor. Oh, they were halcyon days for those who got a part of the graft! Hundreds of contracts on the cost-plus system induced contractors to make everything cost as much as possible and to pay extravagant wages; the greater the cost the more profit to them.

The management of the war from a military point of view is another matter and must be left to the trained historian to review. But it should be said that as in every past war the American soldier, sailor, and marine, officers and men, lived up to American traditions with distinction to themselves and honor and glory to the American nation.

The Sixty-fifth Congress became a war Congress. As

such it was more subservient to the President than any Congress in the history of the country. When war was declared loyalty to the country became the only watchword. Every war measure proposed increased the power of the President. There were protests at times, and there were criticisms of many of the bills sent to Congress by the Administration on account of the provisions they contained which over-rode all precedent, and because they were apparently in contravention of the constitution. In spite of all opposition, sometimes strong and sometimes feeble, these bills were passed, and the country was committed to policies which were never before known, and which if carried on for any length of time would shake the foundations of the Republic.

Legislation for conscription of men to serve in the war aroused stronger opposition than any which President Wilson demanded of Congress. Had it been left to his own party, conscription would have failed, as all of the prominent Democratic leaders were bitterly hostile to enforced military service and endeavored to provide for a volunteer army. Speaker Clark, Leader Kitchin, and Chairman Dent of the military committee opposed conscription with all the vigor they possessed. Speaker Clark said that the impression prevailed that "conscripts were no better than convicts." It was due largely to Julius Kahn of California, the ranking Republican member of the military committee, that the conscription law was passed by the House.

The bill providing for the army also contained a provision which was intended to allow Colonel Roosevelt to organize a division of volunteers and afford him an opportunity to go into the war as a major general. But the War Department was opposed to having any volunteer organizations, and refused to allow Roosevelt to form a military unit such as he proposed, although thousands of men throughout the country, old and young, eagerly volunteered for service under the former President.

The espionage bill was passed after a great deal of opposition in the Senate. It never could have become a law had it not been for the activities of pro-German sympathizers and German agents in the United States, who were doing much to injure this country and help the enemy. Nothing but a war necessity could have induced Congress to place such a law upon the statute books.

It was said a hundred times in the debates in Congress and probably a thousand times elsewhere that there should be no politics in the war. In fact, the pronouncement came from the President himself when he declared that politics was adjourned. But it was as impossible to keep politics out of the war as to keep politics out of any other national or international question. Naturally, the President preferred to deal with and trust members of his own party. It may be said in simple truth that a more partisan President than Woodrow Wilson never occupied the White House. His intense partisanship was shown on many occasions, and he often spoke of Republicans and the Republican party in a contemptuous manner. In the conduct of the war the entire Administration made striking distinctions between Democrats and Republicans. In foreign countries the great war caused coalition cabinets composed of the greatest men of the nations without regard to party. President Wilson did not take Republicans into confidential relations or appoint them to positions of power or influence. It is true that many of the so-called dollar-a-year men were Republicans, but they held no positions in which they could direct and influence the policies in regard to the war. These dollar-a-year men were for the most part men of high standing in the business world, imbued with a patriotic desire to help the Government in its time of need and giving their time and talents without remuneration. In order to get around a statutory inhibition against permitting persons to engage in the service of the Government without pay they were placed on the rolls at the nominal salary of one dollar a year. They were in no sense politicians or statesmen, but simply eminent business men of both parties. They had nothing to do with determining the policies of the Government or the conduct of the war, but their ability and experience were utilized to promote business methods in the organization and equipment of the army.

The President did attempt to hold consultation with committees of Congress composed of both Democrats and Republicans, but these meetings were strained, and during the entire war the Republicans complained that they were entirely without information as to the purposes or plans of the President or of the war authorities. It was only when the Administration sent to Congress measures which were wanted that the Republicans were informed as to Administration policies.

There were two elections held early in the war to fill vacancies in the House of Representatives, one from New Hampshire and the other from Indiana. In filling these vacancies an effort was made by the Democrats, not only to use the war as a test of loyalty, but to assert that Democratic members were needed in Congress to sustain the President in carrying on the war. When a vacancy occurred in the Senate from Wisconsin this idea was emphasized by the President himself, who took a prominent part in the effort to elect Joseph E. Davies, a Democrat, who was opposed by Irvine L. Lenroot, a Republican. It was attempted to show that Davies was 100 per cent loyal while Lenroot's loyalty was questioned. The election of Republicans to the House in New Hampshire and Indiana and of Lenroot to the Senate in Wisconsin indicated that the country did not relish the idea of making the war political.

As the congressional campaign of 1918 approached, it was found that politics could not be adjourned. President Wilson very early took an active part, especially in the primaries of his own party. He defeated for re-nomination to the Senate Thomas W. Hardwick of Georgia and James K. Vardaman of Mississippi. In Michigan, where Henry Ford was a candidate for the Republican nomination, the President sought to have him chosen. Defeated in the Republican primaries, Ford was nominated by the Democrats, but defeated in the election.

Throughout the campaign of 1918 loyalty to the country in the conduct of the war was an issue capitalized by both parties. It was during the canvass to fill the senatorial vacancy in Wisconsin that the President applied the phrase, "the acid test," to the acts of men in and out of Congress in regard to war measures and the conduct of the war.

As election day drew near it became apparent that the election would be close, and each party put forth its best efforts. Then it was that the President treated the country to one of his many surprises. He issued a statement to the people in regard to the coming election in which he said: "If you have approved of my leadership and wish me to continue to be your unembarrassed spokesman in affairs at home and abroad, I earnestly beg that you will express yourselves unmistakably to that effect by returning a Democratic majority to both the Senate and House of Representatives."

The country responded to this remarkable appeal by electing a Republican House with forty-five majority and a Republican Senate with two majority. It was evident that the country did not want to mix politics and war.

The two wings of the Republican party had become united under the management of Will H. Hayes. the new chairman of the national committee.

CHAPTER XXVII

END OF THE WAR

The President Surprises the Country by Going Abroad to Negotiate Peace—Opposition to League of Nations in the United States—Death of Theodore Roosevelt—The President Returns from Europe; Utters a Defiance to the Opponents of the League, and Again Departs for Foreign Shores—Republicans Return to Power in Both Branches of Congress.

FOR some time before the election of 1918 negotiations for ending the war had been under way. President Wilson had promulgated his Fourteen Points. Germany accepted them as a basis of peace and the Allies on November 4 settled on terms of a truce. On November 11, 1918, the armistice was signed and hostilities ceased, amidst a great demonstration of joy in every part of the country. It was quite evident that our people were heartily tired of the war.

As soon as the armistice was signed preparations began for peace negotiations. President Wilson amazed the country by his determination to head the United States peace delegation in person, and left Washington for Paris the day Congress convened.

There was general regret that the President should deem it necessary to take this step. It was said that to fence and parley with the skilled and selfish diplomats of Europe would lower the dignity of the high office he held. He called it "matching minds" with European statesmen. What were the ideals he professed when put in the balance with the international necessities of Europe and national demands of the countries alien to our ideas and our institutions? The Peace Conference, as it passes into history, takes its place beside similar peace conferences which have attempted to make the map of the world for all future time and to regulate governments for generations yet to come.

During the short session of the Sixty-fifth Congress very little of importance was accomplished. Much of the time at Paris was taken up in a discussion of the peace negotiations and particularly the League of Nations, which the President had determined should be first formulated and agreed upon before the real peace negotiations began. The President returned to the United States just in time to see the term of Congress close in a filibuster in the Senate and the failure of many of the supply bills.

Opposition to the League seemed to spur the President to renewed activity. When he landed at Boston on his return from Europe he spoke for the League, and two weeks later when he sailed for Paris the second time his last act was to make a speech, declaring that the League would be pressed at all hazards and so interwoven with the Peace Treaty that it could not be separated from it.

Before this speech was made and the day Congress adjourned thirty-nine Republican Senators of the Sixty-sixth Congress signed a "round robin" protest against the League of Nations as then drawn, and made it quite plain that they would not support it unless it was materially changed. It was also known that a number of Democratic Senators were opposed to the League. From that time forward there was a contest for and against the League throughout the country.

One of the surprises of the Sixty-fifth Congress was the change of the attitude of President Wilson on woman suffrage. He had endorsed the plank in the last national platform which favored equal suffrage to be voted by the states, but when the suffrage amendment was before the House he used his influence to secure a favorable vote. And later, when it was about to be voted on in the Senate, he appeared before the Senate and made an appeal for woman suffrage, saying that it was necessary as a war measure. No votes were changed by the appeal and the amendment was defeated in the Senate. At that time the war was about over and even the President's strongest supporters were unable to link woman suffrage with winning the war.

Among the important acts of Congress was that submitting a prohibition amendment to the states. It had barely two-thirds majority in the House, but passed the Senate by a large majority. It provided that the whole nation should be dry one year after the amendment was ratified. Ratification followed speedily, and by January 16, 1919, more than three-fourths of the states had ratified the prohibition amendment, making the manufacture and sale of all intoxicating liquors unlawful after January 16, 1920.

Following the Eighteenth Amendment came the Volstead law for its enforcement, which, in the discussion of prohibition, overshadowed the amendment. The Volstead law takes its name from its author, Andrew J. Volstead, of Minnesota, and Chairman of the House Committee on Judiciary.

Ten Senators died during the Sixty-fifth Congress, several of whom were men who had been in public life for many years. One of the best known was Jacob H. Gallinger of New Hampshire, the dean of the Senate, who had taken his seat March 4, 1891. He was not a showy man, but a solid, substantial Senator, and always attentive to business. He was an intense partisan, but was none the less respected, because his integrity was a guaranty of his honest purposes. From the beginning of his career he was always a friend of the Great West and among those who sincerely mourned his death were many men from the western states.

Benjamin R. Tillman of South Carolina was one of the most picturesque figures in the Senate. He entered that body March 4, 1895, strong, virile, intensely hostile to everything and everybody, especially the North and Republicans. His last days were sad, for he had become a feeble old man. His view of life had changed. He saw mankind as human beings trying for the most part to do what they thought was right and best. The old intense bitterness died with the fire that slowly burned itself out. Tillman's last days developed within him intense Americanism. He was proud of his country.

Francis G. Newlands of Nevada was a man of vision. He saw farther ahead than any man in public life, and therefore was considered a dreamer and impracticable. He often disturbed his fellow Senators, particularly his Democratic colleagues, on account of his independent methods, but he had ideas of government and the settling of the great problems of the country which will no doubt be adopted in time. The most important of these was a regional railroad system under government supervision, but in private ownership. His other great project was a systematic conservation and utilization of all the national resources of the country, including the water which runs to waste. He was many years ahead of his time, but was always recognized as a man of great ability.

William J. Stone of Missouri died under a cloud. He remained true to his party's pledges of 1916 and tried to make the slogan "He kept us out of war" a reality. He voted against war and honestly believed that it was unnecessary. For that reason he was lampooned, cartooned, and denounced from one end of the country to the other. "Slacker Bill" and "Pro-German Stone" are samples of the names he was called, while epithets of derision and contempt were without number; such was the intolerance of many for a man who voted his convictions and attempted to sustain the declared policy of his party. Stone left behind a career of public life equalled by few men. He had been a Representative in the House, Governor of his state, United States Senator, and at the time of his death was Chairman of the Senate Committee on Foreign Relations.

On the morning of January 6, 1919, the whole country was shocked and stricken with grief when it learned that Theodore Roosevelt was dead. In that hour animosities which he had aroused were forgotten and the country united in paying tribute to his good deeds and wonderful personality. His many achievements were reviewed and the record of his splendid Americanism unrolled. Consensus of opinion proclaimed Theodore Roosevelt the greatest man of his time.

On the morning of the 4th of March, 1919, the Senators began gathering to continue the session which would end at noon that day. The recess which the Senate had taken late in the night was soon to expire, and those who came before that time dropped into different committee rooms and exchanged views. Hoke Smith and myself were talking over the general situation in the Military Affairs Committee room when Senator Reed of Missouri stepped off the elevator and looked in the open door. Everybody knew that Reed had heartily approved of the Lodge resolution of protest against the League of Nations proposed during the night session, although he had not been asked to sign the document then bearing the names of thirty-seven Republican Senators. His position made him one of the most interesting figures on the Democratic side.

"Come in," said the Georgia Senator to the Missouri Senator.

"How do you feel this morning?" asked Smith.

"I feel," answered the Missouri Senator, "just as I would feel if this country had been menaced by a powerful fleet lying off New York harbor and that fleet had suddenly been destroyed by a bold dash of intrepid Americans. I think the men who signed that paper and who saved this country from a great peril are entitled to the highest commendation from the American people."

"I am inclined to agree with you," remarked Senator Smith. "I do not believe this League is going to be approved by the American people."

"Approved by the American people?" said Reed. "Why, when the American people understand this proposition they will bury it beneath an avalanche of votes. I am as you know a Democrat, but if I were a Republican and the issue in the next campaign was the League of Nations, this is the sort of speech I would make." Looking around he saw a staff which was used for raising and lowering the windows and grasping it in his hand, he said, "Imagine this is the American flag and that I am a Republican on the stump in the next campaign. I would go before audiences with this flag in my hand and say:

"'Americans, this is the banner raised and consecrated to liberty by George Washington. It waved over our gallant soldiers while they achieved the victories on lakes and oceans during the war of 1812. It

hung over the cotton battlements at New Orleans when
Andrew Jackson defeated the flower of the British
Army. It was carried to the heights of Chapultepec
by the veterans of General Scott and planted in glory
above the halls of the Montezumas. Abraham Lincoln
preserved it the sacred emblem of a united country. It
has been washed in the tears of all the American mothers
who sent their sons to fight for the preservation of
home and fireside. It is baptized in the blood of the
men who went to death to establish this nation in
liberty and to keep it free alike from the control of
foreign despots and foreign influence.

"'And Woodrow Wilson at the table of Versailles
sought to place the destiny of the American Republic
within the control of the representatives of kings,
emperors, and foreign potentates. He proposed to
substitute internationalism for the nationalism established by our fathers and for a century and a half
sustained by the valor and patriotism of America's
sons and daughters. He undertook to surrender with
the pen what Washington gained by the sword.'

"With that kind of a speech, I could carry every
state north of Mason and Dixon's line and break the
solid South. Indeed, every state of the Union can be
carried if the message might but reach them. What I
could do, thousands of other men can do. If the League
of Nations is made an issue, the Republicans will not
fail to present it in a much stronger light than I have
been able to outline."

It was a very impressive aftermath to the exciting

scenes of the night before. A great many men believed as did Reed, and they were not all Republicans.

There was a bitter feeling between the President and those who were opposed to the League of Nations. It was charged by the Democrats that the Republicans had by a filibuster attempted to force the President to call an extra session of the Sixty-sixth Congress which was Republican in politics. The President did not want an extra session. He did not want to have the League of Nations under constant senatorial fire while he was in Paris completing the peace negotiations. The filibuster was not a party move, but was conducted by three Republican Senators. But even if there had been no filibuster there was so much contention over various provisions in the Army and Navy bills that they and others could not have been passed in the few days that the filibuster lasted. It was absolutely necessary that an extra session be called in time to pass the bills before the end of the fiscal year, June 30, 1919, but the President delayed this call until the middle of May. He was still in Paris when Congress assembled, and for the first time he sent his message by a White House secretary, it having been cabled to this country.

When the extra session assembled the Republicans took control of the House for the first time in eight years. Frederick H. Gillett of Massachusetts was elected Speaker and Frank W. Mondell of Wyoming was chosen majority leader. Champ Clark, who retired from the Speakership, was selected as minority leader by the Democrats.

One of the interesting incidents connected with the meeting of the House was that the rules of the previous Congress were adopted without opposition. For many years, whenever there was a change of parties in the House, the contention over the rules usually had meant a long wrangle and often bitter partisan controversy. At last it seemed that a code of procedure had been evolved which was so nearly perfect that not a dissenting voice was raised against it. The rules now combine the reforms of Tom Reed adopted in 1890 and the reforms of Champ Clark adopted in 1912–1913.

It had been six years since the Republicans had control of the Senate, and when Congress convened in the extra session they took charge with considerable satisfaction. There had been a certain amount of preliminary skirmishing. The old progressive element was still alive and somewhat assertive. Its attack was directed against Senator Penrose of Pennsylvania, who was in line for Chairman of the Finance Committee, and Senator Warren of Wyoming, who was in line for Chairman of Appropriations. Both had held these positions when the Republicans lost control after the election of 1912. But the Republicans kept their fight within their own party. Senator Cummins of Iowa was elected President pro tempore. Senator Lodge of Massachusetts, who had been minority leader, became the majority leader, and after a time the old seniority rule prevailed and both Penrose and Warren were given the chairmanships to which their length of service on the committees entitled them.

The Democrats in the Senate lost their leader and the country a very valuable legislator in the death of Senator Thomas S. Martin of Virginia. He was one of the most indefatigable workers and attentive men in the Senate. Although he had been minority leader during a long period when the Democrats were out of power, the reform or progressive element, flushed with their victories in 1912, concluded that Martin was too much of a reactionary to be leader of the Senate when the Democrats took control and he was deposed. Senator Kern of Indiana was made leader.

The Senate lost another veteran Democrat when Senator John H. Bankhead of Alabama died. Martin and Bankhead were the last Confederate soldiers to serve in the Senate. Bankhead had been in public life continuously for more than thirty years, entering the House of Representatives in 1887, and after twenty years in the House was elected to the Senate.

In a previous chapter I stated that Mrs. Stephen B. Elkins was the one woman who had lived to see her father, her husband, and her son in the United States Senate. When the Sixty-fifth Congress convened Mrs. Eugene Hale achieved the same distinction, as her son, Frederick Hale, took his seat as a Senator from Maine. Mrs. Hale's father was Zachariah Chandler of Michigan. Her husband served as Senator from Maine for thirty years, and her son was elected Senator in 1916 for a six-year term.

Miss Jeannette Rankin, the first woman elected to

Congress, was a Representative from Montana in the Sixty-fifth Congress.

New Year's, 1919, like all New Year's days during the eight years that Mr. Wilson was President, passed without the customary reception. On that day he was in Europe and on the subsequent New Year's days, 1920 and 1921, he was critically ill.

CHAPTER XXVIII

THE PROBLEMS OF PEACE

End of the War Finds the Country Suffering on Account of Its Burdens —League of Nations Becomes a Firebrand—The President Tries to Force the Treaty through the Senate by Direct Appeal to the People—League Hopeless without Strong Reservations, but Wilson Would not Yield—Treaty Defeated—Jackson Day Developments—Treaty Meets a Second Defeat—Why Relations between the President and Colonel House were Suspended—Surprise when Lansing Was Dismissed and Bainbridge Colby Made Secretary of State.

WHEN a war is over the real trouble begins. The statesmen who talk about submitting questions "to the arbitrament of the sword" belong to an age long past. War settles nothing except to demonstrate which nation or set of nations has the longest purse and can put the largest and strongest military force in the field and on the sea. When war ends serious conditions confront all countries that have been engaged in it. This is especially true of a country whose leaders have preached peace, whose people desire peace, and yet are suddenly called upon to blindly follow those leaders into war.

The peace-loving people of the United States awoke one day to a realization that all the preaching and seeming resolve to maintain peace had been mere verbiage. The same leaders who had virtually promised peace had

led them into war. Many people believed that as far
back as the sinking of the *Lusitania*, and all through the
peace campaign of 1916, the Administration knew the
United States was going to get into the European war.
There are reasons to believe, and it has been often asserted, that the President knew that the country was
likely to be drawn into the war when he made his
frantic appeals for great military preparation during the
Fall of 1915 and Winter of 1916.

The United States saved France and England. A
German victory would have brought about the practical
destruction of those nationalities as strong factors in
the world, and the integrity of both is necessary to maintain the equilibrium in Europe—that balance of power
between the forces in all nations which, striving for
control, would create either imperial despotism or democratic socialism as masters of the civilized world. But in
performing so great a service for the human race this
country incurred obligations and assumed burdens
which will make the people sweat for many future
years.

Not alone the burdens in dollars and cents that
the war brought upon America will have to be borne.
Interwoven with them are the serious evils that followed in its wake, the never imagined consequences,
destined to plague generations to come.

The attempt to settle the problems of the war produced a schism in the country. There was created a
line of cleavage wholly unnatural and wholly unnecessary. Up to the time of the peace negotiations there

never had been any serious political differences as to our foreign policy; no division regarding Americanism and the Monroe Doctrine. Even the strife of civil war did not involve the fundamentals which separated this country from Europe.

The great firebrand of 1919 was the Peace Treaty and League of Nations negotiated that year. It set American against American; it divided friends and families; it caused divisions among partisans; it was the greatest common divisor ever known, for it not only divided a whole people, but also parties, religions and communities. The disputes over slavery were intense and bitter, but that was a domestic question; it did not involve other nations. The Peace of Versailles involved the world and threw us into a maelstrom of discussion concerning every part of the civilized as well as the savage part of the globe.

It is not to be expected that any average citizen of the United States will ever understand the Peace Treaty of 1919. Not one in a million has read it, and no one who has read it can explain it. But this we do know, it brought about a state of mind among the people unlike anything ever before known. Concerned up to that time only with disputes over domestic problems, our people were involved in troubles almost wholly foreign in character and relationship.

President Wilson returned to the United States with the League of Nations Covenant and the Treaty of Peace in one document and submitted it to the Senate on July 10, 1919. It had already been printed by order of the Senate and the main features discussed at length throughout the country. Previous to leaving Paris the President had determined to make a speaking tour of the United States in order to explain the League of Nations and secure support for it. He had decided to begin his tour as soon as he landed in this country, but was dissuaded by cables from leading Democratic supporters in the United States. He went to Washington and remained, rather restless, in the White House while the League of Nations was discussed in the Senate.

Gradually the lines of support and antagonism to the League began to take form. A few Senators approved the League because they believed in world peace and thought such peace could be established under the covenant. There was also a large number of Democratic Senators who championed the League because it was an Administration measure and the majority of Republicans had bitterly assailed it. There were Senators in both political parties who were uncompromisingly opposed to the League in any form, and against any agreement which entangled this country in European affairs. There were Senators who were for the League with reservations, and these again were divided into "strong reservationists" and "mild reservationists."

It soon became apparent that the Treaty could not be adopted without strong reservations, and the negotiations were begun with that end in view. President Wilson sent for and held conferences with many Republican Senators, principally those known as mild reservationists. But he offered no compromise of any kind—in fact, from the very beginning of the controversy the President stood firm for the Treaty and League as drawn.

Failing to convince the mild reservation Senators that they should come to his way of thinking, the President decided to start on a tour of the country. About the same time he gave voice to his exasperation toward the senatorial opponents of the League in expressive language. Some of the terms applied to them in public and private were: "Pygmy minded," "lovers of war," "haters of truth," "ignorant fumblers of English," "blind, perverted fools," "deserving of hanging on the highest gibbet," "contemptible quitters," "jaundice-eyed zealots," "pro-German," "disloyal," "dishonest," "cowards," "traitors," "unpatriotic," and "un-American."

The Presidential tour of the western country may have convinced a part of the people that the League was a good thing, but did not change the attitude of the Senators. The tour came to an unfortunate end in Kansas, when the President was taken suddenly ill and was at once hurried to Washington, where he remained in a precarious state for many months. In fact, it was an illness from which he never fully recovered, and for a long time he transacted only business imperatively requiring his signature or sanction. Not more than half a dozen persons were allowed to see him on official business and such conferences were not prolonged. It was believed by many that his disability was such as to require the succession of the Vice President. He was kept alive by the skill and devotion of his personal physician, Dr. Cary. T. Grayson, U.S.N., whom he had promoted to the rank of Rear-Admiral.

But the President held tenaciously to his position on the League. Before he went away on his tour Democratic Senators who supported the Treaty and League, but knew it could not be adopted without reservations, so informed the President, and suggested that certain reservations, which the President could accept and which would be acceptable to the mild reservation Republicans, should be prepared and submitted. They told the President that this plan would split the Republican majority in the Senate and be hailed throughout the country as an Administration victory, whereas if such a plan was not followed the League would be defeated.

"My information is different," was President Wilson's response, and he maintained his position with his usual tenacity. Even after the Senate had rejected all mild reservations and the Lodge reservations had been adopted by a decisive majority, he wrote to Senator Hitchcock, the Administration leader, advising his supporters to vote against ratification if the Lodge reservations were made a part of the resolution.

And so the Treaty and League were defeated, as a two-thirds vote of the Senate was necessary to ratify it. Those who favored the League with reservations were not numerous enough to ratify it, and the resolution of

ratification without reservations was decisively defeated. But the President did not change. Two
months later he wrote a letter from his sick room in the
White House to Jackson Day Democratic diners advising that the fight for the League of Nations be carried
into the Presidential election of 1920, so that the people
might decide the issue. Particular importance was
attached to the message, because William J. Bryan
told those same diners that, as the Republicans were in
control of the Senate and had voted reservations in the
Treaty, majority rule should be recognized and that the
Treaty and League ought not to be carried into the
campaign.

The diverse views of these two men, one who had
been thrice nominated and thrice defeated for President, and the one who had been twice nominated and
twice elected President, caused a very interesting political discussion. It was recalled that Bryan had brought
about Wilson's first nomination and had inserted in the
platform a one-term plank. It also started speculation
as to whether the President, as the proponent of the
League of Nations and its most valiant defender, might
not determine to be a candidate for a third term. This
possibility alone caused a great deal of consternation
among Democrats, because they were perfectly aware
that any President so strongly entrenched in power as
Woodrow Wilson could name the candidate of his party,
even if it were himself for a third term. Democrats
who realized this situation had grave misgivings as to
the election of any man for a third term. So, in spite

of the President's insistence that there should be no reservations attached to the Treaty, negotiations for its ratification with reservations were renewed and urged by many Democratic Senators. The League of Nations was of such tremendous importance that it overshadowed nearly everything else in the special session of Congress.

During the conferences and caucuses over the Treaty there was occasionally some very plain, even blunt, language used. On one occasion Senator Ashurst of Arizona, who had never been a hide-bound Administration man, talked quite plainly to his fellows. The subject under discussion was whether the Democrats of the Senate should support the Lodge reservations, or whether they should follow the President and reject the Treaty if reservations were adopted by the Senate. "I want to say to my fellow Democratic Senators," said Ashurst, "that those who are taking the stand in favor of the Treaty without reservations are either knaves or fools. They are fools if they think they can ratify this Treaty without reservations; and they are knaves if they claim to be supporters of the Treaty and yet vote to reject it because the reservations are attached to it."

Of course such language was wholly unpalatable to the Democrats, and it made Ashurst somewhat unpopular among a number of his fellow Senators, while others entirely approved of the frank way in which he stated the situation.

Early in 1920 a second attempt was made to secure

ratification of the Peace Treaty, but it failed, and the Treaty was returned to the President, with whom it remained until the end of his term. As President Wilson had said in his letter to the Democratic diners on Jackson day that the League of Nations should be submitted to a solemn referendum of the people, the second rejection meant that the League would be a great issue in the Presidential campaign of 1920.

When Colonel E. M. House returned from Paris, after the conclusion of the Peace Treaty negotiations, it became apparent that there had been a break between President Wilson and the only man who had been his personal and political intimate while he was President. Colonel House did not go to Washington, and he maintained the same silence which had made him the man of mystery from the beginning of the Wilson administration.

The story of the severance of the relations between President Wilson and Colonel House cannot be verified, because no such story can be substantiated unless it is agreed to by both parties, but I will tell it as it was told to me, and its probability is confirmed, inasmuch as it emphasizes one characteristic of Mr. Wilson, his determination to keep all important matters under his own control.

Although the President had named Secretary Lansing, Colonel House, General Tasker H. Bliss, and Horace White as members of the Peace Commission with himself, it was a well-known fact that the President was to all intents and purposes the entire American

Commission. It was also well understood among the leading diplomats of Europe that Colonel House was the real confidant of President Wilson, and consequently he was consulted by the prominent men who were conducting the Treaty negotiations. One day, according to the story, President Wilson called at the residence of Colonel House in Paris. He had not been there long when Premier Clemenceau of France was announced. The Colonel told the President that the engagement with the French Premier had been made several days before and was important, but that it would not have been made for that hour had he known the President contemplated calling. He asked the President if he desired to be present at the interview and the President replied in the negative, telling the Colonel to see his visitor in another room and he would wait. The interview with Clemenceau was concluded and the President and Colonel House resumed their talk. They were interrupted again in a few minutes by the announcement that Lord Robert Cecil of the British Commission had arrived. Almost the same conversation and action occurred in regard to the British Commissioner as had just taken place about Clemenceau. The President and Colonel House once more resumed their conference when for the third time they were interrupted by the announcement that Baron Sonnino of the Italian Commission had called to see Colonel House. Again the Colonel apologized and again he was told to see his visitor in another room. But when Colonel House returned from his conference with the last of these prominent members of the French, British, and Italian Commissions, the President had left. From that time the relations between the President and Colonel House were suspended.

Presidents often succeed in making cabinet changes without any explosions. President Wilson made many changes, and all but three were effected quietly. His son-in-law, William G. McAdoo was succeeded in the Treasury by Carter Glass of Virginia. Later when Glass was appointed Senator from Virginia to succeed Thomas S. Martin, Secretary Houston was transferred from the Agricultural Department and Edwin T. Meredith of Iowa was appointed Secretary of Agriculture. In the Department of Justice McReynolds was succeeded by Gregory and Gregory by A. Mitchell Palmer of Pennsylvania. Secretary Redfield was replaced in the Department of Commerce by Joshua W. Alexander of Missouri. Secretary Lane was succeeded in the Interior Department by John Barton Payne of Pennsylvania. None of these changes was of a character to cause undue comment, and none was the result of disagreements with the President.

Garrison left the War Department amidst fireworks, while Bryan retired from the State Department because he was not in accord with the President's views, but there seemed to be only the most cordial feeling between Wilson and Bryan. The second change in the State Department was different. The removal of Robert Lansing was not only harsh, but the method and reasons given caused general adverse comment. During the President's long illness several Cabinet meetings were called by Lansing as premier to consider matters of importance affecting the Government. Suddenly President Wilson asserted that these meetings were an unwarranted usurpation of Presidential authority, and made it very plain that he desired Lansing's immediate resignation, which was tendered and accepted. Lansing had not always agreed with the President. He differed with him about provisions in the Peace Treaty. He was quoted by a witness before the Senate Committee on Foreign Relations as saying in Paris that the Senate would never ratify the treaty, if the Senators once understood "what it let us in for." This statement was never denied by Lansing. That he did not see the President during the latter's protracted illness was rather strange in view of the many important matters in foreign affairs then pending. The President was well enough to see Senators Hitchcock and Fall and discuss the Mexican situation, and to reverse the policy Lansing was pursuing, but he did not consult his Secretary of State. In fact, it developed later that he did not consult any of his Cabinet officers, unless one brief interview with Secretary Glass could be called a consultation.

The selection of Bainbridge Colby of New York as Secretary of State to succeed Lansing was one of the many surprises of the Wilson administration. Colby had been a Republican up to 1912, when he became a Bull Mooser and supported Roosevelt. In 1916 he did not follow Roosevelt back into the Republican

party, but supported Wilson for a second term. It was
a month before Colby was confirmed and he was very
thoroughly discussed by the Foreign Relations Committee. "Do you realize," asked Chairman Lodge,
of a man who urged Colby's confirmation, "that the
selection of a Secretary of State at this time is the most
important ever made in the history of the country?"
When asked to explain he pointed out that only two
lives stood between the Secretary of State and the
Presidency, and that neither the President nor the Vice
President was a strong, healthy man. But Colby was
confirmed, and it was generally believed that the President had at last found a Secretary of State whose
mind would run in the same channel as his own.

The dismissal of Lansing on the alleged ground that
he had called and attended Cabinet meetings during
the President's illness caused consternation for a time
among other Cabinet members. They had attended
these meetings and might at any time be "called on
the carpet," and either dismissed or reprimanded.
Secretary Baker of the War Department confided to a
friend that he did not know for a long time whether he
was to be dismissed or promoted to be Secretary of
State. Lane, who was going out, and Redfield, who
was already out, upheld Lansing, saying all members
of the Cabinet were agreed that the meetings should be
held and were equally responsible. None of the other
members said anything for publication, though once,
in reply to a friend who jocularly remarked: "I see
you are still in the Cabinet." Secretary Daniels replied:

"Yes, and keeping mighty still!" But these Cabinet officers were needlessly alarmed. There was neither dismissal nor reprimand for Secretary Baker, Attorney General Palmer, Postmaster General Burleson, Secretary Daniels, Secretary Houston, or Secretary Wilson. President Wilson had determined before he became ill to dismiss Secretary Lansing. This was one of several matters which worried him at that time and during the early stages of his illness, and which his physician refused to allow him to consider. But it was in his mind and, like the curt notes he sent abroad about this time, startled the country and gave the people notice that Woodrow Wilson had resumed control of the Government, at least so far as concerned the foreign relations of the United States.

Congress in 1919 adopted the Nineteenth Amendment, giving suffrage to women, and it was ratified by the thirty-six states, the necessary three-fourths of the states, by August, 1920. All the women of the country were thus permitted to vote in the Presidential election of that year.

CHAPTER XXIX

ANNO DOMINI 1920

The People Decide to Return to Normalcy—League of Nations Buried by the Voters of the United States in a Solemn Referendum—Harding Elected President—Republicans Win the Greatest Victory Ever Known in Politics.

THE Presidential election of 1920 was the most important political event in the history of the United States, save alone the election of 1860, which overthrew slavery. By many persons it was considered even more important, as it settled the question whether the United States should maintain its independent and distinct sovereignty, or become so deeply entangled with all the other nations of the world as to compel future foreign policies to be guided by the wishes of those nations rather than in the interests of the people of the United States.

Both parties went into the campaign on the one great issue, the League of Nations. President Wilson, speaking for the Democratic party, had submitted the League of Nations to a solemn referendum of the people, and his party, or a large majority of his party, supported him. The Republican leaders, speaking for their party, accepted the challenge. Long before the conventions assembled it was known that the League would be the

paramount issue. The rejection by the Senate of the
Treaty of Versailles as written, and the refusal of
the President to accept it with the Senate reservations,
made acceptance or rejection of the League the one
dominant question to be determined by the voters in
the general election. No matter what may be said as to
the other issues which influenced the voters, the League
was the real issue, and the decision of the electorate
pointed out the policy this country should follow as to
its association with foreign nations. The people did
not want the League as formulated in Paris in 1919.

It is no doubt true that other considerations influenced the voters. Many people were of the opinion
that the intense desire for a change was sufficient to
turn the Democrats out and put the Republicans in.
The high cost of living, the unpopularity of the Wilson
administration, the extravagance and expense of the
Government, necessitating taxation which never before
had been known in the history of the country, all contributed to the great overturn and no doubt would have
elected a Republican candidate if the League had not
been before the people. But, after all, the League was
made the issue, and in spite of efforts from time to time
to raise subsidiary questions to interest the public, the
League remained the one dominating issue throughout
the entire campaign.

After the national conventions were called the interest of the people centered in the candidates rather
than in the issues. The Republicans were first in the
field, and there was a very lively canvass for delegates

© U. and U.

WARREN G. HARDING

in nearly all of the states. All of the Republican leaders knew that a Presidential nomination by the Republicans was as good as an election, and naturally there was the greatest effort put forth by the various candidates and their friends to secure delegates.

Three men at once became prominent possibilities: Governor Frank O. Lowden of Illinois, Major General Leonard Wood of the Army, and Senator Hiram W. Johnson of California. As these three candidates struggled for delegates, another loomed large upon the horizon, and everybody had to acknowledge that he held the most favorable position in case there was a deadlock in the convention. Senator Warren G. Harding was from Ohio; he was a country newspaper man, the editor and publisher of the Marion *Star*. He had owned the paper for thirty years and during that time he had come forward as a political leader. As a state Senator, Lieutenant Governor, and United States Senator for five years, he had attained a prominence which Ohio Republicans believed was sufficient to carry him into the Presidency. He also had the advantage of location. Ohio had elected Wilson four years before—the only state north of the Ohio River and east of the Missouri River which had voted for the Democratic candidate, save New Hampshire. Naturally, it was supposed that the man who could carry Ohio could win the Presidency. That alone was a big asset in bringing Senator Harding forward as a candidate. He was not a dark horse, but a possibility from the first, and yet it was the judgment of many wise political observers up to within a short time before the convention assembled that Governor Frank O. Lowden would win the nomination on account of his personality and because of the splendid record he had made as Governor of Illinois. There were others who were equally sanguine that General Wood had the best chance, because in the primaries it seemed that he had polled a larger vote than any of the other candidates, and also because he was the natural legatee of the Roosevelt strength in the Republican party. Most of the Roosevelt adherents were his earnest supporters, the conspicuous exceptions being the few who had gathered around the standard of Senator Johnson.

When the Republicans assembled in Chicago no one man was sure of the nomination, but it soon became apparent that General Wood and Governor Lowden had been eliminated by the mistakes of their over-enthusiastic friends. Long before the convention met charges had been made by Senator Borah that vast sums of money were being used to promote the interests of these candidates. So specific were the charges that a Senate committee was appointed to investigate them, and before the convention met it was developed that in the primary campaigns to elect delegates the friends of General Wood had spent something like a million and a half dollars in his behalf, while Governor Lowden had spent about half a million dollars of his own money. No particular complaint was made against Lowden for spending his own money, but as men connected with big corporations had contributed to the Wood campaign, it tended to injure him as a candidate. Governor Lowden was virtually put out of the race and no doubt lost the nomination by the development of the fact that two delegates from Missouri had received $2,500 each. While it was shown that Governor Lowden was in no way responsible for this payment to these two delegates, the fact that they were paid the money in his behalf was sufficient to eliminate him when the test came.

More "dream" stories have been written about how the nomination of Senator Harding was brought about than of any nomination that has been made in many years. All these stories have been based on the assumption that there was something mysterious about the nomination of the Ohio Senator. It was stated that it was the result of a conference at 2:11 o'clock in the morning in room 211 of a Chicago hotel; that a senatorial cabal, with others there assembled, agreed that Harding should be the nominee; that they presented their agreement to the thousand delegates in the convention and had it ratified.

Back in 1888 a candidate was nominated by a combination of leading politicians. Since that time, to my recollection, no candidate has ever been named by any coterie of politicians, by any "Old Guard," or by any combination of Republican leaders, unless we should except the selection of President Taft in 1912, and that was more a nomination by a faction of the party than by any combination of a few leaders.

The nomination of Senator Harding was one of those

inevitable political results which follow the course of circumstances. More than a week before the convention met it looked to those who were wise observers as though Senator Harding would be the man, because he had the best position in the race. The use of money eliminated two of the leading candidates and the third, Senator Johnson, never could have been nominated in that convention. Johnson had bolted the party in 1912 and ran as the candidate for Vice President on the Progressive ticket. In 1916 he was elected Senator from California by 297,000 majority, while the state was lost to Hughes by 3,000 majority. Johnson was held responsible for the loss of California to the Republicans and the defeat of the Republican national ticket. And whatever effort may have been made by the Republicans to conciliate and welcome the Progressives back to the party, there was a sufficient number of delegates at the Republican convention in 1920 who did not propose to welcome the California Senator with the nomination for President in a year which was sure success.

When it became apparent that none of the three leading candidates could be nominated, there were efforts made to concentrate on some one of the men who had been considered merely as favorite sons. Governor Sproul of Pennsylvania had the delegates from that state, Senator Miles Poindexter had the solid delegation of Washington as well as delegates from other states. Judge Pritchard of North Carolina had the delegates from his state, Senator Howard Sutherland had the delegates from West Virginia, Governor Calvin Coolidge had the delegates from Massachusetts, as well as others from New England states, and then there was Senator La Follette with the delegates from Wisconsin, but that was the usual thing in national conventions and meant nothing. Plans were laid to stampede the convention for Senator Philander C. Knox of Pennsylvania, with the idea of nominating Senator Johnson on the ticket with him as Vice President. It was made known that Senator Johnson would accept the second place with Knox running as the head of the ticket.

But these efforts were fruitless. The cold logic of the situation prevailed. Ohio had a candidate that was as satisfactory as any of the others mentioned, and Ohio carried by the Republicans would insure the election of the national ticket. Harding was known to most of the delegates. He had been temporary and permanent chairman of the convention in 1916 and had won many friends. He was even suggested as a dark horse in that convention.

As ballot succeeded ballot in the convention of 1920, and it was demonstrated that none of the three leading candidates could be nominated, the delegates naturally turned toward a man who could win. It is true that there were consultations among the leaders. There are always consultations. It often happens that these leaders, catching the drift of the delegates, will quickly get in line and lead the procession. That comes very near to describing what happened at Chicago. The leaders who assembled in any particular room and con-

sulted with each other did not shape the destinies of
the Republican party, because the longer the balloting
continued the more inevitable it became that the Ohio
Senator would win. Naturally, when there were three
other leading candidates, with a large number of scattered votes, it became necessary to open negotiations
with those candidates and with their managers in regard to the breaking up of their following. Governor
Lowden was one of the first to be consulted, and when
he saw that his nomination was impossible, he promptly
offered to release his delegates and urge them to vote
for Harding. Neither General Wood nor Senator
Johnson would follow the lead of Governor Lowden,
consequently the break did not come as soon as expected. But the inevitable in politics happens just as
in nature, and the time finally came when the delegates
turned to Harding and he was nominated on the tenth
ballot.

Governor Calvin Coolidge was selected for Vice President because it was generally believed that he represented the opposition throughout the country to the
increasing usurpation by the labor forces. Nearly
every demand of a national character made by labor for
some time past had been granted or compromised in
favor of labor. Calvin Coolidge was Governor of
Massachusetts when the Boston police went on strike
because they were not permitted to affiliate with the
American Federation of Labor. Governor Coolidge
was credited with the prompt enforcement of law
and order which commended him to the American

people and made him a serious Presidential possibility. Had he been from any one of the states on the Presidential Highway—New York, New Jersey, Ohio, Indiana, or Illinois—he would have been a very formidable candidate for President. Ohio had the preferable position and won the high place; and Massachusetts was given the second place on account of the current of feeling running throughout the country that the time had come when a tendency toward dictation and lawlessness by any class should be curbed.

Next to the selection of the Presidential candidates the most important feature of the convention was the making of the platform, and the difficulty of shaping that document hung solely upon the wording of the plank relating to the League of Nations. The story of the platform would not be complete without a digression concerning the selection of the chairman of the committee on resolutions, with interesting facts bearing upon Indiana politics.

Long before the convention met it was determined that Henry Cabot Lodge, the leader of the Senate, should be temporary chairman. Former Senator Albert J. Beveridge of Indiana became a candidate for permanent chairman. Then followed shrewd manipulation to shut out Beveridge from this honor. Part of the scheme included making Senator James E. Watson of Indiana chairman of the committee on resolutions, and it was a foregone conclusion that Watson would be chosen for the best chairmanship of the convention.

Then when Beveridge was mentioned for permanent chairman the Republican leaders would ask:

"What's that? Does Indiana want everything? Indiana has the chairman of the national committee; she is to have the chairman of the committee on platform; is Indiana trying to grab off everything in the convention?"

The committee on permanent organization was selected with a view of preventing Beveridge from being elected permanent chairman, and it was finally determined that the precedents established at the last two national conventions should be followed and the temporary chairman become the permanent chairman. This procedure conferred new honors on Senator Lodge in national conventions. He had been twice chairman of the committee on resolutions, once temporary chairman, and this last honor made him three times permanent chairman of national conventions.

But the Indiana situation had not altogether cleared up. Will H. Hays, chairman of the national committee, long before the convention met, had appointed 160 different men to make platform suggestions, and had made Ogden L. Mills of New York chairman of this large committee. Hays wanted Mills made chairman of committee on resolutions at the national convention. Consequently he felt obliged to oppose Senator Watson of his own state, and a very interesting Indiana contest ensued. Then it was that the Old Guard, or that element in the party which is so denominated, played its trump card. One of the ablest organizers of political

forces in the country was sent to Chicago to make
Watson the chairman of the committee on resolutions.
His name never was mentioned in connection with the
affair. He stopped at one of the somewhat obscure
hotels where he perfected his organization. He divided
the country into districts; he had his lieutenants visit
the various state delegations, and every delegation was
urged to choose a particular man as member of the committee on resolutions, that man having been selected by
the political manager because he would vote for Watson. When the committee met Watson was chosen
chairman by a large majority.

The selection of Watson, together with the turning
down of Beveridge for temporary chairman, caused a rup-
ture in Indiana politics which lasted until the end of the
campaign and gave the Republican leaders a great many
uneasy hours. There were times when it was feared
that Indiana might go Democratic, and it was often
asserted that Senator Watson could not be re-elected.
Of course, all these assertions were made on the basis
that it would be a normal election and not a political
avalanche.

As the League of Nations was the issue before the
people, and as it had divided Republicans as well as
Democrats, it was natural that the division should crop
out at the national convention. The Republicans in
the Senate had been divided; there were mild reservationists, there were Lodge reservationists, and there were
irreconcilables. Wise Republicans of the Senate early
saw that it was necessary for the Republicans to get

together on the declaration to be made at Chicago. A
draft of a plank on this subject was written and agreed
to. But a surprise awaited the Republican leaders of
the Senate when they reached Chicago. They found
that there was a very important element, backed mainly
by big financial interests, determined to have a very mild
declaration on the League of Nations. W. Murray Crane,
the veteran politician of Massachusetts, then a member
of the national committee, former Governor and former
Senator, was the man who was handling the program
declaring for a League with mild reservations. Never
before at a national convention was Murray Crane
quite so busy as at Chicago in 1920. He pattered up
and down Michigan Avenue between the Blackistone
Hotel and the Chicago Club, dropping into the inter-
mediate hotels, whispering and advising. I do not believe that Murray Crane ever became quite so emphatic
in his declarations as he did on this League of Nations
plank. He was actually insistent at times as to what
should be done, and not in his usual mild and insinuat-
ing manner; he used the word "must" very frequently.

Meanwhile the contest went on in the committee on
resolutions. Senator Borah created something of a
sensation when he announced that the fight would be
carried to the floor of the convention and an effort
made to secure an absolute declaration against any
League of Nations whatever. Then the mild reservation advocates subsided and the committee expressed
hope of reaching an agreement. The senatorial plank
was finally adopted.

I met Senator Lodge later in the day, and he asked me in a casual manner what had been going on outside of the convention, and I replied:

"A most amusing thing to my mind, and the only thing that has happened concerning this convention that has very much real interest—the spanking that has been administered to your former colleague, W. Murray Crane."

At once Senator Lodge showed interest and asked for particulars, and I explained to him that a number of Senators had been in conversation with Crane and told him in emphatic language that he was not running the convention, or the committee on platform, and would not be allowed to shape the terms of the League of Nations plank.

That Lodge was very much pleased there can be no doubt. He knew that Crane knew nothing about the League; he knew that Crane had neither read nor understood the Treaty, and that he was at the convention representing certain elements in the country which were deeply interested in having a League with mild reservations. When Crane and the men he represented were made to understand fully that they would either take the compromise declaration which had been prepared by the Senators, or that they would run the risk of an out-and-out declaration against any League, they yielded and accepted the compromise.

The failure of the large financial interests to secure the mild declaration on the League in the Republican platform recalls an incident when the contest over the

League was at its height in the Senate. Big finance
was for the League earnestly, and became insistent in
talking to Senators. To one of its representatives
Senator Lodge, after listening for a few minutes,
said:

"The time has gone by when large financial interests
can come to Washington and tell Senators how they
shall vote."

In 1912 Theodore Roosevelt went to the Republican
national convention as an active contesting candidate
for the nomination. He is the first, so far as I can
recall, who was purposely present to secure the nomination. It is true that Garfield was a delegate to the
convention which named him for President, but he was
not an avowed candidate. In 1920 all the leading candidates were on the ground, as well as several who were
merely possible as dark horses. Senator Harding,
Governor Lowden, General Wood, Senator Johnson,
Governor Sproul, Senator Poindexter, and Senator
Sutherland were all at Chicago and in frequent consultation with their managers and supporters.

President Wilson could have named the Democratic
candidate for President at the national convention of
1920 if he had cared to exercise his power. He kept
hands off and the convention did what it pleased in naming the candidate. It conformed to the wishes of the
President as to the main feature of the platform. It
endorsed his League of Nations and to that extent hurried on toward the political suicide to which the Paris
imbroglio had foredoomed the Democratic party.

There was nothing unusual about the Democratic convention. For the seventh successive time William J. Bryan was the most conspicuous figure. He did not dominate the convention as he had the conventions of 1896, 1900, 1908 and 1912, but he was present with his extinguisher of Democratic hopes as he had been in 1904. He was there to secure a dry plank and to defeat the nomination of a wet candidate, and failed in both efforts. Afterwards, as in 1904, he took the most effective course to defeat the Democratic ticket.

It is not known whether President Wilson desired or expected the nomination for himself, although there had been a great deal of discussion of a third term and many people thought that, in view of the fact that the League of Nations was to be made the dominant issue by the Democratic party, Woodrow Wilson, its creator, was the logical man to lead the party in the campaign. By nodding his head or giving any other kind of sign President Wilson could have secured the nomination of his son-in-law, William G. McAdoo, who had been one of the ablest men in the Cabinet. It is a strange thing, one of the many mysteries about this mysterious man, that it is still a secret whether or not he wanted his son-in-law nominated as the Democratic candidate. It is doubtful whether any member of his personal or official family knows. Certainly neither hint nor comment, while the delegates were being elected, escaped from the White House. The fact that Wilson gave no indication as to his desire regarding a candidate to succeed him as President has been construed to mean that he felt the party at least owed him a third nomination. But that is wholly a matter of conjecture. His attitude may be explained as comporting with his course throughout his whole Administration, an apparent desire to create a mystery, to cause speculation as to his position, and to so manage it that he might say, in case he chose to comment on his action, that he pursued an obvious and natural course, and to express suprise that it should be considered strange or unusual. As to candidates, what Woodrow Wilson wanted or did not want in 1920 will remain a mystery or await his explanation in his own time.

James M. Cox, then Governor of Ohio, was nominated by the Democrats for one reason only. He was from Ohio. The Democrats had won the election four years before because they carried Ohio. "Carry Ohio," the Republicans said at Chicago, "and we can win with what we had in 1916." "Without Ohio," the Cox boomers said at San Francisco, "the Democrats do not stand a chance of success." And so they nominated Cox on the forty-fourth ballot. It was a prolonged struggle and showed how bitter was the contest for the honor of leading a great party to defeat.

Franklin D. Roosevelt was nominated for Vice President because it was believed the Roosevelt name would be worth 30,000 Republican votes in New York. Roosevelt was Assistant Secretary of the Navy. He was a popular young official, much more popular when nominated than after he had been campaigning for a few months.

An interesting feature of the Democratic national convention was the battle between officeholders. William G. McAdoo, who had the prestige of being son-in-law of the President and formerly Secretary of the Treasury, was made a formidable competitor by his friends. A. Mitchell Palmer, Attorney General in the President's cabinet, was a most active candidate and was at the convention. Both had claims to Administration support, both had support of Federal officials, but not that all-powerful support, the voice of the man in the White House. Gathered in San Francisco were a swarm of officeholders. It seemed as if all the prominent men of the Department of Justice were about the headquarters of Attorney General Palmer. But these were offset by the crowd of Treasury employees who were around the headquarters of McAdoo. Ordinarily officeholders at a national convention are grouped under one banner, but the mysterious silence of Wilson left these heroes of the pay roll free to follow the flag of the men they served or had served. And bitterly did they wage their internecine warfare, these government officials who would have been delighted to fight together under any one flag if Woodrow Wilson had selected the banner. So fiercely raged the battle that each candidate destroyed the other. It must be said in justice to McAdoo that he was only a passive candidate. He had indicated a desire to keep out of the contest, but his former subordinates would not allow it. They hoped to have a wink or a nod from the White House, and so they rallied to McAdoo's support, but without success.

Governor Cox would not have been nominated if any one could have appeared at San Francisco with a word of disapproval from Wilson. But the word was lacking. Note also the mighty change in the Democracy in eight years: Cox was supported by Boss Murphy of New York, Boss Nugent of New Jersey, Boss Taggart of Indiana, and Boss Brennan of Illinois, the latter the successor of Roger Sullivan. All of these bosses were anathema to William J. Bryan. In 1912, when Charlie Murphy cast the vote of New York for Champ Clark, Bryan made the act an excuse to break his instructions and vote for Woodrow Wilson. At San Francisco Murphy and his associate bosses were for Cox and, although Bryan protested earnestly and with eloquence against the selection of the Ohio Governor, Cox won. Ever and again during the convention was heard the braying of that following which in seven national conventions had shouted "Bryan! Bryan! Bryan!" But it was without avail. Still, these persistent persons should not despair. Bryan yet lives, and as long as that silver voice can wake the echoes of a convention hall there will be enough of the faithful to make the welkin ring with the old familiar "Bryan! Bryan! Bryan!"

History in time may be able to make something out of the campaign of 1920, but from a close view there was nothing of real interest in it. The Democrats were doomed to defeat from the beginning, and for several reasons, any one of them sufficient. The most important was the League of Nations. The American people held true to their traditional policy of avoiding entangling alliances with Europe. Next in importance was the unpopularity of President Wilson and his Administration. And not an insignificant factor was the reaction against unwarranted waste and graft in the expenditure of public money. Millions of people, ground to the earth by taxation and the high prices of the necessaries of life, keenly resented the wanton extravagance, the profiteering under the cost-plus plan and many other devices for squandering money which had created millionaires almost over night, and the careless waste that had characterized the disbursement of public funds.

The election of Harding and Coolidge was the most stupendous political victory ever known. It is true that Wilson had more electoral votes in 1912 than were given to Harding in 1920, but two Republicans, Taft and Roosevelt, were running in 1912 and split the Republican party. Even at that Wilson was a minority President, his total vote being 1,323,728 less than the combined vote of Taft and Roosevelt. But in 1920 Harding, running as a Republican against Cox running as a Democrat, no third party of any consequence being in the field, received 404 electoral votes, carrying every northern state, the border states of Maryland, West Virginia and Missouri, besides breaking into the solid south and carrying Tennessee and Oklahoma. Harding had a plurality of the popular vote in round numbers of 7,000,000. He received unprecedented majorities such as 1,089,000 in New York, 715,000 in Pennsylvania, 886,000 in Illinois, 529,000 in Michigan, and in his home state of Ohio, which had given Wilson 90,000 in 1916, Harding had 402,000 in 1920. The slaughter of the Democrats was particularly noticeable in Congress. The Republicans elected 300 members of the House of Representatives out of a total of 435, while the Democrats lost senatorial seats in Maryland, Kentucky, Oklahoma, South Dakota, Colorado, Idaho, Oregon, California, Nevada and Arizona. The Republicans held all seats they occupied, including Missouri. A number of prominent Democrats were defeated, among them, to the surprise of everybody, Champ Clark, who had been Speaker for eight years. I met him in a corridor of the Capitol the day Congress assembled a month after the election. Champ was arrayed in his long statesman's frock coat, looking grave and gloomy.

"What was the matter with your people down in Missouri?" I asked. In a growling voice that was almost a shout, he answered:

"Wilson!"

Senator Harding had said during the campaign that the country wanted to get back to normalcy. And he was right. If there ever was a verdict in favor of a return to normal conditions it was that of the voters in 1920.

With the election came the practical end of the Wilson administration. It still had four months more to serve, but was powerless. The mandate of the American people was so emphatic that both at home and abroad all vital matters were held in abeyance until Harding could be inaugurated. In fact, the outgoing President had been so long in feeble health that he could scarcely have exerted much influence over affairs even had he so willed. The Government had been almost without a head for many months, those around Wilson apparently using his name in many of the Presidential utterances emanating from the White House.

The people had a right to expect much from Warren G. Harding. He was neither an erratic genius of unbounded energy, a profound lawyer of judicial temperament, nor a highly gifted intellectuality sufficient unto himself. A prominent Democrat during the campaign remarked that he was like five million other men of the country. No higher compliment could have been paid him. That is why 16,138,000 men and women of the country voted for him. The period after the election he spent consulting with men of all shades of political opinion, and that was a most promising proceeding preliminary to his assumption of the Presidency. He did not disdain advice, but rather was anxious to acquire information through intimate personal contact with his fellow men. It was like a return to the days of 1896 and 1897 when McKinley was about to begin his successful administration. McKinley did not face the grave problems which confronted Harding. The country was not then overburdened with debt and taxation. Neither was it embroiled in controversies with erstwhile allies of a great war; nor was there a general world-wide unrest disturbing our own as well as foreign nations. The era beginning with 1921 was a time for counsel and consideration, and the more Harding conferred with the ablest men in political and business life the greater satisfaction he gave the people who had elected him.

With serious problems such as few Presidents have had to face waiting for solution, and with the people looking to him for the restoration of the sane and tranquil conditions of former years, President Harding entered upon a period of great opportunities and tremendous responsibility. That he would acquit himself wisely and solely in the interests of the whole country was the expectant hope of the people.

CHAPTER XXX

CONCLUSION

NATURALLY, these volumes contain much about Presidents and their policies. In any nation the head of the government is the most important person in the land. One who writes of Washington in a personal, political, or historical vein must give much space to Presidents and what they do. While no attempt has been made to write the history of the Presidential terms of Harrison, Cleveland, McKinley, Roosevelt, Taft, and Wilson, these six men in the eight administrations of four year periods have been brought prominently forward. I have known all of them well, some of them intimately. What I have written of each or any of them is from the point of view of an unprejudiced observer striving to tell the story as it unfolded.

People are not always just to nor always considerate of, the men they elect to the high office of President. Of the six men who have been Presidents during the thirty-two years ending March 4, 1921, only one escaped the innuendoes of slanderous whisperings concerning their morality. It is a cheering and significant fact that none of these whisperings has ever caused the people to lose confidence in their Presidents. Whenever a President has been rebuked by the people it has been on ac-

count of his policies and acts as President and not for
personal reasons. While it is true that charming personalities like McKinley, Roosevelt, and Taft have left
a pleasant impression upon all who knew them, yet all
Presidents are measured by what they do as chief
magistrates of the nation, and the success or failure of
the administration is determined by the people from
that point of view. Such success or failure depends
upon the ability of the man in office to meet the conditions as they arise and handle them in a statesmanlike
manner and for the best interests of the people of this
great nation.

During the last thirty-two years the Republicans
have been in control of the national government twenty
years and the Democrats twelve years. I have endeavored to set forth how the political pendulum swings
back and forth; why the people, or that controlling
element among them which changes from one party
to another, are influenced to alter their political allegiance from time to time. For every political up-
heaval there is a cause, sometimes plainly to be seen
before the voters register their verdict, always easily
explained after the result is known. Future historians
and all students of politics will be interested in tracing
the causes of these various political changes.

The most important lesson, and one that must be
learned by each generation, is that a long tenure of
power creates on the part of those who rule an arro-
gance and dictatorial policy which the people will sharply
rebuke when the opportunity arises. It is often said

by the leaders of a political party, after they have
gained a great victory, that their opponents will never
win another election. But it never has happened that
either party could continually satisfy the people. The
party in control of the Government makes mistakes,
its leaders assume too much power, elements of dis-
cord are injected, differences within the party develop,
and, finally, some great issue is brought forward with
the result that the party supposed to be so firmly entrenched is overthrown. Continuous control of the
Government by one party is a remote possibility, and,
if such a thing should come about, it would be either
through the development of supermen in statesmanship
or the advent of the millennium.

The third of a century covered in this review has
been marked by many changes. What were considered
extreme and radical legislative proposals in the late
eighties have become the law of the land in these days
of rapid progression. The most striking change has been
the abandonment of a once virile states' rights doctrine
superseded by a current setting strongly towards cen-
tralized government. The tendency of the time has
been in the direction of federalization, diminution of
state power, and elimination of individualism. The
people and the states turn to the Federal Government,
not only for amelioration of their political ills, but for
vast appropriations to carry on their enterprises and
support their institutions. There has been a growing
tendency in these years to have the Government right
all wrongs, provide for all those in want or distress, and

stretch forth its hand to control the police powers and the franchise in the various states. Federal power has encroached not only upon the states, but has extended its control over the business of the country to an extent not dreamed of a third of a century ago. Just what effect this movement towards centralization, and the inclination of the people to look to the Federal Government for succor and support in all emergencies will ultimately have upon the Republic is one of the great problems the future will unravel.

The historian whose narrative covers definite periods, such as the rise and fall of a dynasty or a republic, can conclude his work with more satisfaction than one who essays to write of his own times. The latter is hampered by lack of perspective, and embarrassed because he cannot follow great problems to their final conclusion. He reaches his jumping off place and realizes that he must leave many subjects suspended in the air. He can go back and gather up loose ends as a setting for his beginning, but for his ending he must either break off abruptly or enter the realms of speculation. The author of this work has chosen to end his narrative with the close of President Wilson's administration. The change from a Democratic to a Republican administration at any time is an event, a change from Woodrow Wilson to Warren G. Harding was epochal.

INDEX

A

Adamson law, ii, 312–313–314; in campaign of 1916, ii, 337–340–343

Adamson, William C., Representative from Georgia; Adamson law, ii, 312–313–314

Ainsworth, Frederick C., major general; becomes head of Adjutant General's Department, i, 381–382

Aldrich, Nelson W., Senator from Rhode Island; McKinley tariff, i, 44; calls Carter a "striker," i, 155; Dingley tariff, i., 223; clash with Elkins, i, 224; opposes war with Spain, i, 231; for acquisition of Philippines, i, 283; tariff conference, i, 407; gives rate bill to Tillman, ii, 7; opposes four-battleship plan, ii, 63; his power in the Senate, ii, 63–64; Payne-Aldrich bill, ii, 105; clash with Dolliver, ii, 106; retires from Senate, ii, 120–121

Alexander, Joshua W., Secretary of Commerce, ii, 389

Alger, Russell A., Secretary of War; candidate for President, i, 7; in Cabinet, i, 206; retired from Cabinet, i, 244–246

Allen, John M., Representative from Mississippi; comment on southern elections, i, 60; on defeat explanations, i, 72.

Allen, William V., Senator from Nebraska; talks 15 hours for silver, i, 122; permanent chairman Populist convention, i, 191–192

"Allies," The, ii, 69; join Roosevelt demonstration, ii, 75

Allison, William B., Senator from Iowa; candidate for President, i, 7; McKinley tariff, i, 44; candidate for President, i, 162–172; Dingley tariff, i, 223–172; opposes war with Spain, i, 231; tariff conference, i, 407; railroad rate bill, ii, 8; opposes four-battleship plan, ii, 63; death of, ii, 83–84

"Ananias Club"; founded, ii, 3–7

A. P. A. movement, i, 82–83; sentiment in West, i, 154

Armistice, ii, 367

Ashurst, Henry F., Senator from Arizona, ii, 161; flowery speech, ii, 161–162; opposes repeal canal tolls, ii, 249; plain talk on League, ii, 386

Associated Press; boycott of Carter, i, 47

B

Babcock, Joseph W., Representative from Wisconsin; for tariff revision, i, 406.

Bacon, Augustus O., Senator from Georgia, i, 152; defeated for President pro tem., ii, 220

Badger, Charles J., Admiral; commanding fleet in Mexican waters, ii, 250

Bailey, Joseph W., Representative and Senator from Texas; first appearance, i, 80; supports Bland, i, 183; minority leader, i, 218; leads Democrats for Cuban intervention, i, 232; tilts with Reed, i, 234; encounter with Beveridge, i, 366–367; speech on Texas, i, 408–409; criticises Roosevelt, ii, 61; first resignation, ii, 139; support of Lorimer, ii, 162; resigns from Senate, ii, 203–204

Index

Index

427

Gold Democratic convention, i, 192–193

Gold plank of 1896, i, 174 to 178

Gordon, James, Senator from Mississippi; remarkable speech, ii, 128

Gore, Thomas P., Senator from Oklahoma; starts demonstration for Bryan, ii, 78; mentioned by Clark, ii, 193; resolution of warning, ii, 306

Gorman, Arthur P., Senator from Maryland; voted for silver, i, 37; leads force bill fight, i, 62–63; aids Crisp, i, 78; candidate for President, i, 94; comments on situation, i, 94–95; opposes Wilson bill, i, 126; denounces Cleveland, i, 131; supports amended tariff, i, 133; opposed to Philippine acquisition, i, 282; retired from Senate, i, 317; return to Senate, i, 385; death of, ii, 27–28

Governors' conference, ii, 65

Grand Army; parade 50 years after, ii, 290

Gray, George, Senator from Delaware; against free silver, i, 37; retired from Senate, i, 317; candidate for President, ii, 51–52–79

Gray, Horace, Associate Justice Supreme Court; against income tax, i, 149

Grayson, Cary T., Rear-Admiral; 90-mile ride with Roosevelt, ii, 82; care of Wilson, ii, 384

Gregory, Thomas W., Attorney General, ii, 217

Gresham, Walter Q., Secretary of State, i, 104; restores Queen Liliuokalani, i, 109; differences with Minister Thurston, i, 147

Gridiron Club; burlesques restoration of Liliuokalani, i, 109; hears muckrake speech, ii, 17; Taft and Bryan guests, ii, 71; Ezekiel speech by Penrose, ii, 298

Grosvenor, Charles H., Representative from Ohio; McKinley mathematician, i, 163; opposes intervention in Cuba, i, 232; leads Hawaii annexation, i, 290–291; candidate for Speaker, i, 310; tariff conference, i, 407

H

Hadley, Herbert S., Governor of Missouri; one of "eight little Governors," ii, 170; Roosevelt floor leader, ii, 177

Hale, Eugene, Senator from Maine; opposes war with Spain, i, 231; opposed to Philippine acquisition, i, 282; clash with Newlands, i, 389–390; opposes four-battleship plan, ii, 63; "traded and got cheated," ii, 107–108; retires from Senate, ii, 120–121

Hale, Frederick, Senator from Maine, ii, 377

Hanna, Marcus A., Senator from Ohio; nominating McKinley, i, 164–171–174–175–176–179; chairman national committee, and campaign manager, i, 194–197–198–199; in the Senate, 205–206; opposes war with Spain, i, 231; for Philippine acquisition, i, 280–283; opposes Roosevelt for Vice President, i, 328; Bliss his candidate, i, 333; calls Roosevelt a madman, i, 335; surrenders, i, 341; chairman national committee second time, i, 345; mention for President, i, 376; death of, i, 390; way open for Wood's confirmation and Roosevelt's nomination, i, 390–396; his prominence, i, 396

Hansbrough, Henry C., Representative and Senator from North Dakota; sees omen, i, 73; comment on Roosevelt, ii, 43; Aldrich's chloroform bottle, ii, 64

Harding, Warren G., President of the United States; sworn in as Senator, ii, 292; attempt at hazing, ii, 317; temporary and permanent chairman in 1916, ii, 325; telegram from Hughes, ii, 330; candidate for President, ii, 395–397–398–399; nominated ii, 400; stupendous victory, ii, 411; much expected of him, ii, 413–414

Hardwick, Thomas W., Representative and Senator from

428

Index

Hardwick, Thomas W.—*Continued*
Georgia; opposes ship purchase
bill, ii, 268; defeated by Wilson,
ii, 365

Harlan, John M., Associate Justice Supreme Court; for income
tax, i, 149; comment on insular
decisions, i, 354; swearing in
Chief Justice White, ii, 132–133

Harmon, Judson, Attorney General, i, 105; candidate for President, ii, 186–188

Harriman, Edward H., "private
wire to White House," ii, 19;
$250,000 fund, ii, 41

Harris, Isham G., Senator from
Tennessee; surrenders on silver,
i, 121; floor manager Wilson
tariff, i, 128; leader in silver
movement, i, 149

Harrison, Benjamin, President of
the United States; elected in
1888, i, 3; favors Senators, i, 41;
"free coinage of senators," i,
76; Indian contract schools, i,
83–84; appoints Taft and McKenna circuit judges, i, 84;
break with leaders, i, 85; his
methods, i, 86–87–88; break
with silver men, i, 89; confidence
in re-election, i, 90; Carter for
convention manager, Sawyer
for advisor, i, 91; could not
understand defeat, i, 97; prepares for bond issue, i, 100;
blamed for party defeat, i, 101;
characteristics, i, 101–102–103

Harrison, Pat, Representative and
Senator from Mississippi; opposes repeal canal tolls, ii, 248

Hartman, Charles S., Representative from Montana; bolts Republican convention, i, 179

Harvey, George, proposes Wilson
for President, ii, 13; brings out
Wilson, ii, 181; repudiated by
Wilson, ii, 181–182; return to
Wilson reservation, ii, 256

Hauser, Samuel T., Governor of
Montana; testifies in Clark-
Daly contest, i, 324–325–326

Hawaii; Cleveland reverses Harrison's policy, i, 108–109; monarchy overthrown, i, 147;
wanted by Americans, i, 286;
annexation, i, 290–291

Hay, James, Representative from
Virginia; Chairman Military
Affairs, ii, 149; in Mann-Heflin
clash, ii, 262; opposes Garrison
army plan, ii, 298; President
yields to him, ii, 304

Hay, John, Secretary of State;
Hay-Herran treaty, i, 379;
humorous comment on Roosevelt, i, 380; death of, i, 417

Hays, Will H., chairman national
committee; unites Republican
party, ii, 366; chairmanship
resolutions contest, ii, 402

Hearst, George, Senator from
California; Western Congressional Association, i, 53–56

Hearst, William Randolph, Representative from New York; mentioned for President, i, 375;
nominated for Governor, ii, 22;
criticises Roosevelt in Europe,
ii, 119

Hedges, Job; relations with
Hughes, ii, 323

Heflin, J. Thomas, Representative and Senator from Alabama;
speech on woman suffrage, ii,
205; clash with Mann, ii, 262–263

Heitfeld, Henry, Senator from
Idaho; elected by his own vote,
i, 219

Henderson, David B., Representative from Iowa; candidate for
Speaker, i, 20; opposes intervention in Cuba, i, 232; successful candidate for Speaker, i,
310–312; Cuban reciprocity, i,
364; declines re-election, i, 375

Heney, Francis J., Roosevelt supporter, ii, 174

Hepburn, William P., Representative from Iowa; rate bill, ii, 5–6

Herrick, Myron T., Governor of
Ohio; helped frame gold plank,
i, 174

Heyburn, Weldon B., Senator
from Idaho; pure food law, ii,
10–11; clash with Williams, ii,
156; death of, ii, 202–203

Hill, David B., Senator from New
York; first appearance, i, 81;
candidate for President, i, 94
to 97; opposes income tax, i,
133; reply to Chandler, i, 135;

Index

431

Kyle, John H., Senator from South Dakota, **i,** 82

L

Lacey, John F., Representative from Iowa; stops boom for Dolliver, **ii,** 73

La Follette, Robert M., Representative and Senator from Wisconsin; McKinley tariff, **i,** 44; contestant in 1904, **i,** 394; for tariff revision, **i,** 406; in the Senate, **ii,** 12; favored by Roosevelt, **ii,** 13; opposition to Spooner, **ii,** 35; opposes Payne-Aldrich tariff, **ii,** 105; tariff plans upset by Penrose, **ii,** 154; attacks Taft and Roosevelt, **ii,** 164–165; candidate for President, **ii,** 167; hopes for Wilson's nomination, **ii,** 182; favors ship purchase bill, **ii,** 268; candidate for President, **ii,** 321–399

Lamont, Daniel S., Secretary of War, **i,** 105; close to Cleveland, **i,** 106

Landis, Charles B., Representative from Indiana; stops liquor selling in Capitol, **i,** 367

Lane, Franklin K., Secretary of the Interior, **ii,** 389; upholds Lansing, **ii,** 391

Langley, S. P., inventor of flying machine, **i,** 380; mentioned, **ii,** 114

Lansing, Robert, Secretary of State; appointed Counselor, **ii,** 265; succeeds Bryan as Secretary, **ii,** 275; note of protest to Great Britain, **ii,** 280–281; explains Wilson's peace note, **ii,** 350; peace commissioner, **ii,** 387; removal of, **ii,** 389 to 392

League of Nations, **ii,** 368; opposition to; protest of 39 Republican senators, **ii,** 369; political effect predicted by Reed, **ii,** 372–373–374; greatest divisor, **ii,** 381; Wilson returns with, **ii,** 381–382; Wilson's tour, **ii,** 383; Lodge reservations, **ii,** 384; Wilson and Bryan differ, **ii,** 385; submitted to solemn referendum, **ii,** 393–394; plank in Republican platform, **ii,** 401–403; at Demo-

cratic convention, **ii,** 407; issue in campaign of 1920, **ii,** 410–411

"Leak," on Wilson's peace note, **ii,** 351

Lea, Luke, Senator from Tennessee; in Senate moving picture, **ii,** 264

Lease, Mary Elizabeth; speaks at Populist convention, **i,** 188–189

Lenroot, Irvine L., Representative and Senator from Wisconsin; rules revolt, **ii,** 117; candidate for Senate, **ii,** 365

Lewis, James Hamilton, Representative from Washington and Senator from Illinois; comments on Spanish war, **i,** 233–242; one of Reed's friends, **i,** 306

Liliuokalani, Queen of Hawaiian Islands; dethroned, **i,** 109; restored, **i,** 109; dethroned second time, **i,** 147; reference to, **i,** 286

Lind, John, Representative from Minnesota; McKinley tariff, **i,** 48; encounters Bryan, **i,** 79; Governor of Minnesota, **i,** 270; sent to Mexico, **ii,** 226; Confidential Agent, **ii,** 230; Confers with Wilson, **ii,** 249

Littlefield, Charles E., Representative from Maine; opposes exclusion of Roberts, **i,** 321

Lodge, Henry Cabot, Representative and Senator from Massachusetts; reputed author of force bill, **i,** 60; supports Reed for President, **i,** 162; speech on Cuba, **i,** 166; connection with gold plank, **i,** 177; remarks at convention of 1900, **i,** 338–339–340; clash with Stone, **i,** 386–387–388; Tillman's minstrels, **ii,** 31; permanent chairman; comment on Roosevelt, **ii,** 74–75; tariff conferee, **ii,** 109; extending Monroe Doctrine, **ii,** 163; criticises Taft's Mexican policy, **ii,** 205; favors repeal canal tolls, **ii,** 248; suggested for President by Roosevelt, **ii,** 325; leaves Weeks for Roosevelt, **ii,** 327; withdraws his name, **ii,** 328; strained relations with Wilson, **ii,** 345–346; majority leader, **ii,** 376; reservations, League of Nations, **ii,** 384; temporary and

Root, Elihu—*Continued*
tolls, ii, 248; ends Senate term,
ii, 271–272–273; put forward for
President, ii, 283; opposed by
Roosevelt, ii, 285; candidate for
President, ii, 320; name with-
drawn, ii, 328
Rowell, Jonathan H., Representa-
tive from Illinois; quorum con-
test, i, 33; force bill fight, i,
59; draft of force bill, i, 60
Ryan, Thomas F., delegate from
Virginia, ii, 188; denounced by
Bryan, ii, 191

S

Sanders, Wilbur F., Senator from
Montana; seat in contest, i, 50–
51; Western Congressional As-
sociation, i, 55; comment on
Vance, i, 64; at St. Louis in 1896,
i, 180
Sawyer, Philetus, Senator from
Wisconsin; advisor for Harrison,
i, 91
Sayres, Joseph D., Representative
from Texas; Chairman of Appropriations, i, 119
Scott, Nathan B., Senator from
West Virginia; opposes Wood
confirmation, i, 391
Senatorial stories, i, 167–168
Sheehan, Wm. F., Democratic
manager, i, 404
Sheppard, Morris, Representative
and Senator from Texas, ii, 203;
"Buy-a-Bale-of-Cotton Club,"
ii, 254
Sherman, James S., Vice President;
candidate for Speaker, i, 310;
candidate for Vice President, ii,
73; candidate second time and
dies before election, ii, 201
Sherman, John, Senator from
Ohio; candidate for President,
i, 7; McKinley tariff, i, 44;
success in politics, i, 67; impervi-
ous to criticism, i, 68–69; Secretary of State, i, 204–205–206
Sherman, Lawrence Y., Senator
from Illinois; opposed by Roosevelt, ii, 260; candidate for President, ii, 321; withdraws, ii, 328
Sherman silver purchase law, i,
42; i, 117 to 124

Ship purchase bill; filibuster
against, ii, 267; opposition of
Democratic senators, ii, 268;
"strong-arm" plan, ii, 269
Shiras, George, Jr., Associate
Justice Supreme Court; against
income tax, i, 149
Shively, Benjamin F., Representative and Senator from Indiana;
not Vice Presidential candidate,
i, 344
Shoup, George L., Senator from
Idaho; first term, i, 65
Simmons, Furnifold M., Senator
from North Carolina; critic of
Roosevelt, ii, 62; tariff law, ii,
222–223
Simpson, Jerry, Representative
from Kansas, i, 81; chaffing of
Dingley, i, 313
Smith, Hoke, Senator from Georgia; Secretary of the Interior, i,
105; comment on Cleveland, i,
107; asked by Bryan to be a
candidate, ii, 186; forces reorganization of committees, ii,
219; interest in cotton, ii, 254;
in Senate moving picture, ii,
264; hears Reed on League, ii,
372
Smith, James, Jr., Senator from
New Jersey; opposes Wilson
bill, i, 125; supports amended
tariff, i, 133; retired from Senate,
i, 317; supports Wilson for
Governor, ii, 128; discarded by
Wilson, ii, 181
Smith, Marcus A., Delegate and
Senator from Arizona; Western
Congressional Association, i,
52–54; in the Senate, ii, 161
Smith, Walter I., Representative
from Iowa; opposition to Roosevelt, ii, 88; appointed judge by
Taft, ii, 93
Smith, Wm. Alden, Representa-
tive and Senator from Michigan;
Cuban insurgent, i, 232; Cuban
reciprocity insurgent, i; 365
Smith, William Henry, head of
Associated Press, i, 47
Smoot, Reed, Senator from Utah;
opposed by Roosevelt, i, 375;
opposed by Burrows, ii, 12; on
Finance Committee, ii, 106;
supporter of Hughes, ii, 322